Faith Born of Seduction

FAITH BORN OF SEDUCTION

Sexual Trauma, Body Image, and Religion

Jennifer L. Manlowe

NEW YORK UNIVERSITY PRESS
New York and London

To protect the privacy of the participants, some of the details that could identify them have been separated from the actual interviews and listed in Appendix I. Their names have been changed for the same reason. I am aware that disembodying these voices for "anonymity's sake" poses a danger in that it leaves issues of class, race, and sexual preference unexamined, which is not my intention. My concern has been to protect the participants as well as to make their stories as accessible to as many women as possible.

NEW YORK UNIVERSITY PRESS
New York and London

Library of Congress Cataloging-in-Publication Data
Manlowe, Jennifer, 1963–
Faith born of seduction : sexual trauma, body image, and religion
/ Jennifer Manlowe.
p. cm.
Includes bibliographical references and index.
ISBN 0-8147-5517-8 (alk. paper).—ISBN 0-8147-5529-1 (pbk. :
alk. paper)
1. Adult child sexual abuse victims—United States—Religious
life. 2. Incest—Religious aspects—Christianity. 3. Women—Mental
health—United States. 4. Eating disorders—United States—
Etiology. 5. Body image. 6. Sexism—Religious aspects—
Christianity. 7. Christianity—Controversial literature.
8. Twelve-step programs—Religious aspects—Controversial
literature. I. Title.
BV4596.A25M36 1995
261.8'32—dc20   95-16206
                  CIP

New York University Press books are printed on acid-free paper,
and their binding materials are chosen for strength and durability.

Manufactured in the United States of America

10   9   8   7   6   5   4   3   2   1

Contents

Acknowledgments

I am most grateful to the nine women who participated in this study. Without their courage, insight, and openness this book would not have been so full. I am indebted to psychoanalyst and historian Charles Strozier, who taught me how to work with Robert J. Lifton's psychohistorical method. The people who gave me helpful feedback on my research were feminist scholar Flora Davis; author of *Surviving the Wreck* Susan Osborn; writer and poet Bonnie Kaplan; and psychologist and race activist Janet Davis. I am grateful to Carolyn Fox and Julie Marvin, two copyeditors who helped me make sense to my readers. My psychoanalytic religion and psychology colleagues and friends—Michael Perlman, Elisa Diller, and Pat Davis—helped me deepen my insights into the symptoms of eating disorders. Theologians Catherine Keller and Dorothy Austin helped me to broaden my vision in seeing the gendered and theological nuances regarding food refusal. Each advisor pushed me past my own "anxieties" that go with *being seen* on a written page.

I am grateful to my Ph.D. Foucauldian/writing colloquium and am especially appreciative of Darla Fjeld, Karen Heffernan, Sharon Betcher, Catherine Keller, and Nam Soon Park. For the rewriting of this work, I owe much thanks for their patience and theoretical toil to Jennifer Hammer, editorial assistant at NYU Press, and to The Works Group— Paula Bolduc, William James Hersh, Christian Couto, and Paula Zeuge. Finally, I thank Louise Pavelko at Princeton's Theological Book Agency for her frequent references.

Introduction

Since 1983 I have been exploring the theologies of female survivors of sexual and domestic violence. At the same time I have wondered about the social contexts that sustain and encourage eating disorders in women. In what follows, I explore how three issues—sexual abuse in the family, food and weight preoccupations, and patriarchal religious discourse—interrelate. The relations among Christian religious discourse, incest, and eating disorders have not been traced either in the literature on incest or in the literature on eating disorders. Yet these connections reveal an important, and so far unexamined, psychosocial phenomenon.

Looking at how and where these issues intersect can illuminate some possible sources of female body, weight, and appetite preoccupations. My intention is to offer some social and psychological insights into the multilayered nature of painfully common forms of female suffering—incest and body hatred. I hope such information can awaken and empower helping professionals, advocates, friends of survivors, and, most importantly, the survivors of incest who also suffer from what psychiatrist Hilde Bruch calls "the relentless pursuit of thinness." [1]

Sporadic accounts in the psychiatric literature of eating disorders show that as many as five out of six women in anorexia nervosa treatment programs [2] and seven out of ten bulimic [3] college women report histories of sexual abuse before age twelve. [4] Because my intention was to explore the theology of eating-disordered survivors of incest, I selected nine such women as the subjects for this study in order to explore possible religious links among the women interviewed. All were initially sexually abused before age eight. All reveal that such a history has set the stage for their problematic relationship to their appetite cues (for both sex and food), to their sense of autonomy and personal agency, and to their body-size and shape perception. In fact, there are important links of meaning in the incest survivor's mind between her incest experience and her subsequent eating disorder.[5] These links are also laced with religious content that indict a patriarchal culture. I will show the theological dimension of this cycle of abuse—roots centuries deep in the history of Christianity, especially in relation to Christian women.

In collaboration with psychohistorian Charles Strozier, I created a qualitative, in-depth interview method based on Robert Lifton's work with Vietnam veterans suffering post-traumatic stress.[6] The women interviewed came from the spirituality groups with which I have worked as a facilitator or participant observer.

Each of the nine women I interviewed was molested or raped as a child by at least one older male in her family or extended family; two of the survivors were abused by older females as well. This ultimate emotional betrayal reverberates throughout a survivor's lifetime. It appears in her conflicted relationship to her God, to others whom she would like to trust but can't, and, most insidiously, in her relationship to her body and bodily appetites. As long as the survivor believes she can do something to her body to have power, earn validation and worth, she remains entranced, ultimately a target of further victimization. She is seduced by a false solution.

Important connections lie between a woman's eating disorder, her religious discourse, and her traumatic past. Her abuse is, without question, a horrendous violation with traumatic bodily effects. Her eating disorder expresses both the avoidance of and the wish for redemption from that trauma. I hold that too often her theology, rather than mitigating her trauma, may function as a second source of injury insofar as it enables her spiritualization of her traumatic past and symptoms. I unite these central themes throughout this book, and offer a critique of the theological paternalism found in Christian discourse and in Twelve-Step groups. I believe that as long as the survivor of incest has a paternalistic God who promises to save her if she surrenders her will to Him, her struggle for power and meaning—masked by preoccupation with food, appetite, and weight—will forever be a source of conflict.

A survivor's psychosocial conflict is not about food but about a particularly gendered identity. As a woman, she has been taught, in myriad ways, to hang her security upon external validation. Female redemption is to come from outside herself—from the approval of others, from a male savior, or, in Twelve-Step parlance, from a Higher Power. I argue that a survivor's empowerment process includes disentangling these internalized messages and meanings. As long as survivors of incest are reliant on a paternalistic and transcendent rescue, they are seduced into repeating the paradigm of helpless victim-powerful parent—the paradigm of their abuse. Such a model for "recovery" is a model for a permanent trance which ultimately disempowers the survivor. Her future needs to include affirming relationships that are not dependent on her surrender.

If the significance of these connections becomes apparent it may facilitate empowering new psychological and social approaches to understanding the familial, cultural, and religious sources of female self-destructive "inclinations," specifically those found in women who experience a compulsion to flee from their female flesh through an eating disorder.

Pastoral and secular counselors, advocates and friends, and survivors themselves must not only understand the gendered symptoms of a survivor's suffering—her depriving stance toward her body—they must also work to see behind the disguise of the survivor's eating behavior. For a survivor of incest, food is a "double-edged tool"[7] to block or defend herself from being overwhelmed both by her painful past and by her nonaffirming present. Food intake or food refusal can also be a self-soothing tool. Such an implement works to comfort the survivor. The anesthetizing behavior or ritual can stave off a sense of despair grafted onto her experience through sexual trauma and social gradations of sexual objectification. Food deprivation or purging behavior at times is an act of atonement in some of the survivor's cases. The counselor must realize that until the survivor has more functional means to express her pain, shame, and outrage, as well as fill her emptiness, she will feel compelled to use the methods that have enabled her survival thus far—food refusal, overeating, or binge and purging behaviors. A counselor's role can be to support a survivor through her memory excavation of past traumatic events, and to encourage her to reclaim her present and past power that enabled her to survive.

As these women begin to make their own connections among their abuse, their religious discourse, and their nonconstructive coping behaviors, they can slowly shift from an unconsciously self-destructive relationship with their bodies to an increasingly conscious sense of embodiment. As survivors recognize that they have internalized the voices of the perpetrator and the scrutinizing gaze of a masculinist society—which have taken shape as problems with food and weight—they can begin working together to exorcise the socially and the religiously sanctioned offenses. Instead of seeing their bodily appetites as a source of shame and evil, they can begin to relate to their bodies as sources of power.

I have set up the exploration of these connections in a way that parallels the construction of the questionnaire I used in interviewing the women.[8] In chapter 1, I very briefly introduce the reader to the nine women interviewed and the key concepts employed—*patriarchy, paternalism, incest, trauma, eating disorders,* and *recovery*—and to the method to be implemented (see the appendixes for the questionnaire and for a fuller description of the methodology). In chapter 2, I articulate, in depth, the abuse backgrounds of the respondents.[9] In chapter 3, using case studies, I briefly discuss the most provocative theories connecting eating disorders and incest. Chapter 4 is divided into two sections. In section 1, I trace misogynous themes in Christian theology that divinely license female submissiveness and male dominance in intimate relationships. I also discuss instances within Christian theology that reflect dread of the female body and show, some historical precedents for female self-starvation as, paradoxically, both parody of and resistance to a patriarchal culture. In section 2, I show how aspects of the female saints' ideation in the late Middle Ages mirrors some of the feelings and discourse among modern survivors in this study. In their discourse, some female saints reveal religious, social, and psychological conflicts through their relationship to food, their own appetite, and bodily perception. Chapter 5 is also divided into two sections. In section 1, I follow the development of shared theological themes among some of the women interviewed and reveal a misogynous religious subtext in their language about their bodies and their identities. In section 2, I explore alternative, some might say constructive, coping techniques used by some of the women interviewed. In chapter 6, I demonstrate how Twelve-Step groups offer some survivors more room than their Christian faith-of-origin to define their source of empowerment and restoration to a community and themselves. But I also illustrate how such "belonging" requires a significant sacrifice—they must surrender their will to a "Higher Power." They remain seduced by the paternalistic rescue that their Christian religious traditions offered them—thus leaving them likely to repeat the paradigm of helpless victim/powerful parents, that is, the pattern of their abuse.

In the concluding chapter, I discuss recurring and important themes revealed throughout this project. Food and women's bodies have been given symbolic status in the family, in society, and in religious discourse. Survivors of sexual trauma in this study caricature this misogynous symbolism in their traumatic symptoms—their destructive coping behavior with food. Many cultural and religious forces relay the message that females are less valuable than men and in need of "powerful others" to make them worthwhile—to redeem them. Their justification for existence is to come from outside themselves—from the approval of others, from a male savior, or even from a "Higher Power." In this chapter I promote a critical approach to spirituality and hope. For as long as survivors of incest are reliant on paternalistic and transcendent solutions, they are likely to repeat the paradigm of their abuse. Such a model for "recovery" is ultimately bound to fail the survivor of sexual abuse.

1

Who Are We?

We are everywhere. We are your daughters, sisters, friends, partners, coworkers, lovers, and mothers. We sit next to you on the bus. We're behind you in the line at the checkout counter. We sit beside you in church. We walk in front of you on a crowded sidewalk. Everywhere. More than one source claims that the majority of rape cases occur during childhood and adolescence,[1] more often by someone we know and trust.[2] One out of three of us faces sexual assault in our lifetimes: 61 percent of all rapes occur when we are seventeen years old or younger; 29 percent when we are less than eleven years old; 6 percent when we are older than twenty-nine.[3] Nearly half of the three thousand women surveyed in one college study said they had experienced some form of pressure to have sex since the age of fourteen.[4] One out of seven women report being raped by a spouse.[5] Marital rape remains legal in two states: North Carolina and Oklahoma.[6]

Anti-"rape-hype" commentators like Katie Roiphe have rallied a chorus: "I don't know of anyone who's been raped or molested. Why don't *they* come forward?" Over 85 percent of rapes never get reported, 42 percent of victims never tell anyone about their assault.[7] There is good reason for a victim of rape to be reluctant to expose the sexual crimes against her. Coming forward requires a just context. And history tells us that women are responsible for the sexual crimes against them. Fewer than 5 percent of the rapists who are reported go to jail, and 67 percent of them are repeat offenders.[8] If women are not blamed, then they are grossly trivialized. One Pennsylvania judge who "punished" a man who raped his date decided that a seven-hundred dollar fine would suffice. The money would allow her "to take a short vacation and get over it." No wonder victims of rape are nine times more likely than nonvictims to attempt suicide.[9]

The women interviewed for this study, in a number of ways, could be any woman from the Christian middle class. They are between the ages of twenty-five and fifty-eight. They are college educated and come from East Indian, Native American, African American, and Euro-American backgrounds. Their faith systems are Christian based. Their sexual preferences are diverse. (See Appendix I for more demographic detail.)

Because I am a survivor of incest, a former seminarian, as well as a woman who has struggled with the traumatic symptoms of food, body, and weight preoccupation, I have chosen to include my story as one of the anonymous case studies presented. I felt my story both shapes and reveals the theories I have formulated, and my own example should help sharpen the sense of differences among all the case studies. In keeping with good social-scientific research, I feel it is better to own up to my own hermeneutical perspective rather than make the spurious claim to some unassailable objectivity.

Yet it is not my intention to remain anonymous as an author. When I feel that my own experience challenges or enhances the understanding of a theoretical point, I put it forward directly. The politics of anonymity reflects the way patriarchal cultures have "read" sexual violence as something that victims invite. If I were to report on the religious meaning that survivors of burglaries give to their secondary traumatic symptoms, I could keep the survivor's narrative together and even add her first and last names—for no one would dare blame the victim of a burglary. But where sex is involved, a woman has carried the blame throughout time. Such a misallocation of blame is why my narratives, and those of others, have been "broken up" and are used to show themes in the psychology and socially gendered nature of the trauma, its symptoms, and the religious meaning a survivor gives to it. And because these survivors know all too well the repercussions of public exposure, their names have been changed to protect them.

Definitions

Patriarchy

Because I use the term *patriarchy* throughout this book, it is important that I first define it. I see patriarchy as

a familial-social, ideological, political system in which men—by force, direct pressure, or through ritual, tradition, law, and language, customs, etiquette, education, and the division of labor, determine what part women shall or shall not play, and in which the female is everywhere subsumed under the male. It does not necessarily imply that no woman has power, or that all women in a given culture may not have certain powers. . . . The power of the fathers has been difficult to grasp because it permeates everything, even the language in which we try to describe it.[10]

If we read newspapers or popular magazines, go to the movies, look at how we allocate money for military spending as opposed to social programs and how we treat our natural resources such as earth, air, and water, it becomes clear that our system seeks domination. I believe there is a gendered quality to such destructiveness.

In North America, statistics of murder, rape, and incest are decidedly skewed toward the victimization of females. Over 150,000 females die each year of anorexia, which takes more lives than the AIDS virus.[11] In addition, one cannot help but wonder if the federal government's cutting of seven billion dollars from food stamp programs is evidence that women are undervalued, since 85 percent of the recipients of food stamps in the United States are women and children.[12] In many parts of the world, cultural and religious tradition dictates that women are second-class citizens, and they should not question their status—men eat first, are educated first, and make decisions for women.[13] As feminist philosopher Mary Daly notes,

All of the so-called religions legitimating patriarchy are mere sects subsumed under its vast umbrella/canopy. They are essentially similar, despite variations. . . . And the symbolic message of the sects of the religion which is patriarchy is this: Women are the dreaded anomie. Consequently, women are the objects of male terror, the projected personifications of "The Enemy," the real objects under attack in all the wars of patriarchy.[14]

Because patriarchy assigns a secondary position to women, it creates a hierarchy, in which human value is determined by gender, race, class, position, religion, age, appearance, ethnic background, and physical ability.[15] Thus it promotes the death of *jouissance* (where the pleasure of one is the pleasure of the other), because diversity is lost and people are rendered as objects.[16] And an object is easier to abuse. Most of all, patriarchy has maintained the subordination of women for five thousand years, through manipulation, violence, exclusion from decision-making groups, and economic deprivation. Patriarchy is an ideology and a practice that is invested in keeping women and minorities immersed in self-hatred and apathy. As great numbers of women have bonded together to assume self-determination and equal rights in the past three decades, there has been a terrible backlash[17]—a virtual guerrilla war on women, including higher incidents than ever of rape, incest, battering, control of reproductive rights, pornography,[18] and the feminization of poverty.[19]

Paternalism

Paternalism is a benign mask worn to keep patriarchal powers in place. When I use this term I mean the patriarchal (religious, psychological, and social) forces that in their micropractices condition women to doubt, distrust, even fear their own and other women's power. Such conditioning seduces women (and even some men) to be reliant on the direction, support, and authority of men deemed "in charge."

Incest

Almost without realizing what I was doing, I began to use my particular creativity to explore the incest of which (some would say) I was victim, from which (some would say) I survived. . . . At this point on my journey, I would say we are much more than victims. Survivors, yes, but always damaged, always scarred, most often with wounds forever raw.[20]

Incest is the sexual seduction, molestation, and/or rape of a child by any relative (blood, step, adoptive), trusted care-giver, or friend of the family.[21] The term *victim* is used to identify the one who was sexually abused. The term *survivor* is used by those who prefer to see themselves as having survived sexual victimization. The term I use for parents who were conscious of the abuse but remained silent witnesses is *co-offenders.*

Eating Disorders

I use the term *eating disorder* to describe what seems to be a universal preoccupation among the nine survivors of incest whom I interviewed— whether they are affected by anorexia, bulimia, extensive dieting, or chronic overeating. When I use the term I am referring to the process whereby a woman develops a distorted relationship to food, her body consciousness, and her weight because of living in a sex-exploitive family and culture where her power and worth are defined along a bodily plane. I see these behaviors as *gendered tools* used to manage and express the trauma of sexual abuse. I do not use the term *eating disorder* in the traditional sense (referring to an individual disease) because it categorizes food and weight problems as individual pathologies and deflects attention away from social and traumatic contexts that underlie them.

I use the term *relentless pursuit of thinness* interchangeably with eating disorder. When I do so I do not wish to imply that the survivor's emphasis on slenderness reflects a vain "obsession" with appearance. In fact, throughout I argue that the eating strategies that women develop begin as adaptive solutions to, as well as disguised expressions of, sexual trauma.

Trauma

By *trauma,* I mean a violating experience that has long-term emotional, physical, and/or spiritual consequences that may have immediate or delayed effects. One reason the term *trauma* is useful conceptually is its association with the diagnostic label *Post Traumatic Stress Disorder* (PTSD).[22] PTSD is one of the few clinical diagnostic categories that recognizes social problems (such as war or the Holocaust) as partially responsible for the symptoms identified.[23] One perspective on PTSD is that it "adapts well to the feminist assertion that a woman's symptoms cannot be understood as solely individual, considered outside of her social context, or prevented without significant changes in social conditions."[24] For any woman who develops a distorted relationship to food, to her body, and to weight, introjecting cultural expectations and gen- der-degrading experiences (including the plethora of media images of women as sexual objects) set the tone for how she relates to her self. Sexual abuse in the family further imprints these cultural messages.

Psychohistorian Robert Lifton has delineated five key characteristics of trauma:

1. Trauma leaves an indelible imprint in the form of intense, sometimes repressed, memories that are often death-related. There is no time limit on trauma, and its pain can endure with fresh intensity for a lifetime. There are always residual feelings around the trauma, including anxiety. Sometimes, paradoxically, the behavioral and emotional response to trauma is a mask of invulnerability.
2. Trauma can generate death guilt or other forms of self-condemnation. The victim tends to blame himself or herself for not having done enough to prevent the trauma or the events leading up to the trauma. There is a sense of failed enactment.
3. Trauma creates psychic numbing, the diminished capacity to feel, in its victims. Numbing begins as a necessary form of adaptation. Feelings must be closed out as a way to survive the traumatic experience. Later, however, the numbing itself tends to continue and endure as an inappropriate and self-constricting defensive posture.
4. Trauma profoundly affects human relationships which can become infused with suspicion and vulnerable to disruption. Help or friendship may be perceived as counterfeit nurturance, as insincere and unreliable. Trust in people and one's general community can be impaired and difficult to recover.
5. Trauma brings on a struggle with meaning at various levels of existence. One seeks to give inner form to one's experience. One's sense of personal continuity—indeed one's lifeline—has been interrupted, and there is an effort to find new grounding and connectedness for the self.[25]

Most survivors feel pursued by a chronic sense of loss, what Lifton calls the survivor's *life of grief*.[26] A survivor mourns for lost family, lost faith, lost hope, and her former self—who she was prior to the violations. What has been "taken" from her cannot be returned and will not be acknowledged in a culture that refuses to recognize the atrocity. The concept of PTSD has helped bring the inner reality and the outer reality of the survivor together. It is my intention to draw out the gendered nature of PTSD as it manifests itself in the form of food, body, and weight preoccupations for the survivor of incest. I will also expose the religious roots that often give meaning to such traumatic experiences and symptoms among the women interviewed.

Recovery

Usually when the term *recovery* is employed, it is done so in reference to a chemical-addiction therapy based on a disease (medical) model. One who is "recovering" or "in recovery" is thought to be refraining from using her former addictive substance or habit. Such concepts have been psycho-spiritualized and popularized by the human potential movement and, in particular, by Twelve-Step groups of Alcoholics Anonymous and their offspring—Overeaters Anonymous, Gamblers Anonymous, Incest Survivors Anonymous, Sex and Love Addicts Anonymous, and the like.[27] By actively using such spirituality groups and "working" the steps, one is said to be "on her way to recovery." Since incest is not a disease or an addiction one might wonder why the term "recovery" would be used at all. The women interviewed frequently referred to their "healing journey" as their "recovery." For the sake of this project then, I refer to recovery as a self-oriented vocabulary that reveals the wish to move from victim to survivor. Many sexually violated women prefer to see themselves as no longer victimizable, with esteem reclaimed and bodily confidence reaffirmed, or affirmed for the first time. This language of recovery gives them a sense of hope, a sense of self-empowerment. In later chapters, I will explore to what degree such language is pragmatically helpful.

Sexual Abuse, Faith, and Eating Problems Matched

Below I will briefly describe the respondents and their abuse history, their present faith, their coping techniques with food, and the nature of their present involvement with their families-of-origin. This is to better aid readers in keeping core themes together. In the following chapters, I will go into greater detail regarding each of their narratives.

Cherise calls herself an evangelical Christian. She is a sufferer of compulsive overeating (with bouts of self-starvation in between) and alcoholism. She was physically and sexually abused by her father from age seven until age twelve. She is the only one in her family that has chosen not to kill herself.

Natalie calls herself a Christian who imagines God to be female. She is a sufferer of bulimia who was physically and sexually abused by her father from age two to age five. She has intermittent contact with her family of origin.

Margery considers herself to be a Christian. She is a chronic dieter who breaks her diet with a binge. She was sexually abused by her maternal grandfather throughout her childhood. She lives within a few miles of her family of origin.

Haddock grew up in a cult and now considers herself a Twelve-Stepper. Her faith is in a Higher Power. She suffers from anorexia, bulimia, and compulsive overeating. She also considers herself an alcoholic. She was sexually and physically abused by her father, uncle, aunt, and mother from infancy until early adolescence. She has chosen to cut off all contact from her nuclear and extended families.

Melinda is a former Christian and now considers herself a non-denominationally affiliated "spiritual person." She is a sufferer of compulsive overeating. She has an early history of fasting. She was sexually and physically abused by her father and gang-raped by her older brother and his friends. She remembers the abuse occurring from age four until her early teens. She has attempted to confront her father with his abuse; because he denies the incidents, she has severed all contact with him and her brother.

Janine is a former Christian who now considers herself an agnostic. She has been diagnosed as anorexic with bulimic episodes. She was sadistically tortured and sexually abused by her father, and sexually molested by her step-uncle and a male babysitter. Her first memory of sexual abuse was at age four. She has yearly contact with her family of origin.

Stephanie considers herself a "practicing Christian." She suffers from chronic dieting which she "breaks" by compulsive overeating. She was sexually abused by her maternal grandfather from age four until age eight. She has intermittent contact with her family of origin.

Samantha calls herself a Twelve-Stepper who believes in a Higher Power. She is a self-starver who rarely eats and when she does it's something sweet. She considers herself "a sugar addict" in addition to being an alcoholic and former valium addict. She recalls being sexually abused by her nanny in early childhood and by her father in adolescence. She has yearly contact with her siblings and extended family.

Renita describes herself as a Twelve-Stepper who believes in God as her Higher Power. She is a sufferer of bulimia and anorexia. Her paternal grandfather, her father, and her two older brothers sexually abused her. She periodically lives with her family of origin, in between jobs.

2

A Horror beyond Tears: Reflections on a History of Abuse

It's hard to explain, but a certain kind of horror is beyond tears. Tears would be like worrying about watermarks on the furniture when the house is burning down.[1]

Incest is generally thought of as a rare occurrence in society, yet, it is extraordinarily common. Within the patriarchal nuclear family, approximately 38 percent of girls and 10 percent of boys are sexually assaulted.[2] Every incest survivor with whom I have spoken has reported incest to be a horrendous and disorienting experience whether the incest was committed by a father, a brother, an uncle, a grandfather, a babysitter, an aunt, or a mother. The trauma is immense whether it was done in a manner that was seductive, tender, or brutal, or whether it happened a few times in a short period of time or it occurred over many years.

Incest robs children of their childhoods, of their sexual selves, of the basic ingredients necessary for relationships—trust, bodily integrity, boundaries, security, and self-esteem. One perspective on incest is that it "may result in different responses—sensuous and sexual, fear and terror, powerlessness and loss of self, loss of large blocks of time; but regardless of its form and the child's response, incest is a devastating experience and leaves a devastating mark on its victim."[3]

As a way of coping with sexual abuse, children develop behavioral skills to help them survive their childhoods. "[These] survival skills may include dissociation, hypervigilance, isolation, and/or using sex as a negotiating tool."[4] These techniques are necessary to help the child-victim survive a pathological adult-child relationship and as such are logical responses to chaotic childhoods.

Historical Origins of Trauma

To study psychological trauma is to come face to face both with human vulnerability in the natural world and with the capacity for evil in human nature.[5] According to psychiatrist Judith Herman, "Three times over the past century, a particular form of psychological trauma has surfaced into public consciousness."[6] Taken together, they have deepened our knowledge of contemporary psychological trauma. The first to emerge was *hysteria*, the prototypical psychological "disorder" of women. Most of the patients who were referred to Freud by his colleagues were diagnosed as "untreatable liars." The study of hysteria grew out of the republican, anticlerical political movement of late nineteenth-century France. The second type of trauma was *combat neurosis*. It began to be studied in England and the United States after the First World War and reached its peak after the Vietnam War. The last and most recent trauma to come into public awareness is *domestic violence*—sexual and physical abuse in the home. Its political context is the feminist movement in Western Europe and North America.[7]

Hysteria was called "the Great Neurosis" by the French neurologist and mentor to Sigmund Freud, Jean-Martin Charcot. Charcot focused on the symptoms of hysteria that resembled neurological damage: motor paralyses, sensory losses, convulsions, and amnesias.[8] By 1880 he had demonstrated that these symptoms were psychological, since they could be artificially induced and relieved through the use of hypnosis.

Competition to discover the origins of hysteria was particularly intense between two other famous neurological physicians besides Charcot: Pierre Janet and Sigmund Freud. By the mid-1890s Janet in France and Freud, with his collaborator Joseph Breuer, in Vienna, had each arrived at strikingly similar formulations: hysteria was a condition caused by psychological trauma. Each found that "unbearable emotional reactions to traumatic events produced an altered state of consciousness, which in turn induced hysterical symptoms."[9] Janet named this alteration in consciousness *dissociation*.[10] Breuer and Freud called it *double consciousness.*[11] Perhaps a more accurate label would be *divided self-construction.*

By the early 1890s, Freud had treated eighteen "patients," two-thirds of them women. He soon found similarities among this random sample, especially in relation to how they experienced puberty: "A shrinking from sexuality, which normally plays some part at puberty, is raised to a high pitch and is permanently retained."[12] These patients remained in a state of discomfort into adulthood, "physically inadequate to meet the demands of sexuality."[13] Both Janet and Freud recognized that the somatic symptoms of hysteria expressed disguised representations of intensely distressing events that had been banished from memory. Breuer and Freud, in an abiding formulation, wrote that "hysterics suffer mainly from reminiscences."[14]

By the mid-1890s these investigators had also discovered that hysterical symptoms could be alleviated by a singular solution: when the traumatic memories and the intense feelings that accompanied them are recovered and put into words. This individualistic method of treatment became the basis of modern psychotherapy. Janet called the technique *psychological analysis,* Breuer and Freud called it *abreaction*[15] or *catharsis,* and Freud later called it *psycho-analysis.*[16]

By 1896, after hearing countless patients talk of sexual assault, abuse, and incest at the hands of trusted relatives, Freud was ready to present what he saw as the source of hysterical symptoms in adulthood. In his report on the eighteen case studies, entitled "The Aetiology of Hysteria," Freud made the following important claim:

I therefore put forward the thesis that at the bottom of every case of hysteria there are one or more occurrences of premature sexual experience, occurrences which belong to the earliest years of childhood, but which can be reproduced through the work of psycho-analysis in spite of the intervening decades. I believe that this is an important finding, the discovery of a *caput Nili* in neuropathology.[17]

Freud's "momentous discovery" of the childhood origins of hysteria was met with thunderous silence by his peers, followed by a period of professional "leprosy." He had broken a social code: the prevailing belief among the elite that incest was present only among the lower classes and that it had been conditioned out of "civilized" society. Within a year of Freud's dramatic testimony on behalf of his patients, he retracted his hypothesis. Hysteria was so common among women that if his patients' stories were true, and if his theory were correct, he would be forced to conclude that what he called "perverted acts against children" were endemic, not only among the working class of Paris, where he had first studied hysteria, but also among the respectable middle-class and upper-class families of Vienna, where he had established his practice. This idea was simply unfathomable, beyond credibility.[18]

Freud's disclaimer was written up as "The Theory of Infant Sexuality," a foundation of his life's future work. His previous theory of infantile seduction was revised as *a wish* to be seduced by the parent, not an actual seduction. On occasion Freud would refer to his original theory as "my far-reaching blunder." [19] As for the eighteen patients, they were returned to the category of "untreatable liars."

At the time of these investigations no social-political consciousness existed which would reveal that patriarchal power was being abused in families and was routine in the domestic sphere. Not until the women's liberation movement of the 1970s was it recognized that "the most common post-traumatic disorders are those not of men in war but of women in civilian life." [20]

The most sophisticated epidemiological survey of violence against women was conducted in the early 1980s by sociologist Diana Russell. Over nine hundred women, chosen by random-sampling techniques, were interviewed in depth about their experiences of domestic violence and sexual exploitation. The results were astounding [see box].[21] The box shows a fraction of the shocking statistics Russell and others have compiled.

In a sample of 3,187 women, 1 in 4 had been subject to a completed or an attempted rape; 84 percent of them knew their attackers; 57 percent of the incidents had occurred on dates; the average age of the victim was eighteen and a half.[22]

At least one-third of all females are introduced to sex by being molested by a "trusted" family member.

At least half of all women are raped at least once in their lives.

At least half of all adult women are battered in their homes by husbands or lovers.[23] Eleven to 15 percent of married women report having been raped by their husbands.[24]

Attacks on wives by husbands result in more injuries requiring treatment than do rapes, muggings, and automobile accidents combined; one-third of all women murdered are killed by their husbands or boyfriends.[25]

Woman battering is a major cause of homelessness for women and their children. At least 40 percent of homeless women were abused by their partners, and left. They now face rape on the street rather than battering in the home.[26]

Approximately 85 percent of working women are sexually harassed at their jobs.[27]

According to the U.S. Department of Justice, a woman is beaten in the United States every fifteen seconds; at least four women are killed by their batterers each day; a rape is committed in the United States every six minutes.[28]

Internationally the statistics are not any better. For example, in Nicaragua 44 percent of men admit to having beaten their wives. In Peru, 70 percent of all crimes reported to the police are of women beaten by their partners. In 1985, 54 percent of all murders in Austria were committed within the family, with women and children constituting 90 percent of the victims. In Papua New Guinea, 67 percent of rural women and 56 percent of urban women have been victims of wife abuse. Of 8,000 abortions performed at a clinic in Bombay, 7,999 of the fetuses were found to be female.[29]

Similar to Freud's theories, many psychological models of female development and female "disorders" fail to look closely at what actually happens to girls and women in the nuclear family, which is, in itself, a reflection of and preparation for what happens to women in a patriarchal society: they are often hurt, violated, derogated, and even terrorized in their own homes. They are also limited and constrained by the dictates of traditional femininity, which most religious traditions uphold.

Any psychological approach to understanding gender problems (such as eating disorders) must include not only the early years of childhood but it must also consider social and religious influences on a female's development. An approach that fails to integrate these data and this crucial aspect of women's experience is, at best, myopic.[30] A survivor's social, theological, and familial context as well as her experience of that context are instrumental to understanding the multiple layers of meaning that shape her identity.

Shared Themes

Sexual invasion by a trusted relation goes beyond a physical injury; it is a narcissistic violation. Because these experiences occur early in the development of the child, her sense of who she is in relation to others— her world—is shattered. A core betrayal is imbedded in her memory from the onset of her interactions with her emotionally immature parents and caregivers.

When I use the term *narcissistic,* I refer to a formulation of self-psychologist Heinz Kohut. Kohut came up with the diagnosis *Narcissistic Personality Disorder* when he discovered that disturbed people in his clinical practice had problems that seemed to trace back to their *self-structures* (or their sense of self), which had not properly formed in the first few years of life. Almost invariably Kohut attributes the cause of such defects to be unempathic caregivers who fail to help the child achieve a cohesive self by mirroring the child's accomplishments appropriately.[31] He maintains that today's typical patient is "Tragic Man," child of an unempathic mother and an absent father.[32] Kohut does not believe that this split, fragmented, or alienated self is an inevitable consequence of the human condition, rather, that it is a specific historical formation prevalent in the twentieth century.[33] He does not critique the patriarchal familial backdrop that makes for "Tragic Humanity" but feminists who use Kohut's work often draw out these themes.

Swiss psychoanalyst Alice Miller has taken self-psychological and object relations theory[34]—a theory which gives primacy to interpersonal relations (real and imaginary)—and applied it to children who have been abused or emotionally neglected in the home. Miller's claim is that a child's aim is to please her primary parent because her life depends on it "like a small plant that turns toward the sun to survive."[35] Children look to their caretakers to meet their narcissistic needs: respect, echoing, understanding, stroking, sympathy, and mirroring. These are the same needs that their parents had when they were children. If these needs were not met for them then, they will look to their own children to meet them. Miller calls this dynamic of role reversal *narcissistic wounding.*[36] The adult's narcissistic needs compete with the child's and usually dominate over the age-appropriate needs of the child. In response to the demands that are placed on them, children learn to "take care of" their parents—to develop a false self or "little adult" to survive.

In the case of incest, a child-victim develops a "little spouse" persona to survive. This pattern is passed from generation to generation.

Both Kohut and Miller see the therapist's role as drawing out the troubled person's "true self" through offering empathy and narcissistic reparations. The "true self" refers to the spontaneous aspects of one's personality that would emerge if an environment were, more often than not, safe and affirming. The notion of one "true self" that we could reveal or conceal is a fantasy. More likely, we are a mass of social constructions in which particular situations are continually redefining who we are. We are relational beings who wish to be valued and to belong, and most of us go to various extremes to make such "mattering" feel real, depending on the degree of "not mattering" that we have experienced.

In cases of incest, even if parents are not direct sexual offenders, if they minimize, deny, or resist the knowledge of their daughter's experience of being violated, they collude with the perpetrator in his traumatization of her. Because of this betrayal by parents, the child-victim has to develop ways of dealing with intimate physical and emotional harm and neglect.

In a paper on the "fate of bad objects," W. R. D. Fairbairn, an object relations psychologist, addresses the question of why the child deals with bad objects (negative aspects/memories of the parents) by internalizing and then repressing them, imagining the objects good and the child bad. Fairbairn believed the potency of his answer would best be framed in religious terms, "for such terms provide the best representation for the adult mind of the situation as it presents itself to the child." [37]

It is better to be a sinner in a world ruled by God than to live in a world ruled by the Devil. A sinner in a world ruled by God may be bad: but there is always a certain sense of security to be derived from the fact that the world around is good—"God's in His heaven—All's right with the world!": and in any case there is always hope for redemption. [38]

When Fairbairn was asked, "But could not the child simply *reject* the bad objects?" he answered, "No, for however bad the parents may appear to be, the child cannot do without them; the child "is 'possessed' by them, as if by evil spirits." [39] This claim is demonstrated in the experiences of Stephanie (one of the survivors I interviewed who was raped by her grandfather and ignored by her parents). Stephanie claims that her abuser inseminated her with evil through incest: "It has always been my firm conviction that you were not born sinful, that somebody had to plant a seed of sin deep inside of you."

Fairbairn sees the task of therapy as one of releasing bad objects from the unconscious. For him, the psychotherapist is the true successor to the exorcist. "[The therapist's] business is not to pronounce the forgiveness of sins, but to cast out devils."[40] One among my many aims in this project is to help the reader see that adaptive coping behaviors emerge for the survivor of incest largely to repress the post-traumatic terror—which often feels as real as the atrocious abuse events themselves. A further traumatic sense is due to the terror of betrayal—having no social (outer) acknowledgment of or protection from such a horror. Such adaptive behaviors—as multiple personality disorder, borderline personality disorder, creating a false-self, self-injury, binging, starving, or binge-purging—are often adaptive aspects of surviving a traumatic childhood. Too often the aftereffects and the survivor of incest herself are quickly labeled pathological. Such easy dismissal is tantamount to denying her the integrity of her survival skills and the devastating impact of her incest history.

Early Onset of Abuse

Seven of the nine women interviewed suffered their first sexual violation in the first five years of life. Two remember being in diapers when they were first violated. An early onset of sexual trauma is one shared theme.

"In your memory, when did the abuse start?"

Stephanie remembered being abused at age three. She claims, "It's my first memory ever." She was left at her maternal grandparents on the weekends:

At night my (maternal) grandfather would come in and I would see his face with eyes glazed over, looking at me. His eyes are a particularly terrifying memory to me. This weird smile. He'd then hold a pillow over my face and would touch me with his hand and genitals, and my sister says she's had weird dreams of remembering him doing that to me in the same way, that she witnessed it.

Threats of violence may always be present even if violence is not exercised. Feeling terrorized, Stephanie spoke of feeling "so alone." Stephanie's sister, twenty years later, confirmed Stephanie's experience of incest in the family right after being raped by a stranger—the family abuse memories burst into her consciousness.

Haddock grew up in a family where incest was the way her parents, grandparents, and relatives related to the children. The vehicle for the incest was a religious cult. This cult group performed ritual abuse and held religious ceremonies[41] that usually involved sadistic violence against children and animals. Every adult relative of Haddock's belonged to this cult and participated in sadistic incestuous abuse.

I remember Aunt Maude was masturbating me for sure at 18 months. I don't know—if she's the only memory I have, I just remember her long red fingers inserting themselves inside my little kid vagina. I have no memories of anal abuse, although I was given enemas before the ceremony . . . apparently it was part of their technique to arouse the child so the damage was minimal. Uncle Tom was first. I mean, he—he just shoved it in . . . and there's blood all over the place and I'm *gone*. And then behind Uncle Tom, hidden from my view was my dad, and he's masturbating and he comes up and performs oral sex, and there's blood all over his mouth, and his eyes are like in Mars. He has no—it's like I'm not even a person. Then he puts his penis inside me, and then he thrusts—but he pulls out and ejaculates on the floor. And then—that's the end of the memory. There is blood all over these guys. I only saw my dad excited like that once—once more in my life, it was Aunt Maude's funeral when he was looking at my six-year-old cousin Mike. So I believe dad's a pedophile, pure, plain, and simple.

Emotional numbness, sometimes referred to as *emotional anesthesia* or an "arrest in the development of affect," characterizes the most severely traumatized children. In the worst case, the child may become psychologically dead and psychically closed off. Haddock speaks of being *gone* in reference to how she coped with the horror of her abuse. She then repressed these threatening feelings in childhood because there was no other way to survive them. There was no place for her to be validated in them. She split-off a range of feelings to cope and did not even "know" or remember what happened to her until she found a safe place to go to be heard and supported in integrating these hidden emotional fragments of herself.

In the case of Natalie, she is not able to recall the full details of what happened to her, which is far more common in incest reporting.

I'm not sure exactly when my dad started molesting me. It could have been even in infancy, but I know it was going on when I was about three, and possibly up through five, six, maybe later than that. So I'm not really sure about when it started and when it ended but I know it was happening when I was three, four, five . . . and the way that I know is because I've gotten in touch with that part of me that has body memories. And that's how old I am at that—at that stage.

Many survivors can remember detailed images, feelings, sounds, smells, and tastes as clearly as though the abuse were happening in the moment. Most find their memories to be confusing and vague. Important parts of the story may be missing, and survivors may have difficulty putting the pieces together to form a complete narrative with an accurate time sequence. Although traumatic childhood memories are deeply engraved, they are not stored or retrieved in the same way as ordinary memories. Many survivors have a period of amnesia after the abuse, followed by delayed recall. In a recent, careful follow-up study of two hundred women with documented childhood histories of sexual abuse, one in three did not remember the abuse twenty years later. In 1992, a well-funded organization called the False Memory Syndrome Foundation sprung up arguing that victims of sexual abuse are brainwashed to think they are victims by their support groups and overzealous therapists. Such a group takes the spotlight off alleged perpetrators and places it back on victims of sexual crimes in the family—a familiar focus that keeps the cycle of public and family denial in place.[42]

Samantha also has a vague sense of her incest experience,

I think my abuse was—I think it must have been when I was really, really little. Something happened where I was penetrated orally and vaginally while my diapers were being changed, I think by my nanny—like I have this image of a screaming baby. I mean it's a feeling of terror, you know? Another time, when I was twelve, I can even remember the dress I was wearing. I remember my mom saying to my father, "Samantha is growing breasts." My father got this look on his face that I—you know, once I remembered it, I see it before me. It—this sort of [long pause] ecstatical—it was, you know ecstatic happiness, sort of, "Oh, look, I am going to be a really bad little boy here." I don't know, I can't explain it. And he came over and felt my breasts.

With a deep sense of despair, Samantha sighed, "My whole life has been affected as a result of abuse, and it's hard to know whether the damage was mostly sexual, physical, or emotional, because all of it went on."

Women who abuse children in their care often are reenacting their own abuse or are expressing hostility or projected self-hatred.[43] Other mothers, like Samantha's, do not directly abuse the child but facilitate the abuse of their daughters by the men in their family and minimize the offenses against them by normalizing sexual objectification in the family. Samantha's mother would often bring her son into the bathroom when Samantha was showering. Her claim was that she "knew he would be curious about girls *someday*" and that "it was okay to take a peek at his sister instead." Other mothers of the survivors interviewed were unable to recognize their role in silencing the child who was suffering incest. Note the case of Janine:

When I was four, I was sexually molested, digitally, by my babysitter (a sixteen-year-old male neighbor) and that was my first experience, as far as I can remember. I was also subsequently mauled by my uncle and my dad in sexual ways. My dad was the most offensive. He always made comments and innuendos about my sexual appeal to him; even when I was ten years old he would ask me to try on clothes and string bikinis and model them for him. At other times he would have me perform sexy dance routines. I don't really have memories of not feeling like a sexual object. Of course, my mother was numb to it.

Estrangement between mother and daughter leaves the daughter emotionally vulnerable and without adequate support and protection.

Broken Trust—Felt Powerlessness

Who could abuse a child? A sexual offender is someone in a position of power or authority who exploits that power by manipulating, by seducing, and by sexually invading one less powerful than him or herself. This violating of boundaries and trust can wreak havoc on a child's perception of herself and her world. When a child is given the message that the older people who know her will love her and protect her, and then instead an older, trusted member of her family abuses her and no adult validates the reality of this assault, the child's sense of reality becomes distorted. Such a distortion is narcissistically and socially wounding. A feeling of powerlessness ensues because no one will hear or protect her from the ongoing abuse. The child who has been sexually abused is harmed further if she tells someone and is not believed. She is doubly wounded if she is encouraged to trust in God for her safety. (See more about the devastating role of paternalistic theology in chapters 5 and 6.)

The child who is being sexually assaulted is trapped in a private, impossibly confusing world that gives no validation to the crime of the incest experience. The incestuous intruder into the child's private world is "like a monster that inhabits her closet: He threatens her only when she is alone, and she must find her own ways of coping with his over-powering presence."[44]

"Regarding your abuse, any idea whether anyone else knew about it?"

Cherise told me that the only people who knew about her father's abusiveness have died: "My mother committed suicide when I was seven years old; she was twenty-eight." After the successful suicide attempt by Cherise's mother, her father told her, "Your momma was crazy, and she jumped into Lake Erie, and she's dead. And we'll never ever speak about her again." Cherise told me that his sexual and physical abuse of her began very quickly after her mother's suicide: "Every day he began with degradation rituals." At these times her father would molest, beat, and rape Cherise and then degrade her with a litany of abusive remarks about her body size. Cherise remembers how her grandmother would threaten her father, and felt especially protected from her father when her grandmother was around. She told me she would never forget the day her grandmother died: "But I remember when I was ten, finding out from my father that my grandmother had a heart attack. And—and it was like the gates of hell had opened. I knew it was—this is it, I'm dead—I knew I was dead . . . it was like the one person that was protecting me was gone." Cherise told me her childhood was full of loss, "first my mother, then my grandmother, and to be left alone with my father—my father was psychotic." Cherise later found out from her cousins that her mother was her father's third wife, and that all had committed suicide. She added to her list of loss when she said, "My brother also jumped off a bridge into the same lake my mother did. I'm convinced he took his life as a result of residual effects of years of abuse, absolute years of abuse."

Natalie recalls her fathers's abuse through "body memories." She claims, "I know that I was sexually molested by my dad as a child. I don't have cognitive memories of it but I've had a lot of body memories of it. I tend to think that my mom was kind of turning her back on it." Janine remembers a time when her nine-year-old brother and his friends pulled down her pants in a kind of "we'll-show-you-ours-if-you-show-us-yours" *game*. She says,

I remember running home crying like I was going to go to hell for sure, and I remember telling my mom that this happened, and my mom said, "Don't worry, I won't tell your father." And, it was interesting that it was assumed that *I* really was bad and, like a good Catholic, I got the message that *I was sinful.* She gave me the feeling that I am bad and that she'll keep it *our little secret.* Anything that sexually happened to me or was wrong would have been blamed on me. I got that message very early. I was five years old.

Janine told me that she felt there was no point in telling anyone about being abused; she was sure she'd be blamed: "I thought that the physical punishment would be much worse than carrying around all that shame."

In a patriarchal culture, more often than not, a heterosexual woman's first loyalty is to her male partner, on whom she is financially and emotionally dependent, regardless of his behavior. She sees no other choice. One theory is that maternal collusion in incest, when it occurs, is a measure of maternal powerlessness.[45]

Melinda believed her mother knew about the sexual abuse of her by her father and brother and his friends, though she hesitates to blame her mother: "She never said anything to me directly about it. And I—and I don't remember trying to tell her about the rapes. I—I don't remember. Though it seemed to me that I was screaming it in my body and in my mind, but I don't remember words."

Stephanie spoke of frequently being dropped off with her maternal grandparents for weekend visits. It was during her stay there that she and her siblings were molested by their grandfather. She remembers when her parents would come back to pick them up on Sunday nights: "When they arrived, I wouldn't look at them, and I wouldn't go to them. I was in a shell for a long time. But they don't make any connection with sexual abuse about that, they think it's a kind of *cute little story.*" Stephanie recalls that when she had to stay with her grandparents she felt "horrified." In her words, "I mean I was in absolute terror, just absolute, heart-stopping terror." Stephanie later told me she felt her perpetrating grandfather had the power to kill her: "I think I might have been smothered a little bit by him so that I wouldn't talk or scream or whatever." She told me she felt he had the power to *taint,* even ruin her: "He was decimating me as well." It is clear to me that Stephanie has taken in her offender's shame and gives religious meaning to such shame by calling it an "evil force." In her words, "I felt that this man planted this evil root and that this evil root took hold inside of me because of what was happening. As I child I thought he was a monster."

In situations of terror, people spontaneously seek their first source of comfort and protection. "Wounded soldiers and raped women cry for their mothers or for God."[46] When this cry is not answered, the sense of basic trust is shattered. One theory on trauma and abandonment holds that "traumatized people feel utterly abandoned, utterly alone, cast out of the human and divine systems of care and protection that sustain life. Thereafter, a sense of alienation, of disconnection, pervades every relationship, from the most intimate familial bonds to the most abstract affiliations of community and religion."[47]

Most of the survivors interviewed knew without question and learned through devastatingly painful experiences that nobody would give serious credence to their fears. A mother may have been the most incredulous and punishing after being told, not because she was indifferent to the child but because she has been culturally constructed (and thus psychologically compelled) to protect her trust in the basic decency of her male partner and the fundamental security of adult society. Psychiatrist Roland Summit claims, "Since an adult assumes that other decent adults don't commit incest, and since it is generally believed that children wishfully imagine incestuous experiences or fabricate groundless accusations of sexual assault, it is predictable that most women will reject any hint of incest given by their children."[48] Only an unusually secure and perceptive woman can reward her child for sharing with her the bad news of an incestuous relationship. How many women have networks of support available to help them find safety and shelter for their family and resist further abuse?

Identity Confusion/Divided Selves

Thus play I in one person many people, and none contented."
—Shakespeare, *Richard II*

Because incest is a form of chronic traumatic stress, it can lead to a host of initial and long-term aftereffects. Especially when a child-victim has nowhere to turn for validation of her reality, she may begin to doubt her understanding of that reality. Because she is experiencing one thing (sexual abuse) but is told that she is actually experiencing something else (love, care, protection, or nothing at all), she feels divided in her perception and in her self-construction. This mistrust of her perception often follows her into adulthood. She continues to doubt her perception of the world. Her confusion is felt microcosmically both in her body consciousness and her sense of who she is in relation to others.

Most survivors experience a sense of identity confusion or a *divided self-construction*. One part of the self performs as a "normal" obedient child and the other part or parts carry the child's emotional world, which is the result of her experience of being terrorized.

"How did you cope with these experiences during and after the abuse?"

Haddock gives the following account:

[After my uncle raped me when I was five] . . . the rest of my memory is I'm up to the right looking down on this little kid. At other times when I was being tortured or molested, I would mentally hide behind things and watch or underneath things and peek out periodically.

And Melinda:

I can remember learning how to float up to the ceiling and I could even float out the window, I was very talented. I learned to do that around age four. I remember searching inside myself since I had nowhere else to search, for how to do that. I remember doing that. I split . . . split off from myself. Too, I created parts of myself to handle these things. It's a survival mechanism, and it has nothing to do with your creativity and intelligence. It has to do with a survival instinct.

Both Haddock and Melinda have been diagnosed as having *dissociative disorders*. Dissociative disorders, including multiple personality disorder, are diagnoses particularly applicable to severely abused incest survivors.[49] The DSM-III-R lists the essential feature of dissociative disorders as a disturbance or alteration in the normal integrative functions of identity, memory, or consciousness. The aim of dissociation is *not* to experience, *not* to remember.

Milder forms of dissociation include separating oneself from real and present atrocities through dreams and fantasies. Cherise's story is a good example of a milder form of dissociation:

I dreamed that there was this alien family that would come and tell me that I really didn't belong to this man and they were gonna take me away. I couldn't wait to go to bed at night, it was my comfort, this family. This went on for years. And it wasn't until I was twelve, I—I remember mentioning it to a teacher, we were discussing dreams and how every night we dream and we don't remember. And I said, "I do." She said, "Oh, well tell us one of your dreams." And I told her my dream and she just looked at me. She said, "My God!" And I said, "I've had the same dream since I was eight years old." And the look—it was the first time I realized that this was not a normal dream. And I never shared it with anybody else.

Janine remembers the time she told her mother she was "splitting in half, I mean it . . . right down the middle." Janine recalls her mother's response, "Oh honey, all young kids feel that way during adolescence." It is as if Janine's mother knew firsthand what her daughter was talking about and yet could not validate her daughter's experience, possibly to avoid being threatened by her own memories of abuse. Janine posits her divided self at that time, "I think at that point I was truly living a double existence. On the outside I was this friendly cheerleader-type who was always smiling and affirming everybody, and on the inside I vacillated between crying for help and wanting to die."

One label for this dynamic is called *vertical splitting*.[50] It is thought to be a common response among incest survivors. Currently it is well recognized as a coping mechanism by many clinicians. Dissociating serves many purposes. It provides a way out of the intolerable and psychologically incongruous situation (double-bind), it erects memory barriers (amnesia) to keep painful events and memories out of awareness, it functions as an analgesic to prevent feeling pain, it allows an escape from experiencing guilt, it may even serve as a hypnotic negation of the sense of self.[51]

Most psychologists believe that a secure sense of attachment with caring others is the foundation of personality development.[52] When this connection is shattered, the traumatized person experiences psychic dissonance, she loses her basic sense of self. Developmental conflicts of childhood and adolescence—struggles over autonomy, initiative, competence, identity, and intimacy—are destined to be replete with a sense of powerlessness. Because the developing child's positive sense of self depends on a caregiver's benign use of power and the parent perverts that power by sexually objectifying her, the child never feels an innate sense of self-regard, integrity, value, or self-respect. Her chance for developing a sense of interdependence in relation and personal sense of agency are seriously hindered from the onset of the abuse.

At the moment of trauma, almost by definition, the individual's point of view counts for nothing. In rape, for example, the purpose of the attack is precisely to demonstrate contempt for the victim's autonomy and dignity. The traumatic event thus destroys the belief that one can be oneself in relation to others.[53]

A betrayal of trust also destroys the trust one could otherwise develop in oneself. A hypervigilant preoccupation with one's appetites (both sexual and physiological), seen with women survivors who develop eating disorders, makes perfect sense if we understand the core dynamic to be one of abandonment. Such emotional desertion by caretakers results in an inability to trust and naturally manifests itself in one's relationships to others, the self, and the body.

Psychologist David Finkelhor integrates the dynamics, the psychological impact, and the behavioral manifestations of the effects of sexual abuse.[54] He names these effects *traumagenic* and divides them into four categories: (1) traumatic sexualization, (2) stigmatization, (3) betrayal, and (4) powerlessness.[55]

Traumatic sexualization refers to a process in which an individual's sexuality, including both sexual feelings and attitudes, is shaped in a developmentally inappropriate and interpersonally dysfunctional fashion. This process may result in a premature eroticization of the abused child, who then relates to others in an erotic manner.[56] Traumatic sexualization may also result in the persistent intertwining of sexuality and arousal with the sense of shame and guilt often associated with the traumatic event. And while unsatisfactory resolution of developmental conflicts over autonomy leaves any person prone to shame and doubt, these feelings are felt acutely in the trauma survivor.

Shame is a response to helplessness, the violation of bodily integrity, and the indignity suffered in the eyes of another person.[57] Doubt reflects the inability to maintain one's own separate point of view while remaining in connection with others. In the aftermath of episodes of abuse, survivors doubt both others and themselves. Many diagnose themselves as "crazy."

A related concept is psychiatrist Frank Ochberg's *negative intimacy,* a component of post-traumatic stress that the victim must confront therapeutically to resolve feelings of repulsion and degradation.[58] Negative intimacy is the intrusion of an undesired sexual experience, by someone known to the victim, which invades personal space and provokes associations of disgust and even self-loathing. The one being exploited is made a spectacle not only to her exploiter but to herself. She is forced to watch and experience herself being exposed. Sexual and physical attraction, which in her future might be desirable, is forever tainted by these earlier exploitive experiences. What could be desirable (sexual intimacy) becomes repulsive because of its association with the survivor's past degradation (sexual violence).

Stigmatization refers to the negative connotations (badness, shame, guilt) that are communicated to the abused person by the perpetrator and often are subsequently incorporated into her self-image. His guilt becomes her shame. Many perpetrators disavow their guilt through the use of a variety of strategies including projection, rationalization—"You know you want it"—and denial. If that fails to expunge them of their guilt, they may attempt to justify the abuse on the basis that it is deserved by the victim.[59] The survivor is often overwhelmed with shame and dread about her worth as a result of introjecting the perpetrator's guilt.

Betrayal for abused children refers to the dynamics in which children discover that someone on whom they are dependent (the perpetrator) has harmed them or failed to protect them (the co-offender/silent witness). For adults, betrayal issues tend to relate to a sense of a "just world," wherein victimization does not come to people who do not "deserve" it.[60] Such child-victims often blame themselves and see their environment and even their bodies as having betrayed them. They find themselves feeling chronic vulnerability and a sense of meaninglessness, and often have a self-perception of inefficacy.[61]

Powerlessness is the feeling engendered when a child-victim's will, desires, and sense of efficacy have been overcome or are subverted continually. Issues of powerlessness are particularly crucial for adolescents, who normally are struggling developmentally with issues of dependency and identity, and for children, who are vulnerable in any case. In incest situations, abusers often emphasize the victim's helplessness as a control technique.[62] If the victim resists her attacker/seducer often, the offender will escalate the offenses—becoming violent—to further humiliate the victim into submission. One survivor told me, "He was nice to me when I was very young, and when I reached adolescence and started refusing to play his *games* he got sadistic."

These trauma dynamics are not limited to one part of a linear process. They operate before, during, and after the sexual contact. In a patriarchal culture, where parental power—especially paternal power—is defended at all costs, trauma dynamics surely apply as much to disclosure and intervention as to the abuse itself. Thus much of the stigmatization involved in the sexual abuse may occur after the experience itself, as the child encounters reaction among family, friends, and acquaintances.

These traumagenic dynamics also can be applied to the child's life prior to the abuse. The four dynamics are ongoing processes, and the impact of the sexual abuse always needs to be understood in relation to the child's life beforehand. For example, a child may have experienced a substantial amount of betrayal from other sources prior to the abuse, where the loyalty of significant others was continually in doubt. The betrayal of sexual abuse may be all the more serious because it is a compounding of a scenario that already existed. Traumagenic dynamics can be used to analyze sexual abuse as a process, rather than simply an event.[63]

As I stated earlier, it is a well-known fact that many mothers who do nothing to protect their daughters from abuse are particularly dependent on their partners, both financially and emotionally. Such women often have a history of being raped or molested themselves as children and as a result are particularly needy, insecure in their worth and femininity, and absorbed in their own unmet narcissistic needs.[64] But no degree of maternal absence or neglect constitutes an excuse to tolerate paternal incest (unless one accepts the idea that fathers are entitled to female services from their entire families, no matter what the circumstances).[65] It is precisely this attitude of male entitlement that characterizes the incestuous father and his apologists.[66] Mental health professionals must scrutinize their gendered worldview and check their sexism at the door, if they are to be of any long-lasting help.

Multiple Personality Disorder

If the sexual trauma is chronic, a coping device called *multiple personality disorder* (MPD) may emerge. Not until the early 1980s did psychiatrists make the connection that patients with MPD almost invariably (95%) had been sexually or physically abused.[67] Multiple personality disorder has undergone rapid analysis alongside an exponential growth in known cases. Women with MPD outnumber men by at least four to one.[68]

Fragmentation of the self into dissociated *alters* (inner characters created to carry overwhelming emotions) is the central feature of MPD. The array of personality fragments usually carries shattered aspects of the self, as in Haddock's case. She has a compulsive cleaner named "Priscilla" and an extremely sensitive alter named "little Priscilla" who "carried my pain." Often personality fragments include at least one "hateful" or "evil" alter, as well as one who is an impeccable performer along status quo lines.

While helping professionals should honor the survival techniques employed by each survivor—for they enabled her survival—they must be wary of crossing over into pathologizing or valorizing such symptoms (such as MPD or dissociation). These symptoms emerge as a result of the violence, and because these dissociative devices succeed, a terribly unjust distribution of the emotional burden is carried by the survivor.[69] In Melinda's words, "[A multiple personality disorder] is a survival mechanism and has nothing to do with your creativity and intelligence." Multiple personalities cause the survivor rather than the society or family to bear the burden of her victimization.

Borderline Personality Disorder

Some MPD symptoms are also found among people who have been diagnosed as having *borderline personality disorder*. People with borderline personalities, unlike people with multiple personalities, are thought to lack the dissociative capacity to form fragmented alters, but they have similar difficulty developing an integrated identity.[70] For the borderline patient, inner images of the self are split into extremes of good and bad. An unstable sense of self is one of the major diagnostic criteria for borderline personality disorder, and the "splitting" of inner representations of self and others is considered by some theorists to be the central underlying problem of the disorder.[71]

The common denominator of the two disorders is their origin in a history of childhood trauma. In the case of MPD the etiological role of severe childhood trauma is at this point firmly established. In a study of one hundred patients with the disorder, ninety-seven had histories of major childhood trauma, most commonly sexual abuse, physical abuse, or both.[72] Extreme sadism and murderous violence were the rule rather than the exception in these harrowing histories. Almost half the patients had actually witnessed the violent death of someone close to them, as in the case of Haddock, who not only saw her parents mutilate animals but also saw her relatives, who were part of the same religious cult, take the life of a young black boy and a white teenage girl. In Haddock's words,

My inner kids tell me they saw a little black boy hung—I have reason to believe that the cult members had ties to racial superiority. Another time, I woke up crying one day, I had a memory of a white girl—I was supposed to die but they took her instead. Her eyes were just so sad. And she was maybe fourteen when I was eight. I have memories of my cousin Davey bringing in a dagger—and his hands in my hands bringing a dagger down. I have a personality named Little Priscilla. In the ceremony they had done something to this horse—they killed it. But the head was sort of okay and the body was all bloody and icky and sticky. And it wasn't dead yet, and Little Priscilla went up to it, and it looked at her with its eyes and she just petted its little head until it died. And the fact is, up until I uncovered a personality who carried my pain, I never felt any pain in my life.

Seeing a black child and a young white girl being murdered are early lessons *writ large* that have the intention of indoctrinating, through terror, young participants to respect and observe the gendered and racist hierarchy of their culture. Many cults, besides the Ku Klux Klan, are caricaturing wider cultural values. Melinda also saw animals being killed by her perpetrators and was forced to kill animals herself by the teenage boys who gang-raped her. Her offenders warned her: "If you talk, we'll do the same to you."

Another study found that 81 percent of borderline personality patients have histories of severe childhood trauma. The abuse generally began early in life and was severe and prolonged, though it rarely reached the lethal extremes described by patients with multiple personality disorder.[73] A well-integrated self based upon a whole, stable experience becomes extremely elusive for a woman who has been sexually assaulted and objectified. Instead, her own viewpoint is splintered. She may see herself from the perpetrator's perspective. Her "good" self is an innocent memory (herself prior to the trauma). Her "evil" self is the introjected perpetrator. This splintered experience or divided self-construction is inscribed into her sexuality and is central to the psychological "disorders" to which many survivors are prone, including multiple-personality disorder, borderline personality disorder, depression, and eating disorders.[74]

Broken Narrative

Many survivors have difficulty not only remembering their history but coherently assessing their past. Thus, under the conditions of chronic abuse, fragmentation becomes the central principle of personality organization. Fragmentation in consciousness prevents the ordinary integration of knowledge, memory, emotional states, and bodily experience. Though all the survivors interviewed were able to graduate from college, most felt that their ability to be fully attentive in school was severely hindered by their preoccupation with trying to solve double-binds: "If he loves me, why does he abuse me," or "My family looks normal from the outside, what's wrong with me on the inside?"

A pastiche of inner representations of the self prevents the unification of identity. Such a shattered consciousness is discerned through listening to the survivor's attempt to recall her history. Natalie offers an example of how difficult it is to have full memory regarding an intolerable betrayal by both parents.

One cognitive memory I have—I think this is kind of where my memory is cut—I remember being in bed with my dad, and I *think* my mom was on the other side of me, I was between my mom and my dad. And—and I'm not sure that my mom was there, but I know that my dad and I were in my dad's bed, in my dad's room—[they had separate bedrooms]—and I remember his hand being on my stomach, and it was—it was not right on my tummy, what—I called my tummy then, it was too far down. And I remember thinking, "Oh, my God, he's just an inch from my vagina," you know. I remember feeling that, you know, that—that—kind of terror. Then the memory cuts off.

I use the term *broken narrative*[75] to describe this phenomenon. A *broken narrative* is a sense of being able to summon only parts of a scene from one's past, like having access to only a single frame or two rather than access to an entire film.

Melinda reveals a kind of *psychic amnesia*[76] when she talks about living with her family: "I don't have many memories of being with my family. I don't remember sitting at a table. I don't remember eating with my family until high school. I have no memory. I was really like a walking skeleton. Our house was like Dickens' *Bleak House*. Ironically, that was one of three books we had in our house." When trust is lost, traumatized people feel that they belong more to the dead than to the living.[77] Especially when abuse is chronic, the person may find the notion of death (severing from their lived reality) comforting.

Recurring Trauma

"How did the abuse affect you even when it wasn't happening in the moment?"

According to Melinda,

At age four, I started having this recurring sort of night trauma. Whenever I would be trying to fall asleep, everything would start flipping and spinning, it was very internal. And it was this terrible thing—and it was uncontrollable. I couldn't stop it, I couldn't breathe, I was paralyzed, I couldn't move.

Melinda described her night terrors and claimed at times she could "hear things." At other times she told me she could see things: "At that point it felt so real I thought it was the real thing and it was always a man coming into my bedroom. I would feel an intense fear." Melinda lived with that fear from age four until age forty, at which point she found a medical doctor (and practicing psychologist) who in her words, "understood and was able to help me." She was able to reexperience memories of her abuse in the presence of an empathic listener. Melinda says, "Since I started seeing her [four years prior to the interview] I rarely have this flipping and spinning stuff."

Stephanie had dreams of her grandfather trying to kill her. She recalled:

He was an engineer so he had a lot of electrical equipment and blippy things and stuff like that in his little workroom where we slept. To this day I wake up in a cold sweat remembering the terror. I still get panic attacks when I feel those evil eyes staring at me. I can remember the fear—the fear was especially horrible at night. I would imagine monsters coming. I could see—I actually hallucinated almost—monsters.

To this day Stephanie cannot see scary movies, or read scary books because she "becomes disoriented." She told me, "I lose my sense of who I am. It's almost like being the same terrified little girl that I was with my grandfather and I have to leave and pull myself together. I have to find a place where I can't even hear it going on, I can't hear the music, anything occult just drives me totally back."

Janine told me of a period in her life when she would wake up in the middle of the night, "because I truly felt a dangerous presence in my room. I could hear my father's voice say, 'Shut up you bitch.' " Such *night sounds* occurred right around the first year that Janine had started believing that she was an incest survivor. She said, "I felt I was being tyrannized by his spirit to keep quiet . . . and he wasn't even dead. I rarely slept through the night that year."

According to Judith Herman, many symptoms of post-traumatic stress disorder fall into three main categories: *hyperarousal, intrusion,* and *constriction.*[78] *Hyperarousal* reflects the persistent expectation of danger; *intrusion* reflects the indelible imprint of the traumatic moment; *constriction* reflects the numbing response of surrender.[79] "People with post-traumatic stress disorder . . . have an elevated baseline of arousal: their bodies are always on the alert for danger . . . they take longer to fall asleep, are more sensitive to noise, and awaken more frequently during the night than ordinary people. Thus traumatic events appear to recondition the human nervous system."[80] PTSD, as noted previously, is a result of more than the sexually abusive events. Such traumatic symptoms are socially sustained as long as a survivor feels unsafe, is watched in a voyeuristic way, or feels vulnerable to further attack. Living in a patriarchal and violent culture where one in three women is raped at least once in her lifetime means a survivor must face a traumatic context daily, simply because she is female.[81] Her fears are not without justification. She is not paranoid.

Isolation/Suicidality

"How did you feel carrying around this secret of being abused by a trusted family member?"

For most of Natalie's childhood she blocked the traumatic experience from her memory. However, she could not avoid the memory of molesting her own brother when she was ten and he was five. Such an experience confirmed Natalie's (offender inflicted) sense of shame: "This felt like total proof that I was a horrible person that I could do something so awful. I felt like, I'm perverted in some way, that I'm stained, that I'm no good, that I'm horrible, that I'm a bad person, and that I've got this gunk inside of me, this like blackness, this rottenness." Several times Natalie referred to a "rottenness inside of me that I am to blame for." Clearly, she has internalized the perpetrator's messages and protects him by identifying with his guilt through acting it out.

Renita also articulates the internalized shame of the perpetrator. Such feelings of guilt and shame are taken in through the abuse itself.

After my brother molested me I felt that something just happened to me that I can't tell anyone about. And that changed my relationship with everybody, because now I could never be a part of someone, I am always going to be separate or I am not going to be in one [an intimate relationship]. I mean, no one would want me the way I am. I don't know how to explain it. Like if today my life ended it would be no big deal.

Both Renita and Melinda reveal the predominant dread or the *life of grief*[82] that seems to follow a survivor throughout her lifetime. Melinda claims, "The most painful part of it was that there was nowhere to go and talk about it. And so I had to hold all this in myself." Too often people cannot hear what is happening to a child because the event is too awful to believe or it threatens the family system—the idea that must be maintained is that parents are benevolent and all is right with the world. Melinda articulates how such naïveté wounded her in her family:

This atrocity was happening to me in my own home, in my own back yard. And—and the severe pain of it—physical pain. I mean, I'm just talking about *outrageous* physical pain. There was no place [tearfully]—there was nowhere to go to talk. And so when you're a child, you have to—you have to find a way. And I remember that as a child.

Janine claims she did not know whom to tell or what to tell them; all she knew was that she "couldn't take the falseness anymore." She reported feeling suicidal for six years of her life. In her words, "Several times, after getting my driver's license, I would run stop signs in the hope of being killed. I was afraid to take my own life, though I often wanted someone else to take away my pain by ending my life. Even in college, I often imagined myself walking in front of a truck. Ironically, my dad owned a trucking company."

Passive suicide or indirect self-destruction also reveals (in the extreme) generalized manifestations of trauma: helplessness, lethargy, lack of personal efficacy and depression.[83]

Most survivors who become extremely depressed tend to withdraw from potentially healthy relationships and avoid seeking social or medical assistance. The feeling of being malignantly marked, of being placed outside the covenant of normal social relationships, caused many of the women interviewed intense pain. The isolation they felt was compounded by their difficulty in forming trusting relationships. The legacy of their childhood was a feeling of having been profoundly betrayed by both parents. As a result, they normalized this experience and came to expect abuse and disappointment in all intimate relationships: to be invalidated in their felt experience, as they felt their mothers had invalidated and abandoned them, and to be exploited, as their fathers, uncles, brothers, grandfathers (and in rarer cases, aunts and mothers) used and exploited them. This nightmarish isolation and sequential rejection reinforce what becomes for the victim the most painful reality of incest: "It's my fault. I brought it on myself. I'm so bad I invite trouble and make trouble for others. I'm not worth caring for. There's no place for me in the world of reasonable, decent people. I'll never be reasonable or decent. I'm crazy. I'm nothing but a whore." [84]

A study done by Judith Herman in 1981 with forty female incest survivors found that 60 percent of the incest survivors complained of major depressive symptoms in adult life. Thirty-eight percent became so depressed at some point in their lives that they attempted suicide. Twenty percent had times when they became alcoholic or drug-dependent. To cope with their despair and hopelessness of ever attaining a rewarding relationship with anyone, they vacillated between protective isolation and self-destructive activities. [85]

Of the survivors interviewed for this study, four of the nine are regular attendees of Alcoholics Anonymous. Samantha was drug dependent on barbiturates for fifteen years, as she raised four children. In her words, "I lost so much weight after my last child was born and wasn't sleeping much so my doctor gave me a prescription for phenobarbital. . . . I was hooked on it for fifteen years, plus two martinis with lunch and dinner." Natalie claims she is concerned that she might abuse alcohol and drugs as she did when she was in high school and college—as a way to escape the experience of feeling like a perpetual victim. Natalie used these narcotizing substances to elevate her moods of depression and anxiety, "especially in relation to sexual encounters with the opposite sex." Haddock vacillated between alcohol binges and eating binges for most of her adult life. Melinda begrudgingly attends Alcoholics Anonymous because she knows she "needs support in not drinking," but claims that AA is extremely harsh and the people there lack compassion for her history as a survivor of incest. She has decided never to share the primary reasons she would need to "pick up" the alcohol because she claims she knows she would only be scolded as "a typical alcoholic trying to make excuses for her addiction."[86] All of the above survivors are on psychiatrist-prescribed medication to enable them to cope with the overwhelming feelings of anxiety, a sense of guilt, and depression, the very feelings that set a compulsion to escape (through a mood-altering substance) into motion.

Survivors who abuse substances usually begin doing so as a way to manage the emotional pain, but then the substance becomes a problem in and of itself. These addictive behaviors tend to increase feelings of powerlessness, shame, and self-loathing, which in turn intensify the need to use and abuse substances.[87] Furthermore, abusing alcohol and drugs decreases one's ability to make and implement informed decisions and perpetuates a self-sabotaging cycle. In a climate of AIDS and other sexually transmitted diseases, a survivor of incest who is unconscious of these patterns is, in particular, at risk for infection.[88]

Self-Injury

Abused children discover at some point that the feeling of perceived (and sometimes real, as in Janine's, Haddock's, and Melinda's case studies) threats of death and abandonment cannot be abated with ordinary means of self-soothing. They learn at some point that these overwhelming feelings of fear and despair may be most effectively terminated by a major jolt to the body. Some survivors experience this result through the deliberate infliction of injury. These repetitive gestures and forms of attacks on the body seem to develop most commonly in those victims whose abuse began early in childhood.[89] Observe the cases of Janine, Natalie, Melinda, and Haddock, all of whom were abused by age four.

"Have you ever abused yourself as a result of being abused?"

Natalie answers this way:

I would scratch holes in my skin until I was just bleeding and had horrible scars that became infected. If I got a bee sting or a mosquito bite or anything that was itchy or that was a bump or that wasn't smooth, I would scratch it down to make it smooth you know. Sometimes I would just literally dig holes in my skin [she shows me her right upper arm] and I have horrible scars on my legs and arms from that.

Natalie injured herself when she was feeling afraid or anxious. She said, "Inside I'd get panicky and feel like I was going to be a danger to somebody else; instead I would hurt myself."

Melinda said she is most abusive to herself when she does not reach out for help when she needs it: "I tend to isolate." She did recall a time when she would dissociate from memories through cutting herself.

There were times when I didn't know I was doing this, but I would cut my hand and I wasn't aware of it, it wasn't totally conscious. I would just cut it, my hand, with a knife. Not really severely at all, but just [she shows me by angling her right finger across her left open hand] and then all of a sudden I would—you know, I would—I would wake up or I would notice that my hand had this cut. And you know, for a while I didn't think anything of it. But then it was always like in the same place.

The goal of self-mutilation is usually the act itself (to injure) and not to cause death. A survivor may engage in it to demonstrate control and ownership over her body, to enact the abuse, to prevent further abuse, to feel something, or to feel anything other than the intolerable emotional pain. Haddock indicates a sense of not feeling ownership of her body and face and seems to abuse herself to break her denial.

I'm really surprised that I haven't tried to mutilate my face a lot, because, you know, it's just—I look at it and it's not even mine. I have burned myself but the last time I did it on purpose was on Halloween, the anniversary of my first abuse memory. One of my alters wanted me to burn myself so that I wouldn't feel anything. They used to do this to me without creating any real scars but finally this last time the blister popped and I can finally break the denial when I look at that scar and say, "Yes, it really happened." You know, the blisters that didn't pop you can hardly see. The one that did you can see [she shows me]. Every now and then I just kind of look at it, you know?

"Could harm done to women make them more willing to harm themselves?" A *Radiance* magazine finding showed that 50 percent of anorexics in one clinic had been sexually abused. Plastic surgeon Elizabeth Morgan explored the relationship between incest and the desire for plastic surgery after many of her patients admitted they had been victims of child sexual abuse: "I came to understand that many of them wanted to erase the memory of the children they looked like when they were abused."[90]

There are many reasons a woman who has been abused might injure herself. Janine used self-injury to get her mother's attention. Like Haddock she wanted to break out of the denial.

One time I sprained my wrist doing gymnastics and when I reported the injury to my mom, she said, "This is the fourth time this month that we've had to run to the doctor for some minor sprain or another. If we go to the doctor's this time and he doesn't find anything wrong I'm going to be furious with you!" While I waited in the car for my mom to take me to the doctor's, I lifted my sprained [gestures with arm] wrist and swung it down hard against the dashboard with all my might. The doctor claimed it was just a hairline fracture but I remember feeling relief knowing that there was visible evidence to prove to my mom that I was in fact injured.

Survivors who self-mutilate consistently describe a profound dissociative state preceding the act. Depersonalization, derealization, and anesthesia are accompanied by a feeling of unbearable agitation and a compulsion to attack the body. The initial injuries often produce no pain at all. The mutilation continues until it produces a powerful feeling of calm and relief; physical pain is much preferable to the emotional pain that it replaces.[91] Many do it to prove that they in fact have been hurt. As Haddock says, "I look at that scar and say, 'Yes, it really happened.'" In all four cases cited above, the survivor needed to show me (the interviewer) the reality of her emotionally injured self by showing me where she had physically undergone injury.

Self-injury is also frequently mistaken for a suicidal gesture. Though many (38 percent) survivors of childhood abuse do indeed attempt suicide,[92] there is a clear distinction between repetitive self-injury and suicide attempts. One theory purports that "self injury is intended not to kill but rather to relieve unbearable emotional pain, and many survivors regard it, paradoxically, as a form of self-preservation."[93] Self-injury is perhaps the most dramatic of the auto-destructive soothing mechanisms, but it is only one among many.

Female survivors, socially engendered to be docile, are far more likely to be victimized or to harm themselves than to victimize other people. There are more female perpetrators, however, than are reported.[94] Yet it is surprising that survivors do not become perpetrators of abuse more often. Perhaps because of their cultural devaluation and deep feelings of self-loathing, due to internalizing the perpetrator's perspective, female survivors, unlike males, seem most likely to direct their aggression at themselves. While suicide attempts and self-mutilation are strongly correlated with childhood abuse, homicidality is not.[95]

Re-offended Later in Life

Many child-victims cling to the hope that growing up will bring escape and freedom. But the personality formed in an environment of seductive and sometimes violent control is not well suited to adult life. The survivor is left with fundamental problems regarding bodily boundaries, basic trust, autonomy, and initiative. Living in a patriarchal and offending culture (whether she lives alone or not) means there is no place outside of her fear; there are no gender-neutral domains or violence-free spaces.[96] For all these reasons, the adult survivor is at great risk of repeated victimization in adult life.

"Were you ever abused later in life?"

Haddock told me:

When I was about twenty-three a guy exposed himself to me. I was waiting for the bus to go back to school; I had been in a job interview. When I was twenty-six some guys that my mom said were our cousins took me and my sister to the beach. One of the guys pinned me down and I was knocked unconscious—I don't—I remember kind of coming to—I—I was having my period, I had a Tampax in there. I couldn't get that tampon out for three days. And *I* apologized to *him*, I said, "Jerry, I'm not gonna sleep with you tonight. My sister needs me."

When Haddock went into her sister's room to tell her that she had been raped, her sister responded, "You deserved it." Blaming the victim of a sex crime is certainly common, but when one experiences such blame from a family member the pain and alienation it produces goes even deeper.

Cherise told me of the time she met a street artist who, in her words, "was absolutely gorgeous." She said he was especially sweet to her and seemed to be a very sensitive man. She later found out that he was a rapist.

He was a pathological liar. After he raped me he said, "Well, what are you gonna do? I mean, who's gonna believe you—you should be glad to even have someone like me." On one level I thought he was right. And then on the other level—this was—this is rape, you know, and so I just lived in this confused state, and this is where the whole body images come, because, I, you know, was obese at the time. So I didn't have a sense of ownership of my body, I was like, "Well maybe he's right; I mean how could I ever expect to get a gorgeous man like this?" Never mind that this man refused to be seen with me in public.

Note how Cherise felt a double bind: "On one level he was right" (she was obese and so felt worthy of abuse) and on the other, "this was rape." Cherise reveals a belief held by almost every woman I interviewed, and that is "if I am thin I'm invulnerable." Thinness seems to be a magical defense against violation; it can even give one the illusion that she is "undeserving" of rape.

Janine was date-raped by a man who was a member of an Adult Children of Alcoholics Anonymous group. She reported feeling deeply betrayed by him: "I cared about him and he violated my trust. The day after the rape, I had my first images of my dad sadistically torturing me. I cried as I wrote my ex-friend that I couldn't see him any more because no one was ever going to hurt me again the way my dad hurt me. I got into a therapy group for incest survivors because of all this."

When Margery was in graduate school she had a football player sneak up on her in the dark and attempt to rape her. She says, "I screamed so loud that I fell backward and he ran like hell." Five years later Margery *was* raped by a minister she was dating. She said, "One day he got so angry at me that he pushed me down and anally raped me. That's when all of my history of abuse with my grandfather surfaced. I was a wreck." A common theme that emerged among several of the survivors interviewed was to have a sexual crime in adulthood trigger flashbacks of their sexually abusive childhoods.

Renita illustrates how disconnected she feels to her sexuality and how such a disconnection leaves her open to being used as an object—a common result of childhood sexual abuse. "When Don and I had sex I kind of felt like he used my body for his pleasure—I would just space out while he was trying to get off on me. I didn't even know this was unusual until I told my therapist. And to say it out loud, now, is so scary [whisper]." The risk of rape, sexual harassment, or battering, though high for all women, is approximately doubled for survivors of childhood sexual abuse.[97] In Diana Russell's study of women who had been incestuously abused in childhood, two-thirds were subsequently raped.[98]

Classic psychoanalytic theory has commonly portrayed a woman's repeated victimizations as clear signs of her inherent masochism. The earlier belief was that these women not only enjoyed physical pain but were addicted to repeated abuse.[99] In reality, repeated abuse is not actively sought but is passively experienced as a dreaded but unavoidable fate, accepted as the inevitable price of a relationship. As a result of revictimization in adult life, many survivors experience even greater physical and emotional trauma, lower self-esteem, and a heightened risk of HIV and other infections due to unprotected sex.

Many survivors have extreme deficiencies in self-protection and self-valuation and as such are left with a feeling of a paralysis of will. Because they lack the self-worth, basic communication skills, and experience necessary to set and maintain appropriate limits with sexual partners, they feel they have no option but to tolerate abuse. In the case of Cherise, when her perpetrating father became ill she felt she had to minister to his wishes and needs. Haddock also claimed that if her father wanted her to have sex with him today, she could not say no: "I couldn't refuse him today if he made a pass at me because of the kind of power he still holds over me."

A well-learned dissociative coping style leads survivors to ignore or minimize social cues that would ordinarily alert them to danger.[100] As a result they may repeatedly find themselves in vulnerable situations until they find a safe community or empowering relationships. Supportive and politically active connections may enable them to reconnect to their agent-centered selves and learn that they have rights that must be respected.

3

A Pyrrhic Victory: Contemplating the Physical Cost of Surviving

Eating Disorders and Incest

Anorexia and bulimia are multilayered problems that have no singular cause. Psychological and social factors are generally thought to play key roles in their development. Many psychologists and psychiatrists believe these disorders arise in the context of a process of growing up which has gone awry. A young woman's response to biological maturity and the psychological and social demands of sexual development are widely invoked as being especially relevant.[1] Child sexual abuse is now recognized as a common occurrence[2] with consequences that affect self-esteem, sexual identity, personal competence, and potential for intimacy. A link between such experience and later eating/body-image preoccupations is therefore highly plausible.

As I have said earlier, sporadic accounts[3] in the psychiatric literature of eating disorders reveal that as many as five out of six patients in anorexia nervosa treatment programs[4] and seven out of ten bulimic[5] college women revealed histories of sexual abuse before age twelve. Of the self-selected sample of incest survivors with eating disorders whom I have interviewed, all were initially sexually abused before age eight and all have revealed that this history has set the stage for their distorted relationship to appetite cues (for both sex and food), a sense of autonomy and personal agency, and body-size and shape perception. There are in fact important links of meaning in the survivor's mind between her incest experience and her subsequent eating disorder.[6]

Post-Trauma Manifested along Gender Lines

A persistent problem with eating may disguise a post-trauma response to sexual assault in adolescent girls and women, and as such, can be a gender-specific symptom of Post-Traumatic Stress Disorder (PTSD).[7] PTSD is a relatively recent term first defined in Diagnostic Statistical Manual-III (or DSM-III) (APA, 1980) and redefined in DSM-III-R (APA, 1987) as follows:

1. The person has experienced an event that is outside the range of usual human experience and that would be markedly distressing to almost anyone;
2. the traumatic event is persistently reexperienced in at least one of the following ways: intrusive recollections of the traumatic experience; recurrent distressing dreams of the event; sudden action or feeling as if the traumatic event were recurring (flashbacks); intense psychological distress at exposure to symbolic aspect of traumatic event;
3. persistent avoidance of stimuli associated with the trauma or numbing of general responsiveness;
4. persistent symptoms of increased arousal (i.e., sleep disturbance, hypervigilance, easily startled); and
5. duration of the disturbance at least one month.[8]

More women than men have eating disorders for physiological and socio-emotional reasons. Women are socialized to find value through appearing culturally attractive ("model thin"), a cultural ideal that increasingly demands technological assistance.[9] Two-thirds of adult women report in response to surveys that one of their greatest worries is that they will get fat. Two-thirds have an inaccurate and injurious body image (nearly 95 percent overestimate their body size); 75 percent of adult women within the "ideal" range of weight for their heights still think they need to be thinner.[10] Disorders of eating are so common among women that they could be considered norms rather than disorders.

Cross-culturally, from birth, girls have 10-15 percent more body fat than boys. At puberty, male fat-to-muscle ratio decreases as the female ratio increases. The increased fat ratio in adolescent girls is the medium for sexual maturation and fertility. The average healthy twenty-year-old female has 28.7 percent body fat. By middle age, women cross-culturally have 38 percent body fat.[11] Efforts to be thin are so stubbornly resisted by a healthy body that one who desires cultural value/beauty must police her appetite assiduously.

Social judgment regarding a woman's psychological well-being and essential "goodness" is largely determined by how she looks. Psychologist Ellyn Kaschak maintains, "Becoming a woman involves learning a part, complete with costumes, makeup, and lines."[12] We learn our gender roles through imitation and validation.[13] A female's "beauty" and body size are her cultural currency. Learning to behave like a woman involves learning to sit, stand, and talk in the appropriate (nondemanding) ways that do not take up too much space. Paradoxically she must act her part in a way that appears natural.[14] The ability to diet successfully, as marked by achieving thinness, has been held as a gender-specific key to power, acceptance, and control—a triad that is shattered by sexual assault.[15]

One symptom of sexual abuse is low self-esteem, which often facilitates a personality that seeks to please, for survival's sake. In combination with female socialization, sexual abuse increases the chance that a woman will attempt to resolve a physical boundary violation by attempting to control her body. Some psychologists specializing in eating disorders believe that the psychological and physiological stress created by overvaluation of norms of thinness (which are not consistent with biological disposition) creates a context for restrictive dieting, fasting, compulsive exercise, and even purging. These behaviors that produce caloric deficits inevitably lead to binge eating and/or compulsive eating; purging sometimes develops as a desperate attempt to reverse the error of the binge eating and the fear of further loss of control over the self, and symbolically the environment.[16]

Too often helping professionals and the woman with an eating disorder are distracted by the symptom—the behaviors of the eating disorder—and consequently miss the historical roots of incest that set the symptoms in motion. If counselors and the survivor herself remain distracted by the symptoms the behaviors will intensify. Because this posttraumatic response is cloaked in "normal" female behavior (that is, dieting and/or binging), it is often difficult for both survivor and helping professional to see clearly the connections between her history of abuse and her eating disorder.[17] This connection is vital and must be made if the survivor is to be helped, for a survivor will have a very difficult time giving up any of these behaviors without finding alternative and functional ways of addressing the intrusions and expressing the pain that is the result of her haunting memories. Moreover, she must find tangible ways to feel power in order to let go of her dieting methods—her only physical symbol of power.

Shared Traumatic Themes Manifested in Eating Disorders

Shame

Shame is a common experience of all victimization. It consists in a sense of being brought low, being made unworthy or unfit in the eyes of another.[18] There is a profound sense of self-loathing that is a direct result of being sexually violated. A survivor's attempt to shrink her own body may signal a sense of deeply imbedded shame. At times one is so overwhelmed with the shame feelings that one becomes passive, unable to take action on one's own behalf to put an end to the real sense of shame.

For the survivor of incest, her body is the site of that first shameful experience of abuse. As a child, she may not understand what is happening to her while she is seduced and invaded by a perpetrator. But as she grows up she tries to comprehend the abuse by believing something must be wrong with her body if it was selected to be violated. Something must be wrong with her if she responded to the perpetrator's touch, or that something must be wrong with her if she could not defend herself against the offender's intrusions. A woman may manifest this shame by feeling overconcerned with the size of her body or believing that if she looks a certain way—culturally acceptable—others will not see her core shame. Note Haddock's belief that if she is thin then she is invulnerable to disapproval and rejection—further shame. In her words, "I come to OA [Overeaters Anonymous] because I need a reality check. I need to weigh myself and know that I'm like somewhere around 125 [she's 5'8"]. That way I know that's it. The world has to deal with me as I am and if they run away from me in terror, so be it. It won't be because I am not normal. It won't be because I'm fat."

Guilt

Guilt may be distinguished from shame in terms of its focus. Guilt, according to moral philosopher Paul Ricoeur, is "the subjective awareness of having violated a moral system through having committed a fault or engaged in a wrongful act, and carries with it the anticipation of chastisement." [19] There are two basic ways of acquiring guilt. In the first, guilt is earned through wrongful behavior. In the second, guilt is imposed from an external source.[20] Guilt is imposed on the victim of a sexual crime by the perpetrator and is "taken in" at the level of the perpetrator's offense.[21] The victim then attempts to resolve the guilt by resorting to expiation demanded of her within the internalized moral system.

A survivor's ritual behavior with food may signal how much she has internalized the perpetrator's guilt. His shame of incest becomes her shame. She now holds herself accountable, it is her fault—a result of her sinful nature. As one survivor claimed, "When I break my diet with a binge I feel like I'm shoving food into a garbage disposal."

Self-Blame

Self-blame involves post hoc explanations of how choices that were made led to the victimization experience.[22] The purpose of these explanations is to shift the locus of control of causality from the perpetrator to the victim, thereby giving the illusion of responsibility to oneself for one's fate.[23] Self-blame also functions to protect the self from overwhelming depression, and reduce feelings of helplessness and fear. As one survivor stated, "If I'm responsible for making horrible things happen to me, it gives me some sense I have control." Studies have shown that victims of sex crimes who blame themselves may fare better than those who feel there was no rhyme or reason as to why they were selected. Such findings reveal how psychically powerful the illusion of control is to one's sense of well-being.

Society-Blames-the-Victim

American society reflects the popular notion that "you get what you deserve." This comes out in the common belief that victims are responsible for their plights. Although the public is more sympathetic to victims of sexual abuse and rape than they once were, a female victim's social status is often still lowered—proof of the society's tendency to blame victims for their experience of violation.

Anxiety and depression reflect the survivor's evaluation of her perceived worth to other people. I believe these two emotional states follow a survivor from the first time she was sexually abused. For the core message sent to her is that she has been emotionally abandoned. The accompanying symptoms that reflect her unshakable anxiety and depression are inability to relax, habitual negative self-statements, low self-esteem, psychosomatic complaints (head, back, neck, pelvic, and stomach pain), general passivity, compliance, self-hatred, shame, isolation, and desperate attempts for approval to lift her out of her despair. In Renita's case, issues of self-blame and shame became unavoidable when she first became sexually active. She felt ashamed of her bulimia but also felt it was her only defense against such dreadful and anxious feelings. In her words:

I was really active in my bulimia when [my boyfriend and I] started getting sexually active. There was a definite correlation between having sex and throwing up. I was throwing up every day, even if I ate a normal meal, the whole time that we were going out. And he didn't even know it. I would pretend that I was taking a shower or something and then I would throw up. It was a mess. I am still a mess. I don't really see any—any way out of it. Like this is a lifelong process. Which is scary [whispers].

The woman who binge-eats, self-induces vomiting, abuses laxatives, and fails at dieting uses these behaviors to physically express her feelings of despair—she demonstrates to herself that she deserves lower status in the world. Her inability to stop these behaviors is often used by her to give content to her grief and to make sense of her pervasive sense of shame. She sees it as proof to herself that she in fact did "get what she deserved," according to "just world" distorted thinking. This line of thinking also contributes to further feelings of powerlessness—it's a self-fulfilling prophecy.

For several of the women interviewed, overeating or dieting became their only way to cope with the depression, anxiety, isolation, and self-blame born of their sexual abuse. Renita also illustrates how dieting and appearing thin defend her against sadness and against feeling unacceptable:

Though I was abused from 7 to 13 my anorexia didn't start until I was 18. I was never really aware of the underlying depression that was always there and the food played a big role 'cause, if I didn't eat, I would get high . . . on not eating. And therefore I wouldn't be depressed and I guess if you look good people will think you are fine. But I didn't start throwing up till I was 21. Before that I was totally anorexic and bulimic in terms of exercise. I am still bulimic. I even threw up the vegetables I binged on before this interview.

When I asked Renita what preceded her throwing up, she said, "I feel so depressed with how slow and difficult the process of recovery is— you know—feeling all these feelings and having to remember all these horrible things."

Stephanie shows how compulsive overeating buries her sadness and feelings of emptiness: "Eating still is a way to escape loneliness and a feeling of isolation, being different." Both women's behavior with food illustrate the emotional fallout of trauma. Because most of the survivors interviewed were sexually abused by primary caretakers it makes sense that they developed a primary relationship with an inanimate object, substance, or activity rather than with another person.[24] They found something (food and/or ritual behavior with food) that they could project their needs onto and fantasize having those needs being met. This inner world of the survivor must be kept a secret, however, just like the abuse itself, for she would surely be blamed and disgraced if anyone knew what she did with food, what she did with her father (or other "trusted" offending relative).

Legacy of Repression—The False Self

Many survivors believe they have to keep up a false front regarding the sexual abuse, not only to protect the perpetrator[25] (whose attention they often fear losing), but to defend themselves against blame for the sexual offenses and against the pain of remembering the depth of the betrayal.

When a young girl is sexually abused in her family—objectified and humiliated emotionally and physically—she has two choices: (1) to expose the perpetrator who has betrayed her trust and abandoned the role as protective and nurturing parent, or (2) to "forget," thus silently burying the offender's shameful secret in her body. Unless she is fortunate enough to have a safe person to talk to, she is often forced to make the choice of burying the family member's secret and thus preserving the illusion of a happy family.

To expect a child to tell a family member of another family member's abuse is to expect that same child to risk losing parental love and potentially losing the relationship altogether. Often the perpetrator who is pedophilic may be the only relative who gives attention to the child—thus this incestuous relation, in many cases, is fraught with ambiguity. Often, upon naming the incest, the child may incur the wrath of other family members. More likely, the child will carry the perpetrator's shame inside her body/self—slowly suffocating her spontaneous self. Her pain along with her authentic self are buried in maintaining the offender's secret.[26]

Psychoanalyst Alice Miller claims that most early childhood punishment is tied to bodily deprivation or pain. Children deny the hurtful feelings that they have received through their bodies, especially feelings that are now associated with their earliest suffering. As the child grows she learns to hide the past pain by ignoring the signals given by her body. Eating disorders, a most extreme denial of the body, reveal the power of the defensive self. This part of the self (what Miller calls the "false self") will use physically destructive means to damage or destroy the body because the body cries out to be acknowledged as an aspect of the "true self."[27]

The truth about our childhood is stored up in our body, and although we can repress it, we can never alter it. Our intellect can be deceived, our feelings manipulated, our perceptions confused, and our body tricked with medication. But someday the body will present a bill, for it will accept no compromises or excuses, and it will not stop tormenting us until we stop evading the truth.[28]

I believe the legacy of repressing the incest memory and its accompanying bodily feelings is a form of Post-Traumatic Stress Disorder. Eating disorders are a defensive response that result from the powerful coping mechanisms that many girls who cannot speak about what happened to them employ in order to survive the trauma. Whether one binges, starves, or obsesses about food and weight, all these behaviors and mental activities work to enable the survivor to *dissociate*[29] from the traumatic events of her past. Her eating disorder works to protect her, detaching herself from feeling and, oftentimes, from remembering the event or events. Although this strategy enables her to survive psychologically as a child, it later produces symptoms that block the woman's ability to lead a full and productive life. For as long as she buries the offender's guilt in her body, the perpetrator remains free to re-offend. A therapist needs to remember that the impulse to escape the trauma is what enabled her client to survive as a child. This method of coping that served her once is now most likely serving society and the offender, as long as she remains silent. Such a method of coping is what must be replaced by the survivor—on her terms and in her time—with more functional methods of expressing her emotional pain and outrage.

Damaged Goods

Another sign of post-traumatic stress in relation to sexual violence is the feeling of being filthy and disgusting and in need of ridding oneself of this *contamination*. The survivor of incest often feels at war with her appetite, as if her appetite revealed some deep evil within. As she diets and deprives herself, her physiology fights back to maintain its level of comfort. She grows to dread and fear this cycle of eating and avenging the calories through dieting. Her feelings of vulnerability with food and fat can be a result of her powerless feelings over the perpetrator's (or memories of) invasion. Note Janine's sense of vulnerability:

When I couldn't deprive myself any longer [diet] I would binge on melon or berries or grocery bags full of air popped popcorn. I saw myself as out of control, of course. I saw myself as a mess, chaotic. I was afraid of the power of this out-of-control feeling, of this passionate binge, this indulgence, and this fervor to get what I want and not deprive myself anymore. It was just like, it felt like an elevator dropping—completely out of my hands.

The survivor's use of food-restriction behavior often feels atoning and restorative. She temporarily, psychologically "repairs" her sense of being vulnerable and damaged and expiates her temporary lapse in control over her body. Dieting and purging serve her insofar as they symbolize her control, goodness, and power. What she does with food reveals who she is, her character, her value.

The binge behavior is an appropriate counterbalancing behavior to such rigidity. Her body "presents a bill" to her for the physiological and psychological debt she has accrued in overriding her emotional and physical needs. It is a Pyrrhic victory, a battle that as she fights to win, she loses.[30]

Powerlessness

Powerlessness—complete vulnerability and lack of control over the self or the environment—is designated as the core experience that challenges one's perception of one's world. Powerlessness is a reality for one whose identity, rights, and control over one's body are stripped away by sexual abuse. Psychological impotence surfaces through several symptoms: anxiety, apathy, depression, fear, and passivity. Frequent intrusions, nightmares, or daytime recollections of the trauma heighten feelings of powerlessness over the self. Flashbacks reinforce powerlessness over certain environmental factors and cues.[31]

Incest is a bodily violation that deeply damages one's psychological sense of one's self. Because being a victim often feels as if one has little control over what happens to one's body, an eating disorder may signal a desperate attempt to have control over one's own body—as if control of the physical could shield the psyche/self from further harm. For a survivor of incest ardent attempts to control her body through dieting, fasting, and exercise are efforts to restore the sense of invincibility and omnipotence that is lost in an abusive or assaultive experience, particularly if lost at an early age. Many psychological claims have been made about the double bind of restoring power through weight control for the survivor of incest:

Although dieting, fasting, and exercise can temporarily give rise to feelings of discipline and narrowing control over the environment to her physical self, it is inevitably followed by binge-eating. The brittle rigidity of rules that a victim can construe in an attempt to restore order to her world also contributes to repeated feelings of failure and powerlessness when she cannot conform to these rules.[32]

Melinda reveals how she talks to herself whenever she eats more than she has allotted herself: "I would say, 'You're going to be a pig if you don't watch it.' I'd say, 'You're going to gain weight if you don't watch it.' I'd say, 'No one's going to like you. You're going to be made fun of. You're going to be a target for criticism. People are going to think you can't control yourself.' That kind of thing." For the survivor of incest with an eating disorder, to feel powerless over food is to feel powerless over her self, her perpetrator, and her surroundings. For the nonabused woman to feel powerless over her eating patterns is to feel a threat to her key to power, acceptance, and control. Both groups of women have been conditioned to measure their present value by their culturally defined beauty and thinness; for the survivor of incest, however, this measure of her value is compounded by her belief that her *safety* in the world depends on her control of her body. Recall Cherise's belief that because she was fat—"I did not have ownership of my body"—she was raped.

Quite often when the survivor feels in control of her food and level of fat she feels secure. Margery recalls how confident she felt in graduate school: "I was on this really strict plan where I exercised an hour a day and ate virtually no fat for three years. When I couldn't maintain the diet anymore I would binge and then vomit. [Six years later] I weigh thirty pounds more than I did then and I don't even overeat that much. I think being bulimic really threw off my metabolism." Janine also reveals how she feels "good" when she has maintained her severe dieting regime.

When I was *good* I saw myself as in control and powerful and uncriticizable, invulnerable, admirable, and like someone not to be messed with. I also felt like I have to watch it all the time—no fats, no sugar, no starch—to get that feeling and sometimes be even harder on myself, a little bit harder on myself—no liquids, even water, between meals—to sustain that feeling. I kept thinking that if I do the *right* food and exercise rituals I'll stave off that feeling of being bad— you know—out of control.

Rarely do survivors or their therapists make the connection that the "out of control" feeling has less to do with food and more to do with overwhelming emotions. The survivor feels unsafe, unbearable pain, anger, and shame—all sensations exacerbated by a history of abuse and a victim-blaming culture.

Solitary Source of Nurture

For Stephanie, food still serves as her primary source of nurture: "About 6th grade, I can remember the first time I ate compulsively . . . and it just made me feel so good and nurtured and—and better. It still has that effect." It makes sense that food would become the object that a survivor imbued with unconscious narcissistic meaning—it was readily available to her as a child, in Cherise's words, "It was my drug of choice, it still is a legal drug." Such objects of escape become habit forming; they provide self-calming effects: "The object of an addiction is to perform an important psychological function ordinarily performed by oneself [learned from one's relation to one's caretakers] . . . a self-soothing, self-esteem maintaining function that ordinarily in the course of development is internalized as part of one's own psychic structure."[33] Psychological nuances can be found between compulsive overeaters (or nonpurging bulimics) to purging bulimics. Both symptoms reveal a deep hunger that cannot be met with food. The literature offers support of the theory that binge eating among obese overeaters may be serving a somewhat different self-regulating function than binge vomiting serves for purging bulimics. The overeater seems to be trying to fill a depleted "empty" self, or interpersonally lonely self, via taking food in, while the purging bulimic seems to be trying to reorganize a fragmenting sense of self by manipulating food intake and expulsion.[34]

For the survivor of incest, self-care is not taught or modeled for her by her caretakers. It has frequently been the case that the mother in incestuous families is ill, incapacitated, or for some reason emotionally unavailable to her husband and children.[35] The daughter commonly switches place with the mother and not only fulfills the gender-coded "female" roles of doing housework and child care but provides emotional and physical comfort to the entire family. Sexually obliging the father in the family is one among several of the roles she plays as "the little woman" of the family.[36] In so doing, she not only sets aside the "normal" course of her own sexual maturation, she also suffers narcissistic wounding as the result of losing the experience of proper attachment to and affection from either parent. Through such a role reversal, her emotional needs and experience of power are thwarted.

The narcissistic experience of appropriate parental touch, mirroring, echoing, and affection normally set the example for a child to later meet her own needs in adult life. For the sexually abused child, however, food becomes the sole tool for her to meet her narcissistic needs and the body itself becomes a vehicle for this nurture. Natalie attempts physically to experience safety and comfort through food:

After the abuse I became really shy and really afraid of other people. I think what I did for the most part was avoid them. I really just tried to avoid them. As I look back on it, I think that the main thing that I did was just eat. I've been a binge eater and a compulsive overeater since real early childhood. Whenever I was uncomfortable about anything I would eat and find comfort and security in that. I'd feel a lot of anxiety. It really did relieve a lot of anxiety. Especially if it was something sweet and mushy, it was very comforting.

Incestuous abuse robs the child of power that comes from feeling valued deeply. The exploitation infantilizes her, leaving her one-down—the perfect patriarchal woman: a child-woman, dependent, docile, unable to stand up for herself or to fight back.[37] Because she feels abandoned—deeply unloved and unlovable—she turns to food, bringing to it a "bottomless pit" to fill.

A survivor, in her food behavior, manifests a particular cultural bind. If she wants to be valued in her social environment, she knows she must not threaten her only viable asset—her bodily appeal. But if she wants to avoid being used as a sexual object, she may try to desexualize her body through changing its shape, becoming over- or underweight.

Through violence women are made to fear and distrust their own bodies and feel ambivalent about physically expressing, in dress, movement, or adornment, their own sexuality.[38] Her appearance and her preoccupation with preserving her security then is fraught with conflict. The binge-starve or binge-purge pattern becomes a dance that she feels forced into, much like the incest experience, yet compelled to collude in, for affection's sake. Fellenberg writes, "We see from analytic work with adults who binge with food that the safety of this knowledge that what begins will end and is in their control, is sadly lacking."[39]

Too often a binger has very little confidence that her cravings have an ending. The cues of food cravings get wrapped up in all kinds of complex cravings—for love, autonomy, self-esteem, power, and self-expression. Had the woman with appetite and body distortion received consistent respect for her needs and wishes as a child she would have internalized self-soothing memories and thus would not have to go to such self-violent extremes to create and feel these sensations.[40] Had her physical boundaries been honored as a young girl, she might have been able to trust her own ability to maintain them as an adult. One theory about what's going on in a binge is that

soothing is what the compulsive binger "gains" from the binge. A binge is a substitute for an internal representation which provides self-soothing or other self-regulations. The binger lacks adequate frustration-tolerance and becomes addicted to making an external agent or act do the work that a missing symbolic dimension would do. In short, when the binger feels stress, chances are she will binge or at least overeat. She has no internal structure which allows for self-soothing. The food becomes the consistent object. It never rejects her, turns its back on her or walks away.[41]

Alongside these self-soothing qualities, disordered eating can also work to suppress, redirect, or dissociate the survivor from traumatic intrusions, and insofar as the behavior does so it is reinforced. However, because all of the disordered eating behaviors only temporarily work toward the above ends, an "addiction" or compulsion to repeat this method of coping to fend off intrusions quickly develops; disordered eating becomes more frequent and severe.[42]

By using food to soothe herself from her distress, over time the survivor becomes more distanced from the original trauma; the disordered eating may assume an autonomous function of its own as a generalized coping response to aversive or even slightly negative experiences and feelings. Sometimes intrusions are confined to dreams or nightmares, which explain intense urges to binge eat or purge upon waking.[43]

One of the differences between incest survivors with and without disordered eating is their perception of the origin of their distress. Persons with disordered eating often will perceive disordered eating as the primary origin of their distress rather than the intrusions or flashbacks.[44] Both Haddock and Samantha, self-described "Twelve-Steppers," illustrate how easy it is to see their eating behavior as a sign of their "addiction" or "disease" rather than as a symptom of their trauma. According to Samantha,

I fought back, I thought, by going in to isolation and addiction. I was addicted to anything that gave me comfort. I wasn't allowed to have stuffed animals or a blanket or any of the comfort stuff . . . it was considered *germy*. I got addicted to reading to escape and sugar to nurture myself. I would do both from a very early age. To this day, sugar still makes me crazy. I know when I got a little older, I'd even steal sugar from the pantry.

Samantha's father, a doctor, would often punish Samantha from "out of the blue" for being "dirty." The punishment entailed withholding food from her. She learned very early to seek revenge through sneaking food. She told me that she ate very little as a child and was "a really skinny kid." She says the only foods she really cared for were chocolate, cookies, and candies and that she "could eat the whole bag and nothing else in the course of a day." She claims sweets got her through her childhood and still comfort her through her present depression: "If I can't eat I might as well kill myself."

Haddock claims food was a tool that her perpetrator used to silence and reward her. In her words:

> My Aunt Maude would give me pastries—sugary and creamy foods—after I would be abused and I think that was her way of rewarding me for being compliant—this, I think, set the stage for my compulsive addiction to sugar. I go to Overeaters Anonymous because I am a sugar binger and nothing else. I could eat a half gallon of Cookies-and-Cream ice cream and call that dinner. I did it to give me energy and to comfort me when I was feeling too desperate to reach out for help any other way. I don't do this today but I still struggle to not see myself as obese, fat, huge, obscene.

Compulsive eating, exercise, chronic dieting, and vomiting or abusing laxatives leave a survivor exhausted and relieved of stress—effectively numbing fear, rage, and pain. These behaviors are commonly engaged in to release muscle tension due to the anxiety and irritability associated with hypervigilance.[45] As the survivor binges, her muscle tension is relaxed, and for a while she may feel exhausted and able to sleep, a boon for one plagued by night sweats and flashbacks. Binge eating and compulsive eating may also be used to restore energy for vigilance—Haddock shows this when she says, "I did it [binged] to give me energy."

Extreme eating behavior can be a safe way to express anger. Many of the survivors in my study grew up in homes where expressing anger (or other difficult emotions—sadness, pain, and fear) was not permitted or was violently punished. For the child-victim to express anger directly was tantamount to her provoking an attack. Most people with eating disorders (and victims in particular) are prone to turning anger against themselves rather than toward the people who have harmed them. As they focus on food and self-blame, albeit unwittingly, they join the culture in protecting the offenders.

Undesirability as Vehicle of Protection

According to Cherise,

> I didn't feel anything. I mean, if—if I felt something, I wouldn't have had an eating disorder. My body didn't belong to me, my father had the right to touch my body whenever and however he wanted to. I mean, I never had a sense of

ownership. I was literally trying to survive. I was in a war. I was in a battlefield, so I didn't have the luxury of sitting and thinking about my body. I guess the only times I *did* think about my body was when I had outgrown the chubby clothes from Sears, when I was about to turn 8, and had to move to Lane Bryant [clothes for women size 14 and up]. That was a humiliating day because when I turned 8 years old I was wearing a 22-and-a-half dress size.

For some child-victims, starving to maintain a low weight or binging to maintain a sense of shapelessness are both ways of reversing or diminishing secondary sex characteristics and adult status, an important goal if these characteristics have been misguidedly linked with responsibility of "inciting" the abuser. Subsequently, survivors are able to relax defenses against sexual advances, which they imagine will decrease in frequency because they are no longer sexually desirable.

Although weight gain runs counter to female socialization, it can represent a retreat into safety because fatness is associated with sexual undesirability; therefore, the woman is less likely to need to protect herself against unwanted sexual advances. However, in the case of Cherise, she felt her "fat" provoked an attack because the offender assumed she had "no control" over her body.

Psychologist Elaine Westerlund believes more women retreat into shapelessness (extreme thinness/fatness) to fend off sexual arousal—possible invasion. One woman whom she interviewed gained thirty pounds in one month in the process of remembering her incest experiences. The survivor said,

As my body got bigger, my bones and even my features started disappearing. I was literally burying myself in flesh. And it was a way to cover up, to cover up this incredibly horrible thing that I had participated in, that I must have caused. I wanted to hide my body. I consciously decided, "I don't want a body." And so I made it into a blob. And it was nonsexual. I didn't have a gender.[46]

Remaining obese may also represent a way to establish power to fend off an attack. Ironically, the result of disordered eating is an increase in preoccupation with food and thus a decrease in the survivor's overall alertness. As a woman succeeds in repelling possible perpetrators through obesity or extreme thinness she fails in finding an internal sense of her own power, strength, and beauty. Such feelings will feel elusive if they are dependent upon the kindness of powerful others—more often exploiters of such women.

For the survivor of incest, eating and not eating are infused with her desire to be seen and yet not seen. Her pain over not being recognized as a human being worthy of respect is assuaged through her coping patterns with food, which simultaneously work to self-soothe and block her traumatic memories. Because behaviors with food "work" to aid the survivor's escape from her traumatic past, her anxiety-filled and emotionally deprived present, giving up these behaviors can only be done when more effective coping and soothing techniques are experienced in exchange. Too, when she has a sense that she will be recognized as a person—a full subject and not a sexual object—she may relinquish the only key to power she has ever known.

The women interviewed for this study, out of their despair, have all gone on a spiritual quest to find faith and community that would satisfy their needs in a way that the food behaviors are only partially addressing. All nine survivors experience deep shame and betrayal—symptoms of rape trauma—somatically. As they try to resolve their psychological and social symptoms physically, through controlling their bodies and appetites, they are like hamsters caught on a treadmill—they go nowhere. Christian traditions regarding the female, her body, her appetite, and her nature do not mitigate but may even drive her deeper into her symptoms of post-traumatic stress—shame, anxiety, guilt, and a sense of mistrust of herself.

4

Disenchanting Faith and the Female Body: Deconstructing Misogynous Themes in Christian Discourse

Patriarchal religious messages have been passed down through the ages to define and reinforce women's "natural" inferiority. Such meanings condition women to crave paternal, spiritual, and *bodily* redemption. Female redemption through Christian virtues sets up any woman (or female child) who takes these messages literally to be a possible victim of abuse. Such *virtues* hardly empower female survivors of incest; rather, they enable them to *spiritualize* elements of their victimization.[1]

The legacy of female bodily sin is exemplified in the lives of some medieval female saints. Though an in-depth exploration of the sexual abuse history of saints is not a focus of my work, I suspect that many saints and holy women preoccupied with dominating their flesh also had family backgrounds of physical and sexual assault. Modern survivors of abuse who have eating disorders and medieval saints may have in common not only patriarchal religious themes justifying their appetite dread and body disdain, but possibly previous experiences of sexual violation. Misogynous theology that disdains female flesh and demands female self-sacrifice not only facilitates the "rightness" of violence against a woman, it also sets her up to be in constant need of *bodily* redemption. Such a quest for redemption motivates a victim of sex abuse to mystify her "surrender" to her abuser and her chronic dieting patterns. In the cases of the women I interviewed, these *thin* (and often brief) "redemptions" are losses too heavy to justify.

I. Misogynous Christian Themes

Christian Goodness

I submit that the qualities that make a good Christian are the same qualities that make a female "feminine." Patriarchal religious discourse facilitates self-sacrifice for love, submission to an all-powerful male (or God pictured as male), reliance on external authority for direction, distrust of one's experience as authoritative in itself, and the belief that a male savior will redeem. Such ideals set the wheels in motion for men to abuse their authority and for females to submit to such abuse. The incest perpetrator's acts literally initiate a female into her proper "feminine" role. According to Judith Herman,

The victims of incest grow up to become archetypically feminine women: sexy without enjoying sex, repeatedly victimized, yet repeatedly seeking to lose themselves in the love of an over-powering man, contemptuous of themselves and of other women, hard-working, giving and self-sacrificing. . . . *In their own flesh* they bore repeated punishment for the crimes committed against them in childhood. [Emphasis added][2]

The social as well as the familial contexts into which female children are born set the stage for gender-role patterning. The act of incest both physiologically and psychologically works to mark the survivor indelibly with the lessons of her culture, *writ large:* in order to matter she must *please.* If an incest survivor's environment is a religious one, the images, symbols, rules, and expectations embedded in its values will play a major role in determining how she will "make sense of" her sexually traumatic experience.[3]

Both the psychological literature and my work with survivors in groups support the conclusion that females who are abused as children become more dependent upon and more sensitive to their abusers and, by extension, to other potential abusers. They develop a kind of "sensitivity to the aggressor" that is not mitigated by traditional Christian theology.

My method in deconstructing some of the misogynous themes in Christian discourse is to start by taking some traditional Christian discourse at its word. To gain a larger view I step outside the enchanted forest that has, at one time, helped me and other survivors "make sense" of our victimized pasts.

Most of the survivors interviewed were awakening—still with sleep in their eyes—from an enchanted perspective: one that promises blessings for self-sacrificers, redemption to those who surrender to the Lord, hope in a just future that will be made so by divine intervention, and healing from their "original sin" of being human for those who have enough faith.

Those survivors who remain self-identified Christians have elected to revise the traditional discourse[4] to fit a liberation-theological notion of Jesus as co-sufferer on behalf of justice in the family and advocate for mutually respectful relationships to one's neighbors and to the world. I will not explore how these few Christians can remain Christian; much has been written about how the oppressed work within a Christian framework by liberation and feminist theologians. Rather, I will explore the misogynous flaws that are exposed when Christian discourse is taken at face value.

The Ultimate Crime: Religiously Licensed Sexual Abuse

All of the nine survivors interviewed for this study came out of a Christian context. One of the nine grew up with grandparents who practiced Hinduism[5] but insisted that she and her siblings attend Catholic schools and church. (Because I do not feel qualified to address the nuances of Hindu philosophy upon the developing psyche I have chosen instead to give fuller attention to the Christian theological and psychological influences.)

Feminist psychologists, psychiatrists, and religious scholars have done work revealing connections between patriarchal religion and incest. Some have gone back to biblical and talmudic texts to offer an extensive history of the religious and societal backbone that supports the sexual abuse of children. And others have looked at the patriarchal family and found biblical and cultural support for the notion that children and especially women are subject to the rule and sexual whim of the father. For "without an understanding of male supremacy and female oppression, it is impossible to explain why the vast majority of incest perpetrators are male and why the majority of victims are female."[6]

In patriarchal societies the rights of ownership and exchange of women within the family are vested in the father. These rights culminate in the father's relationship with his daughter. The biblical mandates against incest, in Leviticus 18: 6-18, *omit* any specific reference to sexual relations between father and daughter, while almost every other conceivable breach of the incest taboo is explicitly named and condemned.[7]

There are twelve specific dictates forbidding incest with all female relatives, yet there is no specific mention of incest with the father's daughter. The biblical law is addressed to men. It is assumed without question that men initiate and women submit to sexual relations. The wording of the biblical law makes it clear that incest violations are not offenses against the women taken for sexual use but against the men in whom the rights of ownership, use, and exchange, are vested.[8] Every man is thus expressly forbidden to "take" the daughters of his kinsmen, but only by implication is he forbidden to "take" his own daughters. The patriarchal God sees fit to pass over father-daughter incest in silence. This is a glaring oversight.

Having interviewed several incest survivors in the Netherlands, theologian Annie Imbens and historian Ineke Jonker discovered that when women become conscious of their incest trauma they feel compelled to let go of their traditional patriarchal understandings of God.[9] Such understandings of God posit "Him" as divine judge and patriarch who blames them for their sinful natures.

The nine survivors I interviewed claimed the God they no longer believe in was the God who did not answer their prayers for protection, who called *them* sinful, who demanded *they* forgive and submit to their offender(s), and who required them to remain silent in deference to their parents. In my opinion, this is the very God who in classical atonement theology could not forgive humanity until his own son obediently suffered, even to the point of death, for the promise of redemption. Such a glorified sufferer is the same one who many Christian believers are told to "pick up their crosses and follow."

Religious language which promotes a sacred victim, male authority in the home, church, and state, and a heavenly male savior for long-sufferers, is dangerous discourse because it *spiritualizes* political and social passivity and female victimization in the home.[10] Its impact is felt throughout Western society even in nonreligious homes.

In my research and in the work of Imbens and Jonker, gender roles and the position of the survivors from Christian milieux were very similar to those in nominally and antireligious families. Sexual abuse occurs so frequently that it is clearly indicative of structural flaws in society that legitimate patriarchal domination. However, residual effects of Western religious tradition so sanction female acquiescence and male entitlement in domestic and public spheres that even the nonreligious have a traditional Christian (patriarchal) overlay operating in their minds. Both religious and secular worldviews, which privilege male domination, feed and sustain each other.

Qualification

For the purpose of this study, the question of the values conveyed by Christian religion is crucial. Religious values such as suffering, sacrifice, the role of the female, the role of the child, attitudes toward sexuality, and marriage are all prescribed and proscribed in certain ways within a biblical structure.[11] I do not claim to be summarizing Christianity in total. I am aware that responsible Christian doctrine of suffering is far more subtle than I put forth here. But for reasons of illuminating the dangerous psychological effects of the twinning of literal Christian themes and patriarchal authority regarding "the good female," I have chosen to be "wide-eyed" as I look to lay bare the worst outcomes of such theology.

According to religion scholar Sheila Redmond, children from Christian backgrounds learn five virtues:

1. The value of suffering and self-sacrifice;[12]
2. The virtue of repentance and forgiveness;
3. The necessity of remaining sexually pure (especially for little girls);
4. The fact that they are in need of redemption; and
5. The value that is placed on their obedience to authority figures.[13]

Let us examine each of these shared theological themes.

The Value of Suffering and Self-Sacrifice

I keep praying the Lord will give me His ability to withstand the pain. . . . After all, Jesus requires those who would follow him to deny themselves and pick up their cross. I guess this [the abuse] is my cross to bear.[14]

The view of Christian love, or *agape,* has focused on the concept of other-regard often epitomized by self-sacrifice. Those theologians who emphasize loving one's neighbor as the highest model of Christian love have had a dangerously critical stance toward self-love. This view of *agape* as self-sacrifice is rooted in a Christology that emphasizes Jesus' atonement: his self-immolation upon the cross in obedience to his father's will.[15] Such a "satisfaction theory of atonement"[16] model is deeply problematic for Christian survivors of incest who had to deny themselves in obedience to their father's will.[17] Her self-denial for love's sake takes shape in her stance toward her body and in her stance toward those who promise to love her if she surrenders and obeys. Such self-denial is largely the source of the survivor's psychological, physical, and sociopolitical suffering in her present.

This self-sacrificing ideal causes a woman to develop *morbid dependence*.[18] Karen Horney associated this term with a woman's longing to merge with a powerful other to escape the self (and self-related anxieties). The morbidly dependent "feminine type" places herself in the same danger in an intimate relationship that she fears from the outside world in general. Her dependency upon her loved one is experienced as a matter of life and death, and she complies with humiliation so as not to lose the superior other.[19] The compliance reflects not simply clinging but destruction of her independent will as a condition of the merger. Loss of the desired object (usually an idealized male) causes her panic, for such a loss would mean the loss of the self, a kind of death.

These dependencies are predictable outcomes of feminized socialization but are acutely felt by survivors of incest. Survivors know too well the price they had to pay for parental "affection," and such a price usually felt better than the idea of no love from their parents.[20] When religious discourse romanticizes self-sacrifice by celebrating Christ's death to self as required by his father and on behalf of humanity, a survivor cannot help but *spiritualize* her own self-surrender. Such religious discourse helps a survivor *give meaning* to her passive stance, ultimately facilitating her present and future victimization.

Suffering as Theologically Destined. Justification, or the honoring of suffering more often than not, has a destructive influence on victims of child sexual abuse. The intrinsic value placed on suffering in the Christian context has at least two important implications for survivors. On the one hand, the Christian God is just and merciful: if one has suffered, one must have sinned. Suffering is part of the punishment meted out to those who disobey. And on the other hand, suffering and repentance teach humility and are the way back to forgiveness from this Christian god.[21] There is a sense that suffering must make sense. The notion that "I must have done something wrong to have caused this" is often followed by, "Maybe if I pay my dues, I'll be spared next time." This reductionistic theology is much preferable to the cold notion that cruelty is random or worse, socially sustained.

Many religious and nonreligious people alike subscribe to the same forms of a just-world hypothesis: that you get what you deserve.[22] Self-punishment can also be a vehicle to give content to grief unacknowledged. It is better to feel God is good and that one can earn "his" favor through the right sacrifice than to believe there is no end to suffering. Subsequently, the attempts to restore control in one's world through atonement, in order to prevent further suffering, reflect internalization of this same superstitious popularization of Christian doctrine.[23]

Virtue of Repentance and Forgiveness

The Hebrew term *teshuvah* literally means "return," clearly denoting *repentance*, a return to God after sin. In Judaism there is a distinction between sins against God and sins against people. For the former, only regret or confession is necessary. For the latter, a confession and some form of restitution is standard.[24] In Christian teaching, the Greek word for repentance is *metanoia*, which literally means "to change one's mind"—to have a change of heart or actually a transformation of behavior.[25] Sins against people require admission of wrongdoing, asking for forgiveness of the person wronged or abused, and reconciliation, which can be accomplished only by a change in behavior.[26]

The New Testament passage regarding forgiveness in Matthew reads: "But if anyone strikes you on the right cheek turn to him the other also."[27] This may be the most common biblical passage taken at face value. The Christian emphasis upon a ready flow of forgiveness, responding to *metanoia*, has given rise to a strange distortion of this belief. This literalization, as such, has hampered more than helped the victim of incest. Healthy reactions to sexual assault include anger and outrage over the betrayal of trust and the misallocation of blame. If such anger is not expressed it will surely be somatized. To the survivor, calls for her repentance assume *she* is at fault. Religious mandates that she be forgiving misread the context in which she lives. Such "calls" to repentance should be directed toward the perpetrator. In order to forgive one must not only hear a contrite apology from the one who is at fault, but must also see a consistent change in behavior—which, in the perpetrator's case, demands ongoing mental-health intervention and social support.

Herein lies a paradox. Survivors are often told they should forgive and move on. Even in some incest literature the notion of forgiveness is espoused.[28] We do survivors—and all oppressed people—a disservice by foisting upon them what reveals more about our own uneasiness than about our wish for their recovery. In some traditions (including the Twelve-Step ideology) a survivor is also called to repent or make amends. Such a call is outrageous, and is in my mind a second injury inflicted upon the survivor. Even in the case where a survivor has hurt herself or another, I feel she should be gently guided into forgiving herself and understanding the impossible context out of which such *choices* were made.

Regarding the offender's apology—an extremely rare action taken— many psychologists caution that even the most contrite offender should never be considered entirely "cured." Just as the alcoholic never loses susceptibility to addiction, even after years of sobriety, the offender can never be expected to lose sexual interest in her or his victim. Even after the offender has acknowledged full responsibility for the crime and recognized the harm done, that offender may still crave an incestuous relationship and may attempt to revive it in subtle ways. A person who has had many years of practice excusing and indulging an antisocial compulsion cannot develop secure inner controls in a few months of even the most intensive treatment.[29] Offenders, like their victims, live in a patriarchal culture where child pornography is the largest-selling (underground) pornography.[30]

An offender's abstinence from indulging in the dangerous and de- structive habit of eroticizing and sexually abusing children will require ongoing supervision as well as ongoing social support. While forgive- ness and repentance are two themes that often arise in relation to fam- ily betrayals, in the case of incestuous abuse such themes must be de- constructed for their political content: Who does the forgiving? Who is benefited by such forgiveness? Who does the repenting? What is the result of such repentance? What behavioral changes can be measured?

Female Worth through Purity/Virginity

Women have been taught that their femininity is *pure* so long as their virginity is maintained, and that securing their virginity is their responsibility alone. The physical fact of virginity has historically indicated spiritual valor. For the religious woman a preserved hymen may not guarantee entrance into heaven but the inappropriate loss of the hymen diminishes the chances for eternal salvation. One religious scholar writes:

For the young [religious] virgin, sexual history and spiritual identity are difficult to separate, and when [she] "loses" her virginity because of rape, her spiritual life is damaged or diminished. Virgin rape is as devastating as incest in trespassing the boundary between the personal and spiritual self. The suffering that follows rape . . . is not just physical but also metaphysical and spiritual. The spiritual importance placed upon virginity makes [religious] women especially vulnerable following rape or incest.[31]

The veneration of eleven-year-old Maria Goretti is a modern example of such values. When Maria became a saint in 1950, the Pope spoke of her as a model for all Roman Catholic girls. Maria Goretti was murdered because she refused to be raped. Maria was assaulted by a nineteen-year-old male relative who had already approached her several times before the final assault. She fought her rapist, was stabbed fourteen times, and died later in a hospital. She has been used most recently as a model for Catholic youth in a papal address by Pope John Paul II in 1980. Her shrine was rebuilt in 1979.[32]

In many cultures, a man's honor is contingent upon his control of others, especially in regard to control of "his" woman's sexuality.[33] A woman's honor is associated with her own sense of sexual inviolability.[34] How others treat her affects her sense of self in relation to others. It is virtually a cross-cultural phenomenon that sexual transgressions committed against a woman reflect her own sexual shame even if she did not precipitate the transgression.[35]

Need for Redemption

The Christian focus on the *need for redemption* throws fuel on the already rising flames of a child-victim's sense of unworthiness. For the child who is sexually abused, the abuse can truly prove that she is in need of redemption; it convinces her that she is unworthy of feeling safe or being valued and respected. Lack of validation is one of the deepest developmental deprivations a child can suffer, and yet, because of parental betrayal and emotional abandonment, it is the most common wound known to survivors of incest.

As I have said elsewhere, grief, guilt, and shame are chronic states for a survivor of incest. It is believed that guilt imposed on the victim by the perpetrator is taken in at the level of the perpetrator's offense.[36] He disavows his own guilt and transfers it to the victim who is left with the feeling that it is *she* who must atone for *the offender's* behavior. His sin is now her sin. As children and even as adults, many survivors turn to their perpetrators for forgiveness. Redemption is something a survivor tries to secure by earning her abuser's love through obedience.[37] Like their prayers for deliverance from God, their perpetrator never redeems them. The perpetrator's shame and God's silence leave the child-victim with the sense that she is unredeemable. Ironically, most survivors continue to cling to the hope of an external rescue.

In Christian circles, the child will hear of freedom from suffering only in metahistorical terms. Her present experience must make sense to her, so she believes there must be something bad about her that is worthy of such abuse. Such internalization of someone else's sexual crime halts movement toward resolution of the abuse.[38] It also works to circumvent the process of seeking justice; muteness is always the enemy of authentic change.[39]

When a survivor makes a public complaint or accusation regarding the offender's activities, she defies the perpetrator's attempt to silence and isolate her, and she opens the possibility of finding new allies.[40] The survivor may come to understand her own legal battle as a contribution to a larger struggle, in which her actions may benefit others as well as herself. In later stages in their recovery process, some survivors have found that working within the system to defend the rights of women and children has helped them transform their personal grievance into a focused resistance to all forms of violence.

When a survivor stands up in private, she draws power from her ability to speak the truth without fear of the consequences. She knows that truth is what the perpetrator most fears. As she refuses to obey the offender's rules, she breaks the silence of his secret, and in so doing she may, in fact, redeem herself.

Value of Obedience

Christian discourse frequently underscores the *value of obedience* to authority figures, especially parental or quasi-parental figures. The fifth of the Ten Commandments, "Thou shalt honor thy father and mother that thy days may be long on this earth,"[41] has been proposed to be at the root of Western violence and its attitude toward children.[42] The message relayed to the child is that the adult is not to be questioned, but revered. The foundation for this attitude toward authority is established both in the anthropomorphic conceptions of the Christian deity as male and in the human relationship to this God. Although the Christian theological position of monotheism argues that one cannot assign anthropomorphic characteristics to its God, attempts to "desex" or use multiple anthropomorphic terms for God have been met with strong resistance in much of Western Christian religious practice.[43]

Many feminist theologians have encouraged using alternative gender images for the sake of enabling richer spiritual connections. Carol Saussy writes:

When women image Deity in exclusively male terms, they relate to God (that is, male Deity) as "like the other but not like me." The symbols used of this Jewish and Christian male Deity or God are most often symbols of power and authority: Father, Lord, Ruler, and King. When women image Deity in female terms, however, they relate to Goddess as "like me." Symbols that speak to the Goddess are also powerful symbols but are more likely representative of nurturing and relational power and are perhaps more serene: Earth Mother, Life Giver, Comforter, Wisdom.[44]

Evoking the Goddess can be enormously creative, challenging, and energizing for some survivors. However, replacing male imagery of the divine with essentializing female imagery is not a long-term solution, especially for survivors who were abused or neglected by women. Divinized anthropomorphic solutions are insufficient solutions to facilitating empowerment for survivors of childhood sexual abuse primarily because they sustain a paternalistic paradigm that mirrors the relationship where they were traumatized by betrayal. And such a paradigm is dangerous insofar as it sets the tone as to how a survivor relates to those in authority as well as how she relates to her own authority.

II. No Redemption

The Sin of Being Embodied as Female

It is my claim that men project their fear of death onto women by claiming women are more bodily in "nature." Such myths have convinced women over time that they are innately sinful and their bodily appetites are dangerous. Because "woman" cannot control herself, so patriarchal myths tell us, she must be lead by, dominated if need be, by men. Such discourse supports the "rightness" of violence against her; it also sets her up to be in constant need of *bodily* redemption. Such a quest for redemption is behind both her surrender to her abuser and the chronic dieting patterns of the women whom I have interviewed. These *thin* (and often brief) "redemptions" are false. Theology that does not mitigate dominance against women promotes violence and female passivity. This is seen most clearly in her sacrificing relationship to her body.

Origins of a Cultural Illness

It is striking how often the imagery of anorexics includes Christian/ascetic themes, with a dualistic construction of mind/matter and spirit/appetite coded in terms of purity/contamination, and the ultimate goal of cleansing the soul of desire/hunger.[45] "Out of the earth-womb vegetation and nourishment emerged, as the human child out of the woman's body. The words for mother and mud (earth, slime the *matter* of which the planet is composed, the dust or clay of which "man" is built) are extremely close in languages: *mutter, madre, mater, materia, moeder, modder*."[46]

For centuries the feminine has been associated with the body, nature, and chaotic darkness. From the days of Aristotle (fourth century B.C.E.), nature and body have been relegated to a negative stature opposite to mind and spirit. In her essay, "Is Female to Male as Nature Is to Culture?," anthropologist Sherry Ortner postulates a universal devaluation of women based on a cultural assumption of the hierarchy of culture (the sphere of human control) over nature (spontaneous processes that humans do not control but are dependent on).[47] According to theologian Rosemary Radford Ruether,

Women are symbolized as "closer to nature" than men and thus fall in an intermediate position between culture as the male sphere and uncontrolled nature. This is due both to woman's physiological investment in the biological processes that reproduce the species rather than in processes that enhance her as an individual and to the ability of male collective power to extend women's physiological role into social roles confined to child nurture and domestic labor. Female physiological processes are viewed as dangerous and polluting to higher (male) culture. Her social roles are regarded as inferior to those of males, falling lower on the nature-culture hierarchy.[48]

The Christian tradition has not only maintained this hierarchical order of values but reified them by accepting Aristotle's most harmful charge against female nature—a fundamental weakness in morality.[49] Wrote Tertullian:

You [woman] are the devil's gateway. You are the unsealer of that forbidden tree. You are the first deserter of the Divine Law. You are she who persuaded him whom the Devil was not valiant enough to attack. You destroyed so easily God's image, man. On account of your desert, that is death, even the Son of God had to die.[50]

From a hetero-masculinist perspective everything about a woman is both grounded in and defined by her female body and, in particular, its sexuality, defined as the ability to arouse the male subject rather than to experience desire. Whatever is arousing about her (the female object), and even whether she intends to arouse, is also designated by the male subject. His feelings become hers, his desire her desirability, his admiration her measure of worth, his disdain her degradation, his ridicule her humiliation.[51]

A woman's sexuality, her body and her appetite, have long been considered religiously symbolic. Her body and its cravings have been made to be responsive to the meanings given to them by religious discourse. Women's sexuality has been blamed for the fall of humanity as far back as the first century. The original Genesis story suggests women's co-responsibility for sin. But in the New Testament narrative of 1st Timothy 2:12-14 the blame is squarely placed on Eve: "Eve was clearly the one who was deceived and broke God's law, not Adam."

According to Ruether, women's subordinate status is viewed not only as a reflection of her inferior nature but as "just punishment" for her allowing evil to come into the world, thereby leading to the death of Christ. Read from this perspective, the death of Christ only deepens female guilt, while it absolves Adam (and men in general) of any fault and allows men to represent the male savior as priests.[52]

The fourth-century theologian and "Father of Catholicism," St. Augustine, claimed women lack the capacity in themselves to "image God." They reflect God's image only when viewed together with the male who is their head, but men represent God fully in themselves. In this scenario women are headless without a man.[53] Augustine promoted the Pauline insinuation that only men can represent God fully and be "heads" in the church, in the home, and in secular society.[54]

In the thirteenth century, Catholic philosopher Thomas Aquinas followed in Aristotle's footsteps.[55] He, like Aristotle, claimed woman was defective by nature. Aquinas wrote in the *Summa Theologica* that woman's subjugation existed prior to her sin—it was created by God.[56] Her subordinate status was God's original intention.

Many of these patriarchal theories (in which men are divinely privileged in their capacity to image God in the world) were adopted during the Protestant Reformation of the fifteenth and sixteenth centuries. In Martin Luther's *Lectures on Genesis,* Eve is not considered inferior to Adam in Eden, but because of her willful disobedience she was punished by God, demoted, and all women born of Eve must suffer like her—her subjugation to the male is punishment for her sin. Luther wrote, "The woman bears subordination just as unwillingly as she bears those pains and inconveniences that have been placed upon her flesh. The rule remains with the husband and the wife is compelled to obey him by God's command."[57]

John Calvin, considered (by many Protestant theologians) to be the greatest systematic theologian of the Reformation, saw the hierarchical order of men over women, children, and servants as the original order of creation. Male dominance was seen as ordained by God. For Calvin, "Any woman who challenges this hierarchy or flaunts her will against the divine male authority is sinful, disrupts the order of nature and society, and may very well be a witch."[58]

Having a will and being appetitive, like Eve, who could not resist her curiosity and so ate from the forbidden tree, was surely her (and that of women throughout history) downfall. Two famous Dominican priests, Heinrich Kramer and James Sprenger, also writing in the fifteenth century, link female sinfulness to her "appetitive nature." They write: "All witchcraft comes from carnal lust, which is in women insatiable. . . . She is more carnal than man." [59]

During the period called the Enlightenment, the greatest number of female witch persecutions occurred. Protestants and Catholics were equally involved in persecuting these marginalized women and their children.[60] Women who were not male-dependent—those who owned land, midwives, and herbalists, old and young alike—were seen as a threat to patriarchal rule and were extinguished like a dangerous fire.

When There Is No Outside: Resistance through the Body

Several decades ago, Karen Horney noted that "the prerogative of gender [is] the socially sanctioned right of males to sexualize all females, regardless of age or status." [61] Christian patriarchy has coded women's sexuality, their will, and their appetites as proof of their innate sinfulness. Secular patriarchy has sexualized females through observing, evaluating, and using the female body for their own purposes. Both ideologies merge together in Western culture to give core meanings to male and female, masculine and feminine, in North American society. Although not all men may choose to exercise their theologically divinized right, no woman can choose to opt out of this system. There is no outside of a dominant patriarchal culture which is sustained by misogynous religious symbol systems. All women will be sexualized publicly and privately throughout life, and even if they are discarded or judged negatively, it is still against the standard of the indiscriminate and discriminate heterosexist male gaze.[62]

How such patriarchal traditions, norms, and values come to be symbolized on a body level is critical to explore. Such domination is translated by the incest survivor who develops an eating disorder into an internalized patriarchal voice or gaze that measures her worth by her body size and mastery of her appetite. The myth goes something like this: "If a woman suffers (or more benignly, surrenders) appropriately, she will satisfy the patriarchal tyrant, and be redeemed." *Satisfaction* maintained through bodily control goes against her physical needs and thus must be continuously policed.

Cultural philosophers inspired by Michel Foucault call this self-scrutinizing dynamic the indiscriminate *normative male gaze*[63] which has been internalized by women. One example of this despotic cultural internalization is described by an anorexic woman who speaks of "a dictator who dominates me," or, as another describes it, "a little man who objects when I eat."[64] Such a relationship to food and fat signals *supranormal* feminine behavior.[65]

The woman who is body, self, and appetite policing (regardless of her size) has internalized this male gaze. In Melinda's words,

When I go into stores to buy clothes, the mirrors in the dressing rooms are cruel. They are the most mean mirrors. All I see is flab that's normally hidden under clothes. There are all these layers and layers and even little layers of fat, it's really gross, it's really awful. It must be really awful to sit across from me and look at me all bloated and ugly.

The one who cannot see food and her body without critically commenting on the shape in the mirror or the size of a portion of food has internalized the masculinist voice—offenders in both her cultural and family environment. Gendered self- and appetite-policing has a long history.

Religion and Eating Disorders

Historically, both food and eating have had different meanings for women and men. During the Middle Ages, elective starvation was viewed to be a primary means for women to achieve spiritual purity.[66] In modern Western (and Westernized) societies that emphasize a highly individual and physical/psychological, rather than a spiritual, concept of the self, women still seek perfection through manipulation of the physical. This is a different, yet related, sort of perfection than their foremothers sought. Women's "perfect" body/appetite control is not overtly religious in nature but reveals her covertly sought-after gendered need for redemption. Such redemption is bought at too high a price by ridding her body of its decidedly female features—secondary sexual characteristics such as roundness in hips, stomach, and breasts—in hopes of finding freedom from the sin of being born female.[67]

There are scholars who make connections between patriarchal religion and self-starving females. Religious historian Rudolph Bell coined the term "holy anorexia" to describe the medieval concern over whether such extreme fasting behavior was the work of God or the devil. Nearly half of the forty-two Italian women who lived and died in the thirteenth century and came to be recognized as saints exhibited an anorexic behavior pattern.[68]

Historical research demonstrates women exhibited an ethic that valorized food asceticism more than men. One theory posited is that because women had fewer vehicles for direct power in the church, their bodies became their primary symbol of what they could have control over.[69] According to Caroline Walker Bynum, "Although women were only 18 percent of those canonized as saints between 1000 and 1700, they comprised 23 percent of those who died from asceticism and 53 percent of those for whom illness was central to their sanctity."[70]

Bell expands much of Bynum's research. In his study of female ascetics he examines the vitae of 261 Catholic "holy women" from 1200 to the present. He documents the high number of cases of women for whom self-starvation was central to their asceticism. Bell narrows his focus to the Italian peninsula and to those 261 women recognized by the Roman Catholic church as saints, blesseds, venerables, or servants of God. Bell demonstrates that for 39 percent of these women, an anorexic pattern is evident. The percentage is lower among the Franciscans (32 percent) and highest among the Dominicans (56 percent).[71]

Both Bell and Bynum explore patriarchal contexts that sustain self-starving behavior in medieval women, yet they give little attention to the attempted rapes and family abuses that went on in some of the women's histories. The connections between a woman's self-depriving relationship to her body, her appetite, and her history of religious commitment need to be explored through analyzing her familial and social context.

The value of my work is that I can go into some detail regarding the family background of my respondents.

Survivors of Violence Seek Radical Purity

This soul would fain see itself free, and eating is killing it.

—Teresa of Avila[72]

A full belly does not make for a chaste spirit.

—Catherine of Siena[73]

A purity agenda through food-refusal has historical precedent among Catholic saints of the late Middle Ages. Male biographers (frequently) and female saints themselves (occasionally) suggest that the body should be disciplined, defeated, or even destroyed, in order to release or protect the spirit.[74] Female saints were recorded to be better fasters than males. This difference may reveal the female internalization of a masculine ideal—to be freed from the material, the finite, the body. Such female fasting may have been done to punish the flesh, to destroy or deny its urges, and to repress its sexuality.[75]

Integer, integra, integrum comes to mind. Untouched. A man is more untouched than a woman. He is inviolate; he does not have to be pregnant. A man remains himself, does not have to assimilate, renounce; only women have to do that.
—Anonymous (modern) anorexic[76]

Perhaps such restrictive behaviors among some fasting saints stem not so much from fear of desire but from a deep yearning for bodily integrity (a desire to be untouchable/inviolable). For example, Douceline of Marseilles, Columba of Rieti, and Lutgard of Aywières feared their physical appetites and developed obsessive fears over having any bodily contact. Lutgard panicked at an abbot's insistence on giving her the kiss of peace; Jesus had to interpose his hand in a vision so that she was not reached by the abbot's lips. She even asked to have her own gift of healing by touch taken away.[77] Clare of Montefalco said she would "rather spend days in hell than be touched by a man."[78] Both Columba of Rieti and Lutgard had indeed experienced physical and sexual brutality prior to their becoming fasting saints.[79]

Although there are different reasons for the preoccupation with female appetite in different historical eras, abuse of a woman's body signals the worst (on a continuum) of her status as a sexualized object. This does not mean that any woman's problem with food or her appetite and body perception indicates past sexual abuse, rather, it is indicative of her status as sexualizable object. What is paramount though, and virtually a constant throughout history, is the very fact that it is *symbolism* and *meaning* that must be manipulated for women to seek approval and to avoid humiliation.[80] Most religions demarcate order from disorder and sin from sanctity by reference to the female body.[81] Anthropologist Mary Douglas claims, "The female body, site of processes men have perceived historically as mysterious and potentially dangerous, offers a most graphic symbolism of ultimate concern. Women carry potential for order and meaning and for disorder and chaos in their very bodies."[82]

Menstruation, gestation, lactation, and aging all testify to the triumphs and tragedies of existence. Moreover, because religions choose symbols not only to distinguish order from disorder, but also to effect order and control disorder, the female body often has been religions' symbol of choice. Because the female body is associated most closely with life and death processes, authority asserted over a female body is power asserted over the very forces of human life.[83]

Besides their bodies, women must also accept their appetites as symbolic in a patriarchal culture. Their appetite and eating must be made responsive to the historically contextual *meanings* of weight and of eating itself along with, or instead of, the physiological cues for hunger and satiety.[84]

If a woman can control, shape, *purify* her body, perhaps she can control or overcome the violence against her in her life, the arbitrariness of her gender assignment with all its existential-physical-emotional-behavioral meaning. If she is culturally acceptable (thin and compliant) then maybe she will receive a valued place in her environment. Paradoxically, by gaining control of her body, she succumbs to her fate as a woman. Once again, as she succeeds, she fails. This is a central double-bind of female development.

Indeed, patriarchal religious meanings have seeped down through the ages to make "sense" of women's "natural" inferiority. Christianity's misogynous *virtues*, if taken at face value, can disempower any female. Much of Christian discourse does not mitigate violence against women but rather gives religious meaning to female submission and male dominion.

In briefly examining the outcome of the legacy of female bodily sin I find that a woman's search for spiritual redemption can mask a deep belief in her "natural" inferiority—her sense of sinfulness. Unacceptability is inextricably linked to her bodily nature. One can see these dynamics in the lives of medieval saints as well as modern-day "eating-disordered" women. Both time periods reflect a misogynous dread of bodily desires that are projected onto women because they appear to be more mysterious and body-oriented than men. Both sets of women have responded to that fear and are symbolically expressing that fear with their very bodies. Paradoxically, they objectify their own bodies as proof that they are acceptable subjects—worthy of redemption—in a patriarchal culture. Even as they try to transcend the values and beat the system by *purifying* themselves, they ultimately become victims of a sick system that spells death for those who surrender to its values.

5

A Thinly Veiled Skein: Exploring Troublesome Connections among Incest, Eating Disorders, and Religious Discourse

Paternalistic theology that instills the need for female redemption and promises it via an external rescuer has failed survivors of incest. Yet such a faith still lingers in the language of the survivors. Discern through the following case studies how frequently these survivors reveal psychological and social conflicts, born from their incest trauma, in their religious discourse. A survivor's relationship to her body and to food reveals an abusive past not mitigated by her faith. Religious discourse both shapes and is shaped by her sexually abusive past and at points reflects a double wounding.

Religious language is available to give spiritual meaning to a survivor's post-trauma symptoms. I found the survivors to share a number of religious convictions: the belief that a survivor's suffering has a divine purpose, the notion that praying for reparation will heal her wounded self, a sense of God's silence, a sense that her hunger and food behaviors are symptoms of her evil, the idea that her parent's nature is God's nature, a sense that she is guilty and worthy of blame, and her use of food rituals to find meaning.

I. Shared Religious Themes

God's Will

Long after their liberation, people who have been subjected to coercive control bear the psychological scars of captivity. They suffer not only from classic post-traumatic syndrome but also from profound alterations in their relations with God, with other people, and with themselves.[1]

Many of the survivors initially attempt to make sense of their incest trauma through turning to their religious contexts. Even though only three out of the nine survivors interviewed for this study come from extremely religious homes (where traditions were observed on a daily basis), all went through periods of believing that the abuse was "God's will." To maintain a just omnipotent God, the survivor must blame herself. As W. R. D. Fairbairn has said, "It is better to be a sinner in a world ruled by God than to live in a world ruled by the Devil."[2] In her struggle with her abusive past and painfully compulsive present, Renita saw God as the only possible source of meaning for her life:

I'm more desperate than any normal person, in the sense that I—I really need to believe in God to just—just to kind of make it. If there weren't a God, that would be awful. I mean all this suffering and very hard work has to pay off. If there is a God, then maybe I'm supposed to go through this, then there's some sort of purpose to my life.

When I asked Renita what purpose her life would have without a God, she said, "If there is no God then there's no purpose. I mean if we're all just accidents, then we just come and go, that's all—and my working through the pain of my past has no point. My living today has no point, why bother if there is no reward for all this?" Janine, like Renita, related a desire for a God figure, though she was not able to convince herself that such a figure exists. To hold an omnipotent God would entail holding herself responsible for her past, yet without God life was "painfully empty." In her words, "I ache inside when I think that there's no one out there who cares about me. I mean, why go on if no one's there? I wish I could believe that there was some power that could help me reclaim my own power." Hope depended on help from an outside source for the majority of the survivors I interviewed. Their *horizontal,* human relationships had failed them, so they moved into a *vertical* one. As Stephanie put it, "God's the only one I can trust."

As a feminist working with survivors, I find the practice of seeking the will of an external, omnipotent, masculine God suspect. To the extent that recovery through Twelve-Step programs depends on reliance on a Higher Power, these programs are based on a patriarchal ideology that has no place in female liberation. Twelve-Step groups have been known to save lives. But "surrendering our wills" is at the core of female oppression in patriarchy. Like other feminists in psychology and theology, I believe we need to find an inner will that is both our own voice and part of a collective political movement.

Asking a survivor to search within to find her strength, hope, and courage is asking her to contend with the horrors of memories she has been trying to avoid, to manage through symptoms, or to soothe through her quest for external spiritual meaning. No survivor can empower herself without help from others. Sexual trauma profoundly affects the survivor's human relationships, which can become infused with suspicion and vulnerable to dissolution. Help or friendship may be perceived as counterfeit nurturance, as insincere and unreliable. Trust in people and communities can be impaired and difficult to recover. The survivor's wish for an external redeemer reveals that she has internalized the perpetrator's view of her, and that her religious community does not support her empowerment. Feelings of abandonment fester inside a survivor who has been betrayed not only by the perpetrator of abuse but by her social environment as well. Yet in order to move past destructive patterns, the survivor will need to reach out to others and learn about her rights to physical and emotional respect. She needs support in finding her own voice, her own language; and encouragement to honor her will to survive can help her begin overcoming a wish for paternal rescue.

Prayers for Reparation

At age ten, Janine would pray daily from a devotional book called *My Utmost for His Highest*. She would ask God for "strength to have the discipline to serve only Him." She spoke of writing diaries that were full of prayers that her "selfish nature would be purged . . . so that I could better serve God." She prayed, quoting the New Testament, "He must increase and I must decrease." She "would search in the Bible for psalms and prayers that affirmed celibacy and my wish to eat only vegetables." Her father fought with her over her refusal to eat meat. She told me, "It was a battle that I felt powerful enough to stand up for. I could say no to food but I could not tell my father to leave me alone."

When a father seduces his daughter into sexually earning his favor and the mother does not see such offenses, the survivor realizes that her world offers her no protection. She learns that she will neither be able to get her emotional needs met nor actively participate in life; she must serve the needs of others. All nine of the survivors interviewed had moments when they prayed to God to protect them, to heal their pain, to rescue them from their helpless situation, to guide them in the right way to live so that they would not have to suffer.

Many of these survivors went through periods when they felt something was dreadfully wrong within them as a result of the sexual violation. They pleaded to God not only to protect them, but also to purify them from their essential sinfulness. Stephanie articulates how deeply she feared being tainted by her grandfather's abuse.

I was always extremely ashamed of my body. I had frequent dreams about ugly things growing in my body. I felt my grandfather transmitted his evil inside of me and I lived in terror most of my life waiting for those evil seeds—that evil root—to bear fruit. When I was nine or ten especially, I'd wake up at two or three in the morning and I would open a Bible and—I couldn't understand anything, but I would try to read and would think, if I set the Bible by my bed, it will protect me. And then if I die, they will say the last thing she was did was read the Bible.

Survivors in this study received no reparation until, as adults, they entered socially sensitive counseling. They seemed to know cognitively that the disgrace belonged to their offenders, but their affect, posture, and voice volume revealed a continuing sense of shame and self-blame. Victims of trauma often experience a self-cognition that would be more appropriate to the perpetrator. A culture that blames the victim collaborates with the perpetrator in making it excruciatingly difficult for the survivor of sexual crime to overcome a feeling of sinfulness, unredeemable without the favor of God.

God's Silence

Without the inner picture of caring parents, how can one survive? . . . Every soul-murder victim will be racked by the question "Is there life without father and mother?" [3]

Survivors of chronic childhood trauma face the task of grieving not only for what was lost but also for what was never theirs to lose—the childhood that was stolen from them is irreplaceable. They must mourn the loss of the foundation of basic trust, the belief in a good parent. As they come to recognize that they were not responsible for their fate, they confront the existential despair (a parent and God absence) that they could not face in childhood.[4]

As survivors look to secular culture to aid them in finding meaning, they also find that it is not just their fathers (or just those offending relatives in authority) who experience females as the "touchable class." A female body is both more visible and more humiliating to her simply because the choice to make it visible or sexual is not her own. Hope for being recognized as other than a body is felt by all the survivors interviewed. But most do not "see" the extent to which their God language, the patriarchal culture to which they belong, their incest experience, and their eating problems are interdependent.

Renita recalls times when she would analyze and doubt God's existence:

I start feeling sorry for myself sometimes over having this problem with food and my self-image and then I start overanalyzing everything and then I doubt God—and the meaning of God, and wonder if my life has any meaning really. I think my biggest fear is that there is no God and that we all just die [slight laugh], and then there, you know, I mean we could die today in that case, it doesn't really matter. And that's my legitimate fear, like there is no God—and I wonder about this every day [slight laugh].

Renita is a survivor of multiple molestation by the men in her family. She does not know what it would be like to be out from under a masculinist, minimalizing male gaze. Her plea to God to help her find meaning reveals her core grief born of her incest trauma—which sent the message to her, loud and clear, regarding *her place* of meaning in this society. Kaschak illustrates this point in reference to her suicidal and depressed client Diane. Diane, like my case study Melinda, reported being gang-raped. When the rapists were finished, they laughed at her and said, "I hope you know your place now."[5]

Samantha illustrates the frustration one feels when one prays and nothing changes:

I was wondering where was God when I was being abused? I mean he totally ignored me as a child. Even today, I get the feeling that there is something wrong with me and I am a freak from outer space and all that stuff. A [male] minister at the Twelve-Step meeting once said, "Well, all your Higher Power wants is for you to be happy." And so on and so forth. So, why doesn't my Higher Power *do* something? I don't know, I guess I need more trust.

The temerity of Samantha to ask "Where was God when I was being abused?" is the very courage that she must nurture to move through seeing the trauma as merely a personal injustice. When female/child submission to paternal authority for a sense of protection is exposed as the patriarchal backbone that it is, fewer women will blame themselves for the sexual crimes against them. They will refuse to rely on prayer to change the offender, and will thus be more likely to face the reality of their predicament and speak up for the help they need. They will no longer wait around for their higher power to "do" something.

That Samantha ends up feeling she need only surrender her skepticism to her Higher Power for (usually masculine) him to do his job in empowering her is the core theological point that I find so dangerous. The paternalistic discourse so heavily woven through Christianity and the language of Twelve-Step Anonymous programs is the very discourse that keeps women stuck in cycles of shame, passivity, isolation, and believing that their only real problems are their "addictions" and their "stubborn wills."

For survivors with patriarchally conceived notions of God, especially ones from devout Christian backgrounds, rethinking religious rhetoric and institutions is paramount for overcoming the valorization of female self-abnegation. As survivors question patriarchal notions of God, they move away from giving theological meaning to their abuse experience. They see that such an experience makes sense only in a culture that justifies the sexist allocation of power. For some survivors, to question paternalistic constructions of God and self can provoke feelings of a second abandonment. In facing the truth of their victimized pasts, they have had to leave the enchanted notion of home. In challenging the ways in which their religions of origin and Twelve-Step groups silence them into daughterly obedience to divine will, they confront the possibility of having to leave home—that which is familiar—a second time. As one survivor queried, "How many homes can a person leave?"

A survivor needs ongoing support to deconstruct the governing masculinist worldview that has so gravely encoded itself upon her flesh. Natalie garnered such support by taking a women's studies course.

Because of the breadth of questions she could explore there, she was able not only to ponder the reality of oppression, but also to explore possible ways of dealing with such evil. For a just future, the absence of a patriarchal God seemed to be paramount. In Natalie's words, "After I read Mary Daly, I found myself feeling like how could God allow this to happen to women . . . generation after generation, it keeps happening. Just getting a sense of being overwhelmed with this, and the rage of it, and feeling like if there is a God—that God would either have to be completely powerless, or evil." Natalie eventually dethroned the patriarchal God who does not respond to atrocities against female humanity. She experienced the vacancy that such a dethronement engendered and filled it with her idea of a God who cares about humanity. She made clear that such a God needs allies in the world to bring about social justice.

Imagine the justice that could be brought about if women channeled their dieting rigor—which masks righteous rage—into supporting each other, for instance, in the fight for the passing of the Equal Rights Amendment. Instead of expiating patriarchally imposed shame through their bodies, they could strengthen their bodies, minds, and souls to stand solid with ever expanding political, economic, and psychological weightiness.

Hunger as Indicator of Innate Badness

Those whom satiety drove from paradise, fasting restores.
—Jerome's counsel to a virgin[6]

Like fasting saints of the late Middle Ages, incest survivors experience their bodily sensations—especially hunger—as something that could mushroom out of control. The saints who directed their hunger toward the eucharist did so partly because it was an acceptable object of craving and partly because it was a self-limiting (contained) food.[7] Like contemporary incest survivors with eating disorders, these ascetics felt desperately vulnerable before bodily needs and used food refusal to destroy them. Contemporary dread of female flesh is heard throughout these case studies. It is as if modern survivors can hear through the centuries the internalized religious beliefs held regarding female flesh.

The contemporary survivor's behavior with food reveals her desire to receive that which she felt was missing in her relationship to her parents, to God, and to herself. She both repairs and expresses her damaged self through her food conduct—overeating, binge-purging, chronic appetite policing, or not eating. For Janine, food refusal or eating only selected kinds of food were means of self-repair and purification:

> When I was hungry I felt like I was living right. I even felt better when I would eat only fruits and vegetables, even when hungry. Pretty soon I was able to convince my mind and my body that such feelings of purity were much better than any fattening food. I was on my way to becoming the invulnerable perfection that I really craved. To eat bad foods when hungry would so annihilate my self-esteem that it was never worth the indulgence. If I ever binged it would be on what I called "air foods"—ones that were virtually calorie-less. I believed the kind of food that went into my body had the power to absolve or disgrace me and I would feel these feelings deeply depending on what I had ingested.

What the survivor does with food corresponds to her history of being violated. She *enacts* the violence against her as she binges.[8] What was "put into her" (whether a finger, an object, a penis, or a tongue) in sexual abuse had the power to taint her and make her feel ashamed. The metaphor of food reveals and extends the defiling power that sexual abuse had on her. When she ingests the foods she calls "bad," the degrading memories that she experienced while being abused again emerge. Food refusal, purging, and consumption of only "good" foods regulate these memories' entry into conscious awareness.

Parental Projection as God Image

Sigmund Freud offered important insights into the role of parents in the formation of the representation of God. He posited that God was an "exaltation" of parental images. Too often the notion of God receives little or no attention among mental health professionals. Such an omission means missing an important and relevant piece of information about the survivor's developmental history and her private elaborations (conscious and unconscious) of parental images.[9]

Samantha reacted very strongly to my questions about God. The parental aspects of God seem very clear: "I refuse to use the term God; it's too loaded for me. It's the God of wrath, it's the God of judgment, it's the God of shaming, it's the God of punishment." Samantha told me directly that "as a little kid, my parents were God, always shaming and forever punishing me." She claimed the word "God" was just "too loaded." Instead she used the term *Higher Power*.

Cherise indicated, though unwittingly, that God and Satan were inseparable in her mind from her father. Both her church community and her father left her feeling like "a perpetual sinner." She told me,

My grandmother took me to church and I hated it. I remember people whom I'd never seen before would be telling me I was a sinner, and that I was bad and that it was because of me that Jesus died. I didn't even know who Jesus was, I thought he was the boy down the street and I wondered out loud, "Was he the one who was hit by a car?" They would respond back, "Heathen! Satan has her!" Nobody explained and this made me more confused because Satan I did know—he was my father. My concept of God mirrored my relationship to my father.

Because one's God-image is thought to be formed in relation to early experiences with one's parents, listening to what a person believes is essential to discerning her world of wishes, fears, hopes, and dreams. Discerning the content of one's God-language and religious imagination can aid helping-professionals to gain a wider vision of a survivor's relationship to her parents and social context. Carol Saussy lends an example of the power and process of parental projections when she writes:

One could assume that a child's early experience of her angry, verbally abusive father resulted in a representation of authority as exacting, threatening, and punishing. The child's felt reactions to authority—that is, to her father—take the form of an unconscious representation of ultimate Authority. To this child, father is ultimate authority. The child internalizes, along with bad, frightening father, a negative self-representation: bad me, worthy of punishment. Her negative father/authority representation is in place and will become her unconscious representation of God/authority.[10]

Experience of parental harm and neglect for the survivor then easily becomes projected onto God (bad object/wished-for object) and acted out in food behavior. The survivor's relationship to food and her body not only reveals a conflict born of the trauma of incest, it also reveals a conflict over who she ultimately is, and why she is here. Her sense of meaninglessness does not represent a vague philosophical angst about being mortal, but evolves out of the specific experience of incest, which teaches the survivor acutely painful lessons about the meaning of her life as a woman. The survivors I interviewed all struggled against the lessons that being objectified had taught them. None wanted to believe that the only way she could find relational meaning was through her ability to please. Each one wrestled with these issues through her body, managing conflicts over the threat of meaninglessness by ritually imbuing food with symbolic content that helped her determine her worth and identity.

At times food served as a good God, a wished-for parent. It comforted when she felt lonely, it soothed when she felt anxious, it nourished when she felt emotionally deprived, it rewarded her for coping with a life that could crush a person. At times food functioned as a guide, praising the survivor when she ate the "right" amount of food and wasn't too greedy or self-focused. Not only the larger culture's message about proper female behavior, but also the controlling voice of the offender may be heard in this God. At other times, the survivor's food behavior revealed a cruel God who teased her with temptation and then berated her for having indulged herself. This God too has the voice of the perpetrator, holding her accountable for all her appetites and punishing her with shame. This despotic voice also proclaimed her doomed to a failed future, an isolated life due to her insatiable appetite, which would surely make her repulsive.

Self-Blame

Maria Goretti's story (which I related in chapter 4) is a recent example of religious emphasis on female value through a female bearing responsibility for what happens to her sexually. Yet holding females responsible for sexual activity is nothing new in religious and secular circles alike. The biblical account of creation blames Eve for the advent of universal sin. Her sexualized disobedience was the cause of humanity's fall from grace, the bringer of lust into the world. The message to any child is simple: "I'm a female just like Eve, therefore I too bring about lust." [11]

As a child, and even now, Renita wonders whether her perpetrators, who accused her of being seductive, were right. In her words:

I did feel responsible for what had happened. . . . I start feeling like, "Well maybe they were right. Maybe I shouldn't have tried to look good, or—wear, you know, fashionable clothes." I was always defiant as a child. Like if they said, "Don't wear something that showed my arms or stomach," I'd wear it. So I'd feel like, well if I hadn't done that . . . if I had covered up my body—it wouldn't have happened . . . maybe if I were fat and unattractive, you know, nobody would touch me.

Traditionally, Christian doctrine focuses on overcoming the appetites of body, the sexual act in general, and the female body in particular as the origin of the worst sin. For females raised in the Roman Catholic tradition, as were Renita and Janine (two of the three anorexics in this study), the focus on asexuality, via adoration of the Virgin Mary, begins early.

Focusing on the Virgin Mary as a spiritual figure can be a way a child finds imaginative sexual refuge—for Mary was considered to be the pinnacle of asexuality. Identifying with Mary as an icon can help the child-victim dissociate from her sexuality. Although neither Renita nor Janine explicitly identified with the Virgin Mary, other Catholic women survivors with whom I have worked have identified with "the virgin" as a desire to be impenetrable. But the untenable image of Mary can also work to shame the child who was sexually abused. For no one can be like Mary—a Virgin Mother.

Childhood sexual assault exploits the child by prematurely introducing her to her sexuality. Her body may be involuntarily aroused, and consequently she feels betrayed by and alienated from it. She incorporates these feelings into her developing perception of her body. Eventually the survivor has to realize that the crime was not caused by her sexuality or by her body, but that the sexual relationship was the means through which the offender made use of the child for the offender's own satisfaction.

Crave Sense-Experience of Relief

Because the nine survivors suffered from post-traumatic stress symptoms, they all grew to crave sensations that would provide comfort and relief from shame-producing memories, body-image dread, sense of powerlessness, and a sense of future doom. Samantha told me that "not being able to trust a God or a Higher Power" was a direct outcome of being abused. Yet she felt that such an inability to surrender to this God was the source of her problems today. She said, "I resent having to do it all alone."

Theological paternalism is a faulty vehicle of empowerment. Yet no survivor can empower herself without help from others. Sharing our social contexts and "unpacking" the gender-loaded political meanings that work to keep us cycling in a wheel of self-destructiveness is part of how we assist each other, part of how we empower ourselves. When we rely on empowering ourselves in isolation, despair can be the result. When we are desperate we are more likely than not to turn to some individualized method of coping that works to mask as well as manage the enormity of our pain. Note Samantha's pattern of coping:

The only person I could ever trust was myself, the only person who could save me was myself. My caretakers were either abusive or were not saving me, they were not rescuing me. So I could not trust anyone. I think insofar as I could not turn to any sort of benign God for comfort, I had to be able to do something that I could do for myself—you know—I mean, my parents certainly had no clue how to comfort me. So I turned to food. I had to do it; comfort wasn't one of the options in my family.

Samantha used food to rescue herself when God and her parents would not. Food become a vehicle to transcend her experience of feeling emotionally desolate. Surrendering to a Higher Power is not the solution. Rather, breaking out of isolation with affirming and conscious others is paramount for survivors, like Samantha, who tend to isolate. It seems that dependence on a paternal rescue and isolating and seeking self-soothing rituals in private are two sides to the same culturally gendered "coin."

Food consumption or its refusal can indeed work to displace the anxiety and depression one develops as a result of the trauma of sexual abuse. Self-psychologists Richard Ulman and Doris Brothers define *addictive trigger mechanisms* as "specific substances, behaviors, or persons (e.g., alcohol, drugs, food, sexual partner, or gambling) that are used on a habitual and compulsive basis to arouse archaic narcissistic fantasies and accompanying moods of narcissistic bliss, which in turn provide desperately needed antianxiety and/or antidepressant relief from dysphoric affect states." [12] Samantha used food (as well as drugs and alcohol) to soothe her in ways her parents were unable to. All nine of these survivors reveal narcissistic deprivation due to parental failure. The intrusions of incest reinforce this deprivation, which led the survivor to seek escape. The most tangible escape route a child can find and experience is food binging, which works to anesthetize her deprivation and isolation. As Cherise sees it, "Food is the only legal drug available to a child."

Food Rituals Symbolic of Spiritual Quest

As previously stated, trauma deeply influences human relationships, which can become imbued with distrust and is vulnerable to dissolution. Assistance or friendship may be perceived as insincere and unreliable. Faith in people and one's community can be hindered and difficult to reclaim. Yet for a survivor to overcome some of her more destructive patterns with food and self-blame, she will need to reach out to safe and supportive others. Most survivors initially resist such self-extension for fear of further shame and abuse. The survivors' ritual behavior with food seems to have symbolized what they did not receive from peers, parents, and organized religious institutions.

All nine of the survivors have developed relationships to food that appear to reveal a spiritual quest and a desire for "right" attachment. They bond with food (an inanimate but readily available object to animate in the imagination) as a result of having no one else whom they could trust. What they do or do not do with food is supposed to produce positive feelings of being loved, good, disciplined, valued, comforted, or protected. Their food behavior can also arouse negative feelings for the survivor, such as feelings of being bad, voracious, monstrous, disgusting, repulsive, destined for failure, greedy, and lazy. In either case, food, unlike those closest to her, was an object she could trust and be effected by—it was in her control. She, and her culture, imbued it with meaning.

In all the survivors' case studies it is clear to me that religious meaning or issues of *ultimate concern*[13] are expressed in each survivor's behavior with food: "The anxiety of meaninglessness is anxiety about the loss of an ultimate concern, of a meaning which gives meaning to all meanings. This anxiety is aroused by the loss of a spiritual center, of an answer, however symbolic and indirect, to the question of the meaning of existence."[14] A survivor's relationship to food and her body not only reveals the conflict born of the trauma of incest, it also reveals an existential conflict over her identity—who she is ultimately—why she is here.

For the female survivor who has an eating disorder this identity conflict is intensified. She sees in her eating behavior (like her perpetrator) the power that she cannot master. If she had any pleasurable feelings[15] during the sexual abuse, she interprets this as ambivalence over whether or not the perpetrator was truly in the wrong—which usually is the perpetrator's intention. The food behavior, like her abuse history, is rigorously protected from public view. She guards against it, or finds some way to expunge it from her awareness. To the survivor, this binging behavior evokes and simultaneously numbs her shame. As she diets or purges she seeks to atone for her felt character flaws. Her project of self-redemption becomes a vicious cycle.

Self-destructive religious language, like an eating disorder, can be found among people other than survivors, but for the survivor, I feel these unspeakable concerns are shouted through her body and through her food behavior. As a survivor quests for spiritual meaning in self-help gatherings to aid her in overcoming her eating disorder, she seems to be searching for a faith that will offer her what she is no longer receiving from her eating behavior—an escape from the traumatic and emotionally vacant past and a place to repair and nurture a sense of power, meaning, and value in her present.

II. Alternative Coping Techniques

Nugget Experience

Victims of incest who survive and overcome the pain and neglect of their past often develop techniques to maintain an authentic sense of self. Psychologist Donna LaMar has called such people *transcenders*.[16] They succeed by affirming themselves, by distancing themselves from their families, and by drawing closer to others. "Transcenders as children, learn to nurture and protect themselves on very little. . . . They take in, absorb, and savor tidbits of offerings. These offerings are used for growth over many years."

All of the survivors in this study have come to rely on food to help them *transcend* their unbearable realities. They have narrowed their focus to the fantasy, "I'll be okay as long as I eat only certain foods" (for the anorexic), or "As long as I have something sweet I can tolerate almost anything" (for the binger). Food and food rituals become a very small life-preserver that the survivor holds onto even long after the perpetrator is gone. There is a sense that trauma or death lurks nearby and she must always be prepared.

Some of the survivors interviewed for this study have had a *nugget* experience that they can recall. Such memories may help them transcend their abusive pasts and find connections, besides food, in their future. Observe the responses to the following interview question:

What or who facilitated your survival?

Cherise told me that "out of all that abuse and all of that pain, there still were some nuggets of gold that I've been able to pull on, and to hold onto now. I found those nuggets of gold in teachers and in books. I didn't find it in my faith community." Cherise spoke of precious memories of going to art museums with her mother before she died. As she reflected on her mother's life she said, "My mother, my mother, my mother, I mean, as a woman today I can look back at my mother and say, 'My God, what she must have endured to protect us.' Until she took her own life, I really believe in my heart that my mother did everything she could to keep him from us." She also told me, "My grandmother loved me fiercely."

Books were significant for Janine as well. She spoke of a neighbor couple (therapists) who moved into the house next door to her family's when she was a teenager. She reported:

I would go over to her house and visit and she would recommend books to me and got me involved in a peer-counseling support group. She didn't know about the abuse but she could see I was depressed and for the first time in my life I felt someone could see through me to the half that was not visible. I felt a first sense of connection to someone. Because she and her husband were Christians, I joined their church and the youth group that they led. If I didn't have them as surrogate parents, I don't think—I don't think I would be here. I'm still friends with that woman today.

Melinda comforted herself with music and had a nighttime "secret ritual" that she used to console her until she could fall asleep. D. W. Winnicott would call such a ritual—with an inanimate object—a *transitional object* that works to soothe children as they cope with parental separation anxiety.[17] Melinda's abandonment concerns were quite real at a very early age. In her words,

As a four-year-old, I had this secret ritual of listening to classical music in my bed at night. I would turn up the radio just loud enough for me to hear the music and then I would turn it down and guess who the composer was before the announcer gave the information. Even at age four I would do this and more often than not I would be right. If I didn't have music I don't know what I would have done; music was my reason for living.

Alice Miller claims a key aid for a child-victim's survival is a sense that there is a "helping witness"[18] who does not feel responsible for raising the child and who is not camouflaging cruelty as love because the witness *has* experienced love in his or her own childhood. Such a helping witness usually is someone who knows that the child is special, even remarkable, and can mirror even a modicum of the child's specialness back to her.

Memory of Resistance

Not all of the survivors could remember resisting their sexual and physical violations. Most often the child-victim would freeze off her feelings or envision herself escaping from the abusive event. For example, Melinda remembers using her imagination to escape into a two-foot by two-foot cardboard manger scene that her grandmother gave her. In our second interview Melinda showed me her grandmother's gift and said as she pointed to the display: "I was safe there. Sometimes I'd be Mary, sometimes I'd be baby Jesus. Sometimes the Star of Bethlehem." Melinda's real mother was very sick most of the time and offered very little in the way of protection or nurture to Melinda as a result. Melinda did hold on to a few memories of the times she did see her mother show compassion. "My mom cared for her garden, for the neighbors' plants and their goldfish. Around the house she was numb most of the time." Melinda, who was brutally raped by her father, brother, and his friends, used her creative imagination to build upon positive scenes with her mother and grandmother. Imagination is a vehicle to resist psychological violence. Imaginal musings are all most children can summon when victimized, and not all can muster scenes of compassion. For the few survivors who could remember a time of physically resisting the violence against them, such a memory helped them to recover their integrity in ways that were not as accessible to those who felt too paralyzed to resist. Note the cases of resistance in Janine and Cherise.

Cherise informed me that her father died of alcoholism when she was sixteen. But when she was twelve she recalled the last time her father tried to rape her. By that time she was five foot nine inches and weighed 275. She resisted her father's violence against her by taking on the persona of a "prisoner of war." In her words:

I remember my father coming into my room. My room was always like a fortress. I was always in a state of siege, and all—I—I had the mentality of—of someone in war. I mean I was always [snaps fingers] on alert. I mean I would sleep in my clothes, I would sleep with a hammer under my pillow, I would sleep with knives and food under my bed. I would booby-trap my room—I even had a rock under my sink where I would keep the knives sharp. It's very clear to me that the menace, the terror, was not from outside. When I was 12 my father came in my room, and I very calmly just stood up, and I walked past him, and I went in the kitchen, and I got my rock out, and I took my 12-inch butcher knife, and I started sharpening it. I was very calm. He followed me to the kitchen and I just looked at the knife and said, "Today is the last day you will touch me," and I said, "You come near me, and I will cut your fuckin' throat."

Janine also remembers a time when she was willing to kill if it meant saving herself. She was ten years old the summer her father held her on his shoulders in what he termed "a fun pool game." She told me that he held her legs around him tightly and proceeded to walk to the deepest end of the pool. When she could no longer hold her breath, she tried to wriggle free from this "game." In her words, "I needed air but he held me even tighter and refused to let me go." Janine believed her father was getting a thrill from her fear and powerlessness—"like he had so many times before." She goes on to describe the vivid images that went through her imagination:

I saw myself kicking free and possibly killing this man—my father—in the process. The image frightened me but I nevertheless kicked with all my might. I thrashed about, kicking and beating on him until I was free. That memory gives me courage to this day that I will not be held down by anybody. That next summer, though, he bought me a string bikini—that's when his sadism went seductive.

Once in a situation of danger, most adult women have little experience in mobilizing an effective defense. Traditional socialization virtually ensures that women will be poorly prepared for danger, surprised by attack, and ill-equipped to protect themselves.[19] It is rare for child-victims to feel empowered enough to resist their perpetrators; for those who do, or even attempt to do so, the psychological benefits are enormous. If arming children is the only way to protect them from violence against them in their families, then we are in a serious crisis of values. We are in a serious crisis of pseudo-family values. Laws that do exist must be upheld.[20] Others must be created and used to bring about justice for the victims. Preventive education is necessary but social policy must not leave women economically dependent on men for shelter. Religious and ethical stands must be taken in opposition to violence against children, women, as well as the Earth and all beings. The reality of outrageous sexual crimes against women and children must be articulated and stopped.

Seeking Justice

Survivors of every age and every culture come to a point in their testimony where all questions are reduced to one, spoken more in bewilderment than in outrage: Why? The answer is beyond human understanding.[21]

The arbitrary, random quality of a survivor's fate defies the basic human faith in a just or even predictable world order. In order to develop a full understanding of the trauma story, the survivor must examine the moral questions of guilt and responsibility and reconstruct a system of belief that makes sense of her undeserved suffering. She then must decide what action to take.

Survivors who become politically involved with others in preventing violence in the home often find such involvement extremely empowering.[22] Others find that working with domestic and sexual violence is "too close to home." Such survivors may find other ways to actively engage in making the world a safer place. Those who do become politically active often feel that their chronic despair lessens.[23]

Having identified the patriarchal order, especially as it operates within families, is not enough. Real insight implies commitment to changing the destructive situation, and the implications of this are not comfortable. For the person who has learned to *see* the reality of living in a sexist culture, nothing can ever be the same again. In Daly's words,

[T]here is hope involved in the insight into sexism. This hope has its basis in the fact that those who are oppressed live in a dialectical relationship with the privileged group. The status of the latter requires the consent of the former to the oppressive situation. Recognition of this is redemptive and revelatory knowledge, pointing the way to "salvation" from the dehumanizing situation. The beginning of an adequate response is a will to integrate and transform the heretofore divided self.[24]

Women must be careful to check out their methods of repairing their divided selves born of social, familial, and religious double-binds. They need to ask themselves, "Is this relationship truly empowering? Do I feel I can have all my power here without penalty or guilt, or is this dynamic like the one I knew as a child?—one where I have to play a role and stuff my experience (opinions, needs, desires, and limits) to get along."

Role of "Right-Relation"

Audre Lorde writes: "When I speak of the erotic, then, I speak of it as an assertion of the lifeforce of women; of that creative energy empowered, the knowledge and use of which we are now reclaiming in our language, our history, our dancing, our loving, our work, our lives."[25] It would be a mistake to think one could heal one's "divided self" in one act—for truly healing insight involves a will to change that which externalizes itself in continually unfolding action.[26] Such work cannot be done alone, it depends upon some kind of "right-relation." Right-relation describes a norm of relationship based upon love and justice. It is *eros* that moves us to seek union with others; justice requires that this union be shaped by mutuality, safety, trust, choice, responsibility, and respect for bodily integrity.[27] In gender role-bound behavior, seen most clearly in violence against women by men, there is a core *disconnection:* we become cut off from the possibility of mutuality and joy. This disconnection deeply affects our self-conception. For the self is literally constituted in, by, and through relation.[28]

The role of reaching out to others and building "right relationships" has been the singularly most politically, spiritually, and physically empowering move that all nine of these survivors have made. When I asked Renita what interrupts her self-abusive thoughts or impulses to binge, she told me, "When I get desperate and needy, and I can't ground myself, the only thing that can pull me out of the spiraling down is a phone call or maybe seeing one of my roommates at home." Renita spoke of feeling as if she were in a trance of sadness. She claimed, "The only way out is by going to a meeting and then seeing someone I know there or meeting someone or hearing something I need to hear there. I really can't say that I have consciously gotten myself out of it. It's more like someone has broken my isolation trance, and [snaps fingers] snap, I feel significantly more hopeful."

Natalie responded to the same question by telling me she has been most helped by Twelve-Step groups "because of the peer support." She went on to say:

I have grown to feel a spiritual connection to these people in ways that I've not known in my past—not that I never had connections with friends in my past— it's just that to be able to really trust people without the real danger of merging and me losing myself or becoming abusive or manipulative in some way that didn't happen on a consistent basis with people until I started coming to groups for adults from dysfunctional families.

The role of mutually empathic relations appears to be a powerful vehicle to healing for survivors who are able to reach out to others. A few of the survivors, like Margery and Samantha, appear to be too steeped in shame—still under the weight of the perpetrator and the larger culture's blame—to reach out for group support. Survivors making "right-relational" connections alongside micro- and macro-political connections to their abuse and self-abuse histories seem to me to be the real "food" that most of them crave and by which they could be sustained.

Women who begin recovering from the incest trauma of their history do so when they call the patriarchal God of their oppressor by name and in doing so realize on which side this God stands. Then they can learn to let this God go.

Courage to See

Letting go of a patriarchal God demands courage. Existential courage, as a dynamic, has two sides: the courage to be as *a self* and the courage to be as *a part*.[29] This idea truly applies to survivors of incest, for it will take courage for them to find and firmly be themselves, and it will take participating in a supportive community to excavate a sense of agency. She will need support to be courageous and will need to be brave to reach out for support. Such efforts are extremely difficult for survivors, so steeped in years, layers of shame. But in my experience, it is the beginning of a survivor's "self" excavation. Such work will entail disentangling the mass of social constructions that already define her. Daly discusses radical courage as the *courage to see,* to no longer be eye-less/I-less.[30] This courage is expressed by those who dare to defy their patriarchal context by naming their experience and expressing opinions that threaten the dominant order. Both the *courage to see* and the *courage to be* are necessary to a survivor's empowerment process.

Many of the survivors' mothers were eye-less/I-less and thus not able to see the atrocities occurring in the home nor to offer their daughters a sense of self-respect that may have enabled them to report the abuse. These women were often the patriarchal female ideal: submissive, docile, obedient, selfless, as well as male idolizing. These women obeyed the cultural ideal to remain eye/I-less; they were supranormal mothers in a patriarchal culture. Without role models with the courage to see, it is a wonder that these survivors were able to develop sharp and courageous sight. Throughout the interview process I consistently witnessed ever-increasing courage in all nine of the survivors. The ones who sought contexts of support, I believe, were better able to strengthen their sense of eye/I-sight.

The importance of nurturing this *courage to be* as well as this *courage to see* is paramount for lasting survival. In failing to advocate such decisive action, traditional Christian discourse grossly failed these survivors of incest: believing that God might have a plan regarding their abuse did not empower them. Holding on to the notion that God would respond to their prayers and make their offenders change did not help them. Believing that their behavior—being "good," that is, self-sacrificing—might "turn God around" and give them the love they craved did not work.

What did seem to facilitate some of the survivors healing processes were their memories of resistance, their sense that someone loved them, their memory of at least one positive experience, relation, or ritual, their experience of becoming involved in justice-seeking, and their gaining support as they discovered both the *courage to be* and the *courage to see.*

6

Self-Help or Self-Harm? Analyzing the "Politics" of Twelve-Step Groups for Recovery

My relationship with my Higher Power is based on what I used to look for in men.

—Renita

All of the women I interviewed for this project were involved with Twelve-Step spirituality groups at one time. Such groups are based on the program of Alcoholics Anonymous (see Appendix D). Seven of the nine are still involved in some form of Twelve-Step spirituality group. A core element in a Twelve-Step approach to "recovery" is the notion of *surrender*. To heal from your addictions, and the pain of your past, you must "surrender your will to God as you understand Him." Serenity as well as *sanity* are promised to all those who surrender to this external (nearly always understood as male) God or Higher Power.

Theological paternalism is a theology that ultimately fails survivors of incest and compounds their setbacks, especially those who suffer from decidedly female compulsions—food, weight, and body preoccupations. For such theology repeats the paradigm of an abusive past. In the survivor's history the redeemer and the perpetrator are one; both invite the survivor to surrender her will for healing and to have value.

A Community of Peers

The core experiences of psychological trauma are disempowerment and disconnection from others. Recovery, therefore, is based upon the empowerment of the survivor and the creation of new connections.[1]

Psychotherapeutic counsel has significantly helped all nine of the survivors interviewed for this study come to terms with their traumatic pasts. However, all see their present task as one of creating a functional future with the help of peer support. Such a self-validating future can take place only within the context of relationships—not in isolation. It is only through relationships that the survivor can rebuild the bases of human connection, such as trust, autonomy, identity, and intimacy which were destroyed by the abuse.[2]

Self-help groups modeled on Alcoholics Anonymous offer a place for a survivor to find helpful connections. Though not all of the survivors I interviewed found Twelve-Step groups to be liberating, the majority of those who do believe that it is possible to "take with them only what is helpful and to discard the rest." They are unaware of the multiple social constructions that are upheld in such groups.[3] Such constructions cannot help but psychologically and socially influence a survivor's burgeoning identity.

The "addiction" anonymous groups do not focus on in-depth exploration of the incest trauma itself, nor do they analyze the underlying dynamics of eating disorders—a therapy group for incest survivors or a therapist who specializes in sexual trauma and eating disorders are the places a survivor (who can afford to) turns to engage in such work.[4] The anonymous groups do, however, offer a cognitive framework for understanding symptoms that may be secondary complications of the trauma, such as substance abuse, eating disorders, and other self-destructive behaviors. They also offer a set of moral guidelines for personally assisting survivors and for restoring their connections with others, instructions known generically as the "Twelve Steps" (see Appendix C).

What's Going On?

A psychological dynamic of the Twelve-Step program seems to be a kind of *theological transference*. In psychoanalysis, *transference* refers to the therapeutically invaluable tendency of the patient to see the therapist as a reincarnation of some important figure in the patient's childhood and thus to reenact this past relationship in the therapist's presence.[5] Survivors who have left their "organized" faith-of-origin, or those who have felt left out of their congregations—chilled by the lack of acceptance there—seem to come to the anonymous programs to experiment with separating both from their family-of-origin as well as from their patriarchal faith-of-old. They experience, in Winnicottian terms, the *transitional sphere*[6] of the supportive, nonhierarchical meeting rooms.

In these meeting rooms survivors come to believe in a power greater than themselves that is of their own understanding (or creation). Through the help of their *Higher Power* (transitional or good object) they are enabled to separate from their past betrayers, both internalized and real. These betrayers are internalized as bad objects, the cruel voices born of abusive relationships from the past. These betrayers are, more often than not, those authority figures who have gravely let the survivors down in both their church and family.

Sociologically, a Twelve-Step group acts, in Van Gennepian terms, as a *liminal sphere.*[7] That is, the survivor is personally not what she was (a victim) and not yet what she hopes to be (an agent in her own life), she is "in between": surviving but without a solid conviction of herself as powerful.

Goals of Rituals for Survivors

Though individual meetings may vary, Twelve-Step rituals usually include the opening of every meeting with the reading of the Twelve Steps and Twelve Traditions, a description of addiction, as well as each member's introduction of himself or herself, for example, "Hi. I'm Jane/John and I am an addict/incest survivor." The group meeting may include a speaker, listening to a tape about addiction, writing about a step, or a discussion of one of the twelve steps. The second half of the meeting allows time for sharing how each person experiences addiction in his or her life and how each is "recovering" today. The meetings end with the request to honor each member's anonymity, and hands are linked while reciting the serenity prayer.[8]

"Change brings with it risk—either in the movement itself, or in the new relationships and possibilities brought about by it. It should not surprise us, then, that socially significant movement is often regulated by ritual."[9] Ritual is a necessary and important form of social and self-communication for people overcoming early sexual and psychological trauma. Changes are aided and sustained by self-affirming and self-expressing rituals. Rituals, or purposeful actions whose intent is healing transformation, are a significant part of Twelve-Step meetings. They work to reshape and reaffirm each member's personal and collective identity. The ritualizing community promises to help persons troubled by "addictive" behavior move from being victims of their past to becoming survivors in their present.

For an eating-disordered survivor of incest in particular, the Twelve-Step group Overeater's Anonymous enables her to make the move from being soothed through narrow and isolating behaviors with food and food rituals to being soothed and supported by relying on her "Higher Power" and the community of peers. Too, where she uses food to assuage her guilt (the concomitant effects of self-blame/social shame), she is offered in exchange the fourth and fifth steps to give her vehicles to speak the truth of her past and confess any harm she may have done to others as a result of being victimized. The group and her faith in a Higher Power are offered as identity-shaping forces in exchange for her dependence on the magical and atoning powers of food.

How Rituals Work

Twelve-Step groups can be ritualizing communities. Ritual theorist Arnold Van Gennep has outlined ritual processes that accompany "life crises" in the following stages:

1. Separation (pre-liminal);
2. transition (liminal); and
3. incorporation (post-liminal).

A *spatial passage* across a threshold symbolizes social passage through life crises.[10]

The woman who has been sexually invaded and narcissistically wounded as a child is, in a way, making spatial transitions by disengaging from present and past abusive settings and abusive person(s). As the woman becomes conscious of the dynamic by which she was trained (through the incest experience) to respond passively to another's exploitation of her, she may work also to separate from her internalized accusers. By becoming conscious of the messages she was given by both her perpetrators and her culture regarding how females should respond to males (or others) in authority, she makes a necessary separation from a victimizable role.

By participating in safe constellations of relationships, many survivors begin experiencing support from others like themselves. The Twelve-Step member simultaneously makes a *social passage* through life crises into what can be a first stable relationship with self and others. Both her habits with food (eating and/or not eating) and her involvement in anonymous programs have ritual qualities. But the anonymous program has the potential of helping her connect with a community—it offers possibilities to repair narcissistic wounds (needs for mirroring, touching, echoing, affirming, listening, trust building) in relation to others—something no food or drug could ever offer her.

I have adapted Van Gennep's rites of passage to fit the ideal context of the Twelve-Step spiritual support group. To be a member of a Twelve-Step group, one need only *want to separate* from past abusive patterns of behavior and relationships. This begins the *transition process,* giving one time to reassess goals and needs in the company of others who share a similar quest. Finally, the group *incorporates* the individual into a way of forming "healthier" relationships. These three definitions are not "states" but demarcations of movement over the course of one's participation in a ritualizing community.

Designated passages mark important points in a survivor's transition. First, she separates from a past identity as a victim of abuse (pre-liminal). With this move, former socializations, introjections, and community loyalties are examined and, quite likely, brought into question. Second, during the period of liminality, "a period of betwixt and between,"[11] the survivor is neither comfortable with her old values nor has replaced them with new ones.

The survivor is no longer unconsciously in a destructive relationship with food or with violating others and is not yet a person consciously coping on her own (liminal stage). The final phase may be a time of reaggregation during which the Twelve-Step member reestablishes a new "assumptive world"—a new belief and value framework that creatively challenge aspects of old values, while locating new ones that have been more freely chosen.[12] The adult survivor then prepares to incorporate herself into a valuable self-image that will better deal with the world outside the group's "practice setting" (post-liminal).

Unlike Joseph Campbell's monomythic hero cycle (separation, initiation, and return),[13] in the survivor's cycle she does not return to the same setting as a changed "heroine." The survivor in recovery more often will choose to move into finding relationships and settings that reflect her internal change. Self-value and bodily respect (not self-sacrifice or abuse) are the survivor's guides. Such internal (Higher Power/Self) and external guides (the group and its steps) may lead her to seek and sustain relationships that reflect a more empowered model.[14] As ritualists cross the threshold, they temporarily exit from the status system and find themselves in immediate, nonhierarchical contact with their *compadres*. A prime quality of liminality is an I-thou ethos which Turner calls "communitas."[15] In this liminal moment distinctions of wealth and class are suspended in favor of equality and homogeneity.[16]

For Turner, *communitas* represent those who exile themselves and call into question the whole of normative order.[17] They are volunteers who "pull out" of the status quo to reach meaningful planes of existence and follow "higher callings"—mystic life-styles, counterculture groups, or socialist bastions. Incest survivors seeking healing through Twelve-Step spirituality groups may fit this definition of *communitas* insofar as they refuse to remain ashamed and silent regarding the abuse they have experienced in their family of origin. In many ways, the woman who rejects violence against herself and names this violence is not only a survivor but a revolutionary against hierarchically gendered family systems and sexually abusive family secrets. By their resistance to violence and their newly found solidarity with other resisters, they invite all who will listen to rethink traditional "familial" arrangements.

Communitas—like Twelve-Step groups—have a unifying element that works to make the group cohesive. All members have been "wounded," in one way or another and feel there is nowhere else to turn for help. In Turnerian perspective, the Twelve-Step group models *communitas,* in that "their rituals involve [sharing] cooperatively," and "secular distinctions of rank, office and status are temporarily in abeyance or regarded as irrelevant."[18] In a Twelve-Step group, each member speaks on a "feeling" level—status, position, or title remains anonymous. "It is in liminality that communitas emerges . . . if not as a spontaneous expression of sociability, at least in a cultural and normative form—stressing equality and comradeship as norms."[19]

In North America, whose citizens are relationally hungry and lacking in meaningful ritual, it is not surprising that so many people find comfort in Twelve-Step meetings. The groups provide a predictable format where people can attempt to be relatively honest and open about who they are and from where they have come. This may explain in part why so many people stay in groups for so long. There are few other places for them to find authentic interaction and support.

How Twelve-Step Groups Help

A Place to Share Feelings

The white fathers told us, "I think therefore I am," and the Black mother within each of us—the poet—whispers in our dreams, "I feel, therefore I can be free." [20]

Twelve-Step groups have helped survivors by offering them a financially cost-free environment where they can gather and receive psychosocial support. For many survivors of incest who attend anonymous meetings, such an environment also facilitates their breaking the silence of their incest history. A slogan of the groups is "To heal you must feel." The groups offer the survivor a place to share feelings that were not safe to express in her family-of-origin. For most of the women interviewed for this study, a multiplicity of feelings was bottled up for years and consequently manifested in a somatization—the survivor's self-destructive relationship to her body and to food.

Emotional venting is only a small part of what the Twelve-Step program offers. The focus in meetings remains largely on learning from a common source of instructions (the Twelve Steps and Twelve-Step literature). Sharing day-to-day experiences in such groups reduces shame and isolation, fosters practical problem-solving, and instills a sense of possibility for a more functional future. Through the sponsor program, the survivor is able to connect with like-experienced others who promise to support her in maintaining her "sobriety" (nondestructive behavior with food or other symptomatic habit).

Through listening and connecting her own story to the stories of "recovery" told by other survivors who struggle with food problems, she gives language to these experiences. In such a group a survivor may be inspired to break the destructive coping habits fueled by isolation. In some anonymous groups specifically for survivors of incest (Incest Survivors Anonymous [ISA] or Survivors of Incest Anonymous [SIA]), members are permitted to share their sexually traumatic history, their relationship to a present habit/addiction(s) that they use to avoid the pain of their past, as well as to safely rage against their offenders. ISA/SIA groups reframe the Twelve Steps of Alcoholics Anonymous by saying, "We admit we are powerless over our pasts," thereby giving themselves frequent reminders that they were not responsible for the sexual violence against them. Unfortunately, this language does nothing to equip survivors to resist future violence against them.

Anonymous programs are places where many survivors seeking spiritual help look to imagine a nonoffending spiritual power that can give them courage, strength to resist further abuse, and hope for "right" relationships.

When I asked the survivors how they were helped by the Twelve-Step program, they gave me the following accounts.

Spiritual Strength

Cherise believes "there's no other way to explain how I survived other than direct intervention from God." She also claimed her "willingness to ask for help has grown as a result of being a member of several Twelve-Step groups." In her words:

I *am* a miracle. . . . My faith is everything. I came into Overeater's Anonymous four and a half years ago, and I have four-and-a-half years of abstinence. I came in weighing over 320 pounds, wearing a 30-and-a-half dress. I've lost about 160 pounds; I wear a size 12 dress. At that time my blood sugar was 280; today it's 80. My blood pressure was 200 over 110; my blood pressure today is 120 over 60. I had arthritis, I had a cane; I walk 2 miles today. I couldn't tie my shoes, I can tie my shoes, I play tennis. All of these miracles have come about because of the Twelve Steps of Overeater's Anonymous that are spiritually based principles.

Janine seemed to find more support from the Feminist Step group to which she belonged. She described what she liked about the group: "Though I still go to OA, I find I like the Feminist Step group better; it's based on a spirituality from within." When I asked Janine about the step that requires turning one's will and life over to the care of God, she told me this: "I'm uncomfortable with the wording in that step. Rather, I try to transform myself—to turn the abusive voice within into an advocate."

Melinda reconstructs the Twelve Steps to resonate with a more creation-centered spirituality.[21] When I asked her what she meant by the word *spirituality,* she said:

Spirituality is a sort of integrated sense of myself, and of all my qualities, good and bad, you know? It's the ability to perceive all of myself with compassion and a sense of connection with all of life actually, you know? And the bottom line is I see sort of like hands holding it, you know, caring hands holding the whole earth. A sense of caring for all that is, whether it's a tree, or whether it's a deer or someone in Brazil or wherever. It's—it's life. And it's that sense of reverence for it and a desire to do whatever one can to protect and cherish it. Whether it's someone else's life or my life, that's what spirituality is to me . . . a sense of dignity or integrity towards the uniqueness of all those lives . . . allowing them to unfold in their own way and in their own time with their own mistakes.

It is clear that these survivors are searching for some power to aid them in finding hope. Whether it is direct intervention from "God," the nurturing quality perceived in compassion for all beings, or an advocate voice within, the desire to find courage to resist despair and further violence against them is paramount for these survivors. Such "liberating ideology" may even be shared. In the case of Melinda, she deeply wants "to find a safe community where I can experience and share the reverence for life that I have known." Janine also claims: "I want to help others find their own 'inner advocate' and I want to participate in groups where people are being self-affirming, actualizing themselves, and letting their true power emerge in ways that are ultimately empowering to many."

Social Skills and Support

For some survivors peer support was never part of their childhood, due to their deep sense of isolation and shame. The Twelve-Step groups seem to be places to practice relating to male and female peers. Samantha says: "I have gained support. Some social skills. The feeling that I'm not alone, you know, other people have these issues. It's a very slow process. You know, trusting. Trust is a real huge issue, trusting people." Samantha, like Cherise, has a sense that the meetings are giving her the safe—nonsexual—opportunities to learn to trust.[22] She told me she prefers the Feminist Step group because "there are things that I can say to females that I can't say to males. I feel more comfortable with women than I do with men."

Renita told me that what she really likes about the Twelve-Step programs are "the phone calls [laugh]." Somewhat nervously she said, "Just knowing that there are other people out there like me. And it's okay. You know, I'm not the only one who sticks her fingers down her throat [laughs]. That's a big one, I think. And then just knowing that, you know, I can talk about something, there's somebody who cares, or somebody who's 'faking it till they're making it.' " For Renita and for many survivors, Twelve-Step groups are more functional than the family they grew up in. Problematic rules of "keeping up the appearances of a happy family" do not apply at the meetings and are in fact exposed as a destructive force that has worked to keep the survivor alienated and ashamed for her anger at familially imposed silence. In these groups she can make connections with other survivors and strategize on how to cope with traumatic experiences (flashbacks, numbing, hypervigilance, mistrust of others) as well as how to deal with basic elements in life and relationships—something many of these survivors were never taught in their families-of-origin.

Exploring Incest and a Wounded Sexuality

Haddock told me the following:

The group that's been the most helpful to me is Sex and Love Addicts Anonymous (SLAA). It's basically a group for grown-up incest survivors. Once you get through the tangible Twelve Steps, you've gotta deal with the intangible. And the reason I'm not saying Survivors of Incest Anonymous is 'cause I've very seldom seen people there who wanted to get well, they just wanted to wallow in it. And that's all AA is, I would say. At SLAA everyone there is looking at their adult dysfunctional sexuality, and how it relates to God. And how it's an outgrowth of the incest. I would say very few people [in SLAA] don't know that they're incest survivors. I'm sure they all are, but 95 percent of them admit it and are working on it.

Ideally, a group facilitates a survivor's constructive survival instincts, resulting in a collective wisdom that is greater than the sum of its parts. It takes everyone beyond where they started. For a group to be effective,

There needs to be a balance of structure, receptivity to change, creativity, and room for individual differences. Groups operate at both a conscious level and an unconscious level, where people's buried or repressed needs operate outside their awareness. It is important to realize the power of group norms. People have been lifted to new heights in groups, and they have been abused and led to violate their own values.[23]

For one lesbian survivor I interviewed in this study, "coming out" in these groups "was not an option." She told me, "The one time I did share that I was a lesbian I had two people come over to me and invite me to lunch so they could help me see what they termed 'my sinful lifestyle.' " There are Twelve-Step groups for lesbian and gay people as well as for bisexuals. But such groups are usually found only in metropolitan areas.

The two women who stated that they felt confused about their sexual identity said they could never explore their sexual ambivalence in meetings. "The heterosexism is in the air in most meetings in my town," said one of the survivors. The group Sex and Love Addicts Anonymous is a spin-off group of regular Twelve-Step meetings. Though the preamble does have a caveat that "renders sexual preference irrelevant," such a message seems to work as a euphemism: "Don't bring your specifically Gay/Bi/Lesbian concerns to this meeting." However, sexual conversations are more often limited to examining that which is pathological about one's sexual appetite. Such groups are not seen as places to explore sexual desire, expression, and identity.

Traditional anonymous groups work toward the goal of making conscious the narrowly personal and pathological. They leave the rest unconscious. That is, influences other than the narrowly defined personal ones remain obscured. Feminist Step groups, now burgeoning all over the country, involve an awareness and understanding of addictions and everyday experiences, as organized according to gender and other culturally salient variables. As sociopolitical meanings are changed and explored in the groups, the invisible is made visible. This is not a simple cognitive experience, but one that is embodied and highly full of feeling. It is consciousness as used by Paulo Freire[24] and certain feminists, the making visible of women externally and internally, in society and to themselves. Such goals should be a major aspect of feminist therapy and of support groups for women in general.

How Twelve-Step Groups Hinder

Individual Disease/Individual Cure

There is no doubt that Twelve-Step programs have helped people get through a lot of days. But they do nothing to decipher or change the larger context in which time passes, especially in a "Just Say No" culture that would like to wipe out progressive gains for good.[25]

Such groups fail female survivors of incest (and people outside the dominant power structure) by placing too much emphasis on self-blame and self-responsibility. The Twelve-Step programs' core concept—personal accountability for one's actions—is decidedly acontextual. The responsibility for both addiction and recovery rests squarely on the individual. In particular, according to social theorist Ellen Herman, "The programs' philosophy that addiction is a disease emphasizes the person and problem in isolation from any outside social forces." [26] This may ease some of the guilt that people feel for pain that they and others have experienced, but it can be debilitating to one who may have logical and adaptive reasons to turn to methods of escape. Cherise's case illustrates the damage one can undergo through privileging a disease or sin-redemption model for addictions:

Everything I do is God-centered; I am very theocentric. Everything I do is spiritually based. I have a disease that is self-centered; my disease wants me to stay here all day and think about what I don't have. So I don't have a telephone. Fine! I have a house, I have food, I have friends, I have help, I have my love. I'm in a program that tells me to do a verbal gratitude list. I don't care what you don't have; everybody knows that, you tell them.

The facts that Cherise has been on welfare and is a single mother (as well as a survivor of incest and sole survivor of a suicidal family) are never taken to be sources of her destructive use of food and alcohol; rather, the problem is her "cunning and baffling disease." If Cherise were to emphasize her particular history, she would be considered to be begging for a "pity party" or "rationalizing." [27] Many Twelve-Step members believe that exploring the "whys" of addiction leads to making excuses that will inevitably lead to "picking up"—indulging in their destructive habits. Individual disease language, and the Twelve-Step groups themselves, frequently refer people back to themselves with the message that their "grandiose will" and "old negative ways of thinking and behaving" are the sources of their pain. Consequently, only new, positive approaches, nurtured by the programs themselves, are thought to produce "serenity." As one member said: "The primary focus in Twelve-Step groups must be on the addiction and not on any group's social inequities that the program is not designed to cure." [28] Involvement in social change as part of "recovery" is left unexplored. Forget about instigating a social revolution!

Speakers in most meetings—whether recounting stories of assault, struggles with work, or relationships—rarely mention directly the realities of physical power, economic inequality, homophobia, racial bigotry, or sexual coercion, even in instances where these were clearly being described. When incest is mentioned, unless that is the groups' particular focus (as in Incest Survivors Anonymous or Survivors of Incest Anonymous), and even sometimes when incest is the focus, sociopolitical analysis is not encouraged. Rather, "naming" the particular offender and "letting go" of her personal shame is seen to be the aim of recovery, as if a social focus and personal accountability are mutually exclusive dynamics.

Linking the micropolitics of a survivor's emotional pain and destructive coping habits to the politics of her family-of-origin is not enough. She must also see the connection between her incest history and her consequent survival skills as revealing the macropolitics of a sexually oppressive and violent culture. In my belief, social consciousness-raising is a necessary step for a survivor's empowerment. She will be better able to find "serenity" if she sees that her "sanity" (in Twelve-Step jargon) is not dependent on her atonement, through taking her personal inventory, nor through redemption by God or Higher Power; rather, she is not to surrender her will and self but reclaim her will and self through making these larger connections to her "personal" behavior and history. Such connections may inspire her to feel the righteous rage that may motivate her to take action toward social change. This insight can also deepen her compassion toward her coping history and her process of finding support in the present.

Polly Young-Eisendrath, in her article "Entanglements: Food, Sex, and Aggression in Female Development," discusses what women need to do to overcome the double-binds placed on them in a patriarchal culture. These binds are that whether a woman resists her socialization and asserts her right to be authoritative, or accepts the effects of her culturally displaced authority (onto men and God), she will feel and hear she is wrong. Either she will be too demanding and too dominant, or too helpless, too dependent. There is no way to get it right.[29] "Double-binds drive women to destructive behavior with food. Since there is no way to get right within the binds it is necessary first to reveal them, and then to step outside them. By acknowledging you *can't* get it right, it becomes easier to respect and value the choices you do make."[30] Twelve-Step groups, far from offering women a place to deconstruct the sociocultural and psychological double-binds in which they feel stuck, instead offer false solutions: "If I surrender my will to a Higher Power, I'll be healed from my addiction. If I'm healed, I'll be free."

Distrust of the Demonic Ego

Another central problem with Twelve-Step ideology is its emphasis and distrust of the "willful" ego and the need to surrender one's will to that of one's Higher Power—who ultimately "knows better." The sin-and-redemption theme of Christianity in the Twelve Steps focuses on deflating the ego and does little to activate the will and internal power necessary for self-respect and appropriate self-defense.

The surrender of the ego/self and distrust of personal will are built into the Twelve Steps and are visible throughout the literature. There is an emphasis on "being willing" to take a "fearless moral inventory" of all one's character defects—as if all present suffering with one's addiction (destructive behavior) is about one's own character flaws or burial of those flaws. There is no sense that destructive behavior patterns might be the result of being raped or exploited. The source of one's "addictions" is seen to be one's stubborn will to control one's own life. As I have said before, it is in surrendering one's will that one is promised redemption—freedom from abusive relating. Personal desire is frequently seen at odds with the Higher Power's will. As in many cults and even in much Christian discourse, self-skepticism seems to be the rule rather than the exception.

Problems with food and weight are seen as the result of being permanently and individually diseased, stubborn, and "unteachable," rather than as adaptive reactions to unbearable pasts.[31] The solution to this "disease" is promised to all who sincerely put into practice, "in all their affairs," the Twelve Steps and their principles—it is an individual-based solution.[32] There is no acknowledgment of a social context or lack of a social context that might be part of the problem. Rather, the Twelve Steps, with their focus on personal faults, shortcomings, and surrender, pathologize the survivor and keep her energy directed inward. She is discouraged from making broader connections to social politics in the world around her. Not only is an apolitical meeting politically and psychologically disempowering to a survivor of incest, it can work to narrow her contact with the world around her. In Käsl's words, "While people gain support in meetings and have loving experiences and are encouraged to help other (addicted) people, the basic construct of the program does not provide a path toward a transcendent kind of love embracing all people." [33] An attitude of suspicion is taken toward those people who are not in Twelve-Step recovery programs. They are often referred to as "earthlings." Severing ties with people outside "the program" is seen as part of a sound and sustainable recovery.

Loyalty and Unity

Loyalty to the ideology of the Twelve Steps (rather than expressing conflict) are also built into the "Twelve Traditions." [34] Group unity (rather than personal opinion) and remaining apolitical are required under the guise of remaining focused on one aim: remaining sober (nondestructive with food or a destructive habit). In fact, avoiding public controversy at all costs is one of the most trenchant features of such programs. It is as if the only logical way to preserve internal cohesiveness and prevent groups from being diverted from their purpose by secondary issues is by repressing conflict. Such guidelines not only parallel the rules of most families where abuse goes on, they mirror the discourse and practices of fascistic nations. As these guidelines are rigidly adhered to, they reflect a *loyalist faith* [35] or a stage of development reflective of early adolescence. This is a stage when people shift their loyalty ties from parents and teachers to their peers, which acts as a salve in times of dramatic change (liminality). [36] Belonging and acceptance help build a sense of security, of course, but too often people in Twelve-Step groups (whatever their age) are already stuck in adolescence, due to past abuse. They may really be needing communal help to move into a more self-empowered interdependence. Nurturing their inner authority, expressing a wide range of emotions, tolerating gray areas in their behavior, and learning to connect to their power are all necessary steps that can help a survivor build a center of meaning.

Below, I asked each survivor what she would change about her Twelve-Step group.

Blames the Victim

Cherise sighed nostalgically as she recalled her history of attending Twelve-Step groups. She resisted offering any criticism of the program and called such attempts "the grandiosity of my disease." What Cherise wanted Overeaters Anonymous to be rougher on its members. In her words:

I'm saddened by the lack of recovery in OA, particularly in [my town]. It breaks my heart to hear people say I must be one of the ones who can't be helped by the program due to "unteachability". And the reason that I see that in my four-and-a-half years here in OA, that it doesn't happen, is that we don't use the literature of AA. We baby one another here. I mean addictions to food are a form of suicide and it takes years to recover. What we do to ourselves are degradation rituals, but we do it to ourselves because we've been told by some perpetrator we should.

It is clear, in the case of Cherise, that being "held accountable" for self-destructive behavior has been an important aspect of her recovery. However, the connections she makes from her destructive behavior to her perpetrator needs to be explored further. Cherise's story reveals to me that her "Higher Power" is imbued with qualities of her perpetrator—the image is unsympathetic, policing, and positive that her will is, at base, evil. Too often Twelve-Step groups see comprehending the sociopolitical context of one's history as irrelevant to recovery. Having empathy for a survivor's traumatic past can be dangerous if it "coddles the addict." Such empathy is thought to give the addict fuel to justify "using"—returning to her addictive behavior. This harsh attitude blames the victim and seldom facilitates longer-term empowerment for the survivor.

Diet Mentality Maintained

Abstinence or swearing off certain foods, eating plans, and weighing and measuring food are behavioral coping techniques sometimes suggested for bingers or self-starvers in Overeater's Anonymous. Such plans may aid a survivor in a short-term crisis, but in the longer term such techniques will not facilitate a survivor's move toward freedom from the tyranny of slenderness or the repressed feelings embedded in her body from a sexually abusive past.

Understanding what motivates and sustains an incest survivor's behavior and preoccupation with food, weight, and shape perception is central to moving from symptomizing her gendered and abuse-related stress. A program for addiction recovery is the wrong model for dealing with the reality of incest. Incest is not a disease, habit, or addictive trait—it's a social crime with immense traumatic effects.

Abuse of Power

Renita recalls: "In Alanon [an anonymous group for adult-children or partners of addicted people], I've often had too many leaders who talk too much; I think they've got a lot of anger. I feel like leaders abuse their power." The lack of prescribed ways to voice uneasiness when people are offensive or abusing their authority is intensified in Twelve-Step programs primarily due the subjective messages for handling tensions that arise: "Remember to put principles before personalities," and "Don't take anyone's inventory, focus on your own character defects." Both guidelines encourage people to set aside differences and conflict for the common good of the group.

In Renita's case she is thrown back into a pattern much like her family of origin, in which she must deny problems, avoid talking about them, and keep the anxiety about abuses inside her body. When a group colludes in the denial of a problem, it is tremendously scary for a member (especially if she has a history of being abused) to say out loud what everyone is denying. Much like a cult or fundamentalist religion, Twelve-Step groups encourage loyalty, discourage questioning, and see themselves as above reproach, which leads people to set aside their skepticism or forget to trust their own instincts.[37] Loyalty, self-sacrifice, passive-dependence (on a powerful other), and self-doubt are exactly the opposite traits a survivor of incest needs to nurture. Questioning the status quo and challenging her social "feminine" conditioning are paramount features to a former victim's liberation.

Unsafe Open Policy

Natalie reported feeling uncomfortable with the open-meeting policy: "Sometimes I feel like anybody can come, and so it can be a really scary place to be because people who aren't at all safe can come, 'cause the only requirement is a desire to, you know, desire to stop eating compulsively, a desire to stop drinking or a desire to have healthy relationships. There's no screening at the door." Natalie had experiences "where people just really weren't too safe," and said quietly, "I felt really uncomfortable in the meetings with volatile people in the rooms. I don't know how I would change that though; I mean, I wouldn't want to deny anybody the experience of being able to recover." Such altruism on Natalie's part can be dangerous; the reader may remember that Janine was raped by a fellow Twelve-Stepper from Adult Children of Alcoholics Anonymous meeting.

Because most Twelve-Step groups do not restrict membership or attendance at meetings, the group boundaries may be too flexible for someone who is in the beginning phase of her "recovery" or memory retrieval. The survivors of sexual trauma who are just beginning to remember their history are usually extremely frightened and flooded with intrusive symptoms, such as nightmares and flashbacks. Hearing the details of others' experiences may trigger her own intrusive symptoms to such a degree that she is able neither to listen empathically nor to accept emotional support. Survivors are advised to wait six months to a year before considering joining a group.[38]

Both Natalie and Samantha told me that they were also in closed therapy groups with six to eight other female survivors. Samantha informed me that her therapy group work was initially fairly cognitive and educational. It provided a forum for exchanging information on the traumatic symptoms, and sharing strategies for self-care and self-protection, before it preceded deep-memory retrieval, and later, social-assertiveness strategizing.

I believe the power of having female survivors work together to "hear each other into speech"[39] is the most helpful model for mending her sense of living a divided life. A survivor's trauma is imbedded in her body, and her habit is to rectify such trauma by focusing on purifying and escaping herself through "fixing" her appearance. Both the female body and female appearance are charged with conflict that is best dissected among equals, without the gaze of a male observer. Even a benevolent male therapist is not recommended during the first two years of a survivor's memory retrieval, if she was sexually abused by a male. The politics of empowerment can be hindered in therapeutic arrangements that mirror her traumatic past. Too, having a male therapist—a culturally empowered other—can keep her in a romantic-like arrangement that may not mitigate her fantasies of being rescued/redeemed by a powerful other.

In a Twelve-Step group there is no guarantee that the survivor will be protected against being flooded with overwhelming images and feelings or boundary crossings by other members. Therapist-led or self-selected support groups give a survivor more of a feeling of control regarding her safety. Thus, she is better able to insure that the environment will be consistently safe and one that fosters the development of her strength and coping abilities as well as self-protection.

Though Twelve-Step groups have guidelines against verbal boundary violations ("no cross-talk")[40] there is no protection against physical boundary exploitation. For many survivors, saying "no" to any physical advance by another is not in their repertoire of experiences. Same-sex incest groups exist but many of the Twelve-Step groups are mixed. Because physical boundary violators come in both genders, there are no guarantees regarding safety. The majority of these groups are all-inclusive, "there is no screening at the door"; a survivor must be very wary.[41]

Too Much God-Talk

A key agenda in Twelve-Step recovery groups is that each member "come to believe in a God of their understanding" who "can restore them to sanity." In the following case studies we see that the notion of a God (let alone one with omnipotent diagnostic and psychiatric skills) is problematic for some of the survivors.

Janine claimed she disliked her Twelve-Step group's emphasis on needing a Higher Power "to get out of the mess they're in." She said she felt pressured to believe. Janine understood the need for help but could not consistently "believe in an omnipotent God as a personified being that's external to me that is in control or has a plan for my life." She described her understanding of power as "something neutral." Power could be abused or used to "create fairness."

Trusting God or a Higher Power was also a painful impossibility for Samantha: "The only problem I have is in trusting a Higher Power. *Only!* But I don't know whether I would actually want to change the language or anything. The language is what's hard for me about the Twelve Steps." Perhaps because people feel their own recovery to be fragile, problematizing the traditional discourse is anathema in meetings.

Melinda said she would change the concept of a Higher Power as "something that cannot be personified." She resists the Twelve-Step caveat regarding the unformed nature of God: "Even though they say your God can be 'a God of your understanding however you want to define Him' I have a problem with still referring to it as 'him' or 'her' for that matter. God is not a person—that's too limiting. I even hate the word God, come to think of it . . . it's too limiting too. Even Higher Power is too limiting." Melinda said she preferred the notion of a *higher consciousness:* "I think it's inherent inside people somehow. I can't believe in a male God with a beard in heaven. I've—I've never been able to do that. Even as a child." As a child Melinda saw Jesus as an invisible brother who comforted her. Melinda's real brother, four years older than she, joined his friends in gang-raping her. She went on to say: "I don't feel right about worshipping any person and that's where the Twelve Steps disappoint me most."

Melinda, Janine, and Samantha articulate the problem of the Twelve Steps' double message about God: "Made a decision to turn our wills and our lives over to the care of God as we understood Him." The wording of this step is slippery. One is limited in one's choice if God is to remain a "He." Others may have a completely different concept of a higher power—as female, genderless, or a life energy/spirit. In the case of Janine and Melinda the terms "God" and even "Higher Power" are so problematic as to be useless.

For these three survivors, the notion of passively and mindlessly turning their wills and lives over to the care of God or a Higher Power is tantamount to turning their lives and wills over to the care of male doctors, clergy, husbands, politicians, or other authority figures—it is disastrous. It reinforces obedience to male authorities and sets up further Cinderella complexes in which women are indoctrinated into trusting that men will take care of them, when in fact they more often exploit or control such women.

Paternalism Unchecked

Analysis of the rampant paternalistic messages or the politics of one's God image is rarely, if ever, encouraged in traditional Twelve-Step groups. Women like Renita could benefit from analyzing the psychosocial politics that lay behind their self-image and the image of their Higher Power or God. In her words: "My relationship with my Higher Power is based on what I used to look for in men. My Higher Power is my support, my place where I get validation of what I am. The relationship we have helps me define me every day in terms of how I see myself. It's a more completeness of me. That's where my purpose, I think, comes from." Notice Renita refers to herself as an object, she is a "what" rather than a "who." In her home, she lacked affirming relational *mirrors* to give her purpose and validation and so sought to earn such meaning from men outside of her family—securing their favor through a thin and culturally attractive body; that failing, she sought it through her Higher Power. The social and psychological sources of her search must be explored if she is to deconstruct the multiple layers of her adaptive and destructive patterns with food and relationships.

Consciousness-raising that helps Twelve-Step members understand the classed, raced, and gendered nature of their plight and their struggle might aid them to find power to become politically involved in standing up for their and other women's rights for economic, racial, social, and relational respect. In the groups I have observed since 1985 I have never heard anyone explore the politics behind their God/Higher Power imagery. Or if they did, it was met with sententious responses: "You must have faith," "Just trust H. P. (Higher Power)," or "Remember it's not thy will but God's will." Or as Samantha heard from a Protestant minister who runs several Twelve-Step meetings in the church over which he presides, "All your Higher Power wants is for you to be happy!" In other words, "Don't speak up about your socio-personal discontent."

When Janine spoke at a meeting about never being able to forgive her family for the abuse and abandonment she felt in relation to them, she told me, "A long-time Twelve Stepper spoke after me, claiming 'recovery is about faith not feelings!' "

Self-Blaming

"The last thing women and minorities need to do is hand their wills over to others to control. To do so is at the heart of oppression. Our will is the source of our power for good." [42] Most of us need to expose the anti-power messages that we have received from traditional sin-redemption theology which proposes that we were born sinful and are in need of (external) redemption from our wicked flesh or devious wills. According to Samantha:

I think that the Twelve-Steps have a certain amount of blame. The notion of "taking a fearless personal inventory" and focusing on changing yourself to fix the source of your problems seems a bit harsh to me, especially if you've been victimized and your pain is not about self-pity. Because you are not responsible for your abuse when you are a little child; you can't do anything about it.

What is problematic with the "fearless" moral inventory idea is that it assumes the one with chronic destructive behavior ("an addiction") is morally guilty. This may be applicable for some who attend Twelve-Step programs (e. g., perpetrators of assault, narcissists with grandiose egos), but for marginalized people and particularly for survivors of abuse it is counterproductive.

A moral inventory was a core element of the moral rearmament movement (from the Oxford Group—the parent group of AA), which proposed that leaders and businessmen and those who held open power in government assess the harm that their need for money, status, and control has done to other people. Victims of oppression are rarely in such power positions as to analyze how they have abused their power. Most people, particularly the oppressed, tend to blame themselves for their abuse, and this step often reinforces self-blame.[43]

Recovery also includes reclaiming and enlargening one's inner strength and will, not surrendering it. Most survivors who have survived have not been encouraged to notice the powerful resources within them that have enabled such survival. Self-confidence is seen as a slippery slope to sin (addiction) in much Christian discourse as well as in many Twelve-Step meetings.

What Can the Church Do?

For both Stephanie and Margery, belonging to a Twelve-Step group was not effective support. In Margery's words, "I could never open up in those meetings especially when the group members were always changing." Stephanie claimed, "There is no way my recovery could include powerlessness. Forget it—I've already done powerlessness as a child!" Instead, both women sought female support through friendships in their denominational churches. Natalie seemed to rely on a therapist group and Twelve-Step group for her empowerment but remains a member of a Christian church. I asked the three women the question: What would you like to see change in your church to facilitate healing from sexual abuse? Stephanie answered this way: "I don't have any real hope that the church can do anything. I mean there are some people who preach against violence in the church and that's a little point of light, but it's not gonna have any effect. The church is dead [long pause]." And Margery:

> I would like to see people lift up the issue so it's not a secret anymore, even hear sermons that deal responsibly with the issues. Pastors should know the police, attorneys, Youth and Family Service agencies, shelters, so they can resource women and children. They should also have safe places to offer women and children fleeing abusive settings. The church could be a real resource if pastors made the effort to be informed on the issues. I know a couple of pastors who have done this and though it's a lot of work it is necessary work.

Natalie sees it this way:

> I'd like to see the church liberated from patriarchy. Oh, gosh! Well, it wouldn't even look like the church any more. I'd like to see the church be a place where the abuse that does go on in the world is talked about openly and honestly. And, what else? Just that other people's realities be taken as just as valid, whether they're women, physically disabled, or who are a different color or ethnicity, or you know, where everybody's truths are just as valid [her voice hoarsens here], that it's not just one person's set of ideas or truths that everybody else has to follow. I could go on forever about the church being liberated from patriarchy, but I'm losing my voice.

Pastors and pastoral counselors can be a resource (through referral) to people involved in sexually and physically volatile household climates. They need to immerse themselves and deconstruct the legal aspects, the gender politics, the psychology, as well as the theology of the issues surrounding abuse and its prevention.

Politically Empowering Spirituality

The traditional Christian sin-and-redemption model sees humans as born sinful and in need of salvation—baptism, confession, deflation of self—a politically empowering spirituality sees all beings as born worthy of respect and wholeness. Instead of fearing that our passions and desires will run wild, we can consider them part of a whole, to be enjoyed in balance with responsibility and care. Thus politically empowering spirituality takes us past fear, control, and duality toward integration.

> [Erotic or life-loving spirituality] takes us beyond "recovery narcissism," where people become obsessed with recovery perfection, ridding themselves of charac-

ter defects and shortcomings, and constantly analyzing their behavior. They lose perspective of the external world, the naturalness of imperfection and the wonder and mystery of life. What is needed is a balance between inner understanding and outer connectedness.[44]

The word *spiritual* is such a loaded term in any case—a term so disembodied by Western philosophical and religious thought that it is hard to understand spiritual identity as part of our bodies and our social and emotional lives. Philosophy and religion scholar Tess Tessier uses the term "spiritual" to refer to "our most fundamental identity and connections to ourselves, to others, and to the world, whether or not that identity involves a relationship with some transcendent power." [45]

When a spirituality group underemphasizes the political and psychological reality of the past, it grossly discounts the reality that childhood sexual abuse affects a survivor at her very core of being as well as the deep effect on every relationship she has. They support society's refusal to acknowledge its complicity in facilitating a male-dominated culture (where women's and children's bodies are objects of male entitlement).

A survivor's relationship to food and her body reveals most vividly her sociopolitical and spiritual fragmentation. Spirituality must serve an empowering role by connecting the survivor to her self, to nurturing relationships, to her body, to her memories, as well as enable the integration of her trauma. Such work can then facilitate the important element of reconnecting to a community that offers her faith in her strength and "right" relationships, affirmation of her struggle, and reclamation of power, as well as its participation in the political resistance to further violence against women. A community that only offers a survivor support in "abstinence"—self-restraint—grossly neglects her developing a fuller sense of her power.

Counsel to Counselors

What counselors who work with women survivors of incest or eating problems can learn from Twelve-Step groups is the crucial role that nonshaming and safe peers have in nurturing self-compassion in the survivor. There is a parallel relationship to food abuse and sexual abuse. The degree of self-destructive behavior often parallels the degree to which a female has internalized the cultural and familial messages of her sexual devaluation and objectification. The chronicity of her eating problems often mirrors the chronicity of her sexual objectification in the home and family. The significance of these connections may facilitate new approaches to understanding the social and religious sources of female self-destructive impulses, specifically those found in women who experience a desire to flee from their female flesh through an eating disorder.[46]

Counselors and advocates who work with empowering women survivors of incest and eating problems must not only understand the gendered symptoms of a survivor's suffering—in her depriving stance toward her body—but they must also work *with* the survivor to see behind the disguise of her eating behavior. For a survivor of incest, food is a double-edged tool to block or defend the survivor from being overwhelmed by her painful past and to carve out ways of mattering in her culture—which usually includes self- and bodily-deprivation. The counselor must realize that until the survivor has more functional tools to express her self-power as well as her pain, shame, and anger, she will feel compelled to use that which has enabled her survival thus far—food refusal, compulsive overeating, or binge-purging behaviors. A counselor's role can be to promote the survivor's empowerment through validating her remembering and naming her incest experience.

The first gift a counselor can offer is the most obvious—she or he can ask the question, "Has anyone in your past touched you in ways that made you feel uncomfortable?" If the survivor answers in the affirmative, and indicates incestuous or invasive touch, it is a good idea to take that claim seriously, and work with her, if necessary, to find a counselor who deals specifically with incest. Such a counselor should also be sensitive to the issues of eating disorders, post-traumatic stress, and gender socialization.

A combination of quality one-on-one incest therapy and conscious same-sex feminist support groups may be the context out of which a survivor will be encouraged to *see* social and interpersonal connections. Such work involves not just naming the unnamed but the unnamable, speaking not just the unspoken but the unspeakable, exposing the impossible values that keep women living divided lives and in double-binds. Socially empowering support groups should work to return a survivor to her own vision, and, in this way, she will be able to contribute to a feminist cultural vision. For once a survivor is encouraged to see for herself; nothing ever looks the same.

Theologically, a pastoral counselor who is counseling a Christian survivor has an important role in facilitating her spiritual reparation. The pastoral counselor may feel like a punching bag for the patriarchal mistakes of Christianity; nevertheless, such a counselor can be a powerful balm to the broken-hearted and enraged sufferer of incest. Such a counselor will need to make sure she has a quality network of support and a life-style that is socially and physically nurturing; this work is quite draining and can be a theological challenge to even the most well-balanced "person of faith."

If the pastoral counselor is male, and the survivor was abused by a male, he may want to support the survivor by helping her find a female therapist (preferably feminist) who is conscious of incest therapy and same-sex group work. The survivor should be asked what she would prefer and encouraged to take her time in finding a qualified therapist who feels safe and theologically open-minded.

Imagine hearing what Stephanie told me: "When I was six years old I often told my brother how much I hated Jesus. Once I told him I saw Jesus nailed upside down on the cross by his penis and that he died struggling to free himself. My brother begged me to stop telling him any more about Jesus' death." Working to support survivors as they retrieve memories and express outrageous pain, shame, and rage about their past does indeed require helping professionals who are socially empowered, ones who are supported in processing the trauma of hearing survivor's horrendous histories and painful coping styles.

Space to express her history and a nonjudgmental (empathic) *witness* to her present experiences are the best gifts a pastoral counselor can offer a survivor. An incest survivor must be given the theological room she needs to free herself from her painful experiences not mitigated by her religious upbringing. "A survivor needs to be able to express her negative feelings toward the church, her faith, and God. Counselors of incest survivors must be able to accept this. If they are unable to do this, they must be able to say so and to help the woman arrange for other counseling."[47]

When pastoral counselors are unable to understand the way a woman views God and her religious tradition, and consequently launch into a defense of both, they cannot give the woman the room she needs to let go of those aspects of religion that oppress her.[48] Very often a survivor who feels straightjacketed by the patriarchal doctrine of her history will turn to self-help settings (like Twelve-Step anonymous programs) to gain a kind of critical freedom.

Twelve-Step spiritual recovery programs have saved many survivors from taking their own lives. The fellowship, the spiritual "hope" offered, and the ongoing support groups at no cost have been life-saving for many male and female survivors who seek spiritual community and help from a nontraditional spiritual practice. Ironically, such a program offers theologically little that is different from the patriarchal elements of Western and other religious traditions.

It is a good idea for a survivor who is spiritually inclined to find a politically empowering spirituality group—one that may lead her to an involvement in claiming her political power through activism and consciousness-raising. Political consciousness-raising must be seen as part of any therapeutic approach, especially in later stages of therapy. Initially, the micropolitics of incest and a woman's eating disorder must be ferreted out of the macropolitical situation in which she lives.

The survivors who are waking up—and wiping the sleep out of their eyes—seem to be moving beyond the patriarchal language of male divinity/hierarchy, sin-redemption, and self-blame for social ills. In so doing they seem better able to make connections between their abuse, their religious discourse, and their self-destructive behaviors with food. As connections are made, survivors can begin to move from having their bodies be the locus of their decidedly gendered conflicts. Instead of being motivated by an unconsciously self-destructive relationship to their bodies, as they are helped to claim their sharp I/eye-sight, they move to an increasingly conscious sense of embodiment.

As survivors recognize that they have internalized the patriarchal voices and gaze of the perpetrator and society, they can begin working together to exorcise the social, the specific, and the religiously sanctioned offending messages. Instead of seeing their bodily appetites as their source of shame and evil, they begin to relate to their bodies as a source of power. With their newfound insights they may seek to enable other women to find freedom from dependence on offenders and fantasy males who will rescue them from their socially enculturated shame.[49]

7

Summary of Key Findings

I have come to recognize sexual trauma as a common theme among women who have eating disorders. My results reveal that the particular form of the eating disorder not only expresses the particular conflicts born of the sexual trauma but reveals the religious (cultural) and social context of women's trivialization and objectification (as bodies that exist to arouse the male subject). Most importantly, I found, through examining the literature, that among the general population, sexually traumatized women suffer from eating disorders more often than not.

It is not surprising that "recovery" in a patriarchal context is unlikely to feel stable—such a woman will find little support for reclaiming her power and an affirming relationship to her body; she remains one among the sexually colonized. Survivors are usually complimented for their ability to restrict their food intake, especially if they are "thin." "Fitting in" a size that's too small is the patriarchal key to belonging to which women who do not want to be ostracized must aspire.

Symbolic enactment of the sexual trauma manifests itself in a woman's relationship to food and her sexuality. Although my study did not include analyzing the sexuality of survivors, I explore the gendered, traumatic, and religious meanings a survivor (along with her culture) gives to her appetite and body. How sexual trauma and its psychosocial conflicts manifest themselves in one's sexual expression and experience of one's self are subjects I would like to explore in my future work.

Sexual abuse comes in many varieties: seductive, sadistic, and under the guise of experimentation, education, or "innocent play."[1] I have found that sexual abuse is socially and religiously sanctioned insofar as it is minimalized and "overlooked." This "averting of the eyes" is a gender-specific lesson for all females from an early age. Females in particular (like children in general) are taught not to *see* clearly the violations done to them in the name of male/parental authority and entitlement.

The survivors in this study reported haunting dreams around the time of the onset of trauma memory. Most did not remember having positive dreams until at least two years after the onset of flashbacks—until the worst of the post-traumatic stress symptoms were worked through and they developed functional techniques to manage these troubling memories. Women who remembered some form of resistance to sexual violence and memories of the same were better able to imagine themselves standing up for themselves in the present. This may also point to society's condemnation of those victims who respond in fear by freezing and are thus considered to have *wanted* the abuse.

My findings have helped me understand the psychology of victimization and how vulnerability and shame follow a survivor throughout her lifetime. Her relationship to food reveals a complex social psychology that appears to have religious overlay. Her eating behavior can function as an atoning device through which she purifies herself from guilt and shame that grew out of not resisting, possible bodily reactions that confused her, or degrading and blaming messages sent by her perpetrator and by her culture. Food and eating behavior can also be a two-pronged tool that soothes her as well as helps her keep her focus off her traumatic symptoms of self-hatred, body-dread, flashbacks, distrust, hypervigilance, and fear of death. But ultimately, in using food and a body focus to avoid working through the traumatic memories, she weakens herself, making herself a more likely target of violence and shame. For an escape or a defense through an "addictive" habit locks a survivor into a cycle of shame, isolation, and even more self-blame—both the culture and the perpetrator are let off the hook.

A survivor's impulse to psychologically escape (through an eating disorder) is initially a healthy one, especially as a child. As a child she could not physically leave nor tolerate the reality that there was no one "out there" for her. As she introjects the "sin" of incest, her offenders remain protected. The illusion that they care for her is preserved insofar as she keeps their secret and shame. As she carries the perpetrator's guilt, she lives in a chronic state of needing redemption. Until she has support and help in learning new tools of coping with the real trauma of her past and meaninglessness in her present, she will not be able to let go of her atoning and coping habits with food—be they compulsive overeating, binge-purging, fasting, or, more commonly, chronic dieting. In order for a survivor to reclaim her power she must come to see the dynamics of the incest—to let the crime fall upon the offenders and the offending culture that aids her in seeing her value through her sexual (physical) currency. My belief is that those who know they are innocent (or that their involvement was the product of the psychology of seduction) will probably not manifest "atoning" or escaping symptoms like eating disorders.

The survivors' theological discourse did surprise me. I was expecting to find more identification with Jesus as role-model/martyr. But Jesus Christ was not a key figure in these interviews. What emerged instead was an enchanted and paternalistic theology. As I listened closely I heard some conflict over the women's wish to be rescued and made valuable through an external God or power, but the desire seemed to emerge in almost every case. In Renita's words, "What I look for in God is what I used to look for in men: protection, love, a sense of myself." The incest survivors interviewed for this study differed from the battered women I interviewed several years ago. At that time, I found that Christian women who could not leave batterers more often than not had internalized a "Christlike" self-sacrificial identity. They believed their battering spouse/partner could be redeemed by their love and self-sacrificial behavior. They would often quote Scripture regarding Jesus' model. One woman said, "God has put my husband in my life for a reason. I am leading him to Christ by my example." The cross of Christ was a vehicle through which she justified, even divinized, her own suffering.

Survivors whom I interviewed for this study relayed a different theme to me. They seemed to want to *be* redeemed rather than *to* redeem. There was a greater religious passivity (almost childlike in tone) in their theological discourse. Surrendering their will to a Higher Power seemed to be their key to redemption. Though many felt ambivalent about such a gesture, all seemed to feel it was what would free them from the shame of their past and the tyranny of food and thinness. Waiting for an external power/redeemer seemed to be a core theme. My point is that incest can do that. Sexually violating a child who needs your love, as all children do, by promising her more love if she surrenders her power often is the dynamic of the crime. Incest is a powerful betrayal that affects the child's entire worldview and sense of meaning in relationship and will taint all bonds she will make in her future. The core betrayal follows her throughout her life and will emerge most insidiously in her God language and body suffering. Relationships with humans will always be fraught with distrust and conflict. Dependence on fantasy or fantasy objects will often feel safer. It is as if her vulnerability and hunger for love, soothing, and meaning are better spent waiting for a miracle. Who wants to face working through the grief of the reality that no one was there and no one will ever be able to fill up the cavity at the core of her self?

Too often survivors are fed hollow spiritualities that promise external redemption. When one's spirituality or recovery program includes surrendering one's will to a Higher Power, one repeats the model one knew as a child victim of incest. Such a model is ultimately disempowering.

Surrender, like spirituality, is a slippery term. After all, needing to "let go" is quite human and certainly a key feature in most mystic traditions. Christian mystics and especially female saints have emphasized surrender because of the inadequacy of reason to achieve their aim—oneness with God or Christ. Zen koans and Sufi stories are often deliberately cryptic. They defy rational or intellectual analysis, and that may well be their function: to challenge the mind in ways that force it to abandon its normal habits of thinking.[2] These mystical exercises do enable one to escape the self temporarily—which can be an empowering outlet—to give the rational mind and self-preoccupations a rest. Yet such "rest," when done to avoid emotional memories and pain, can keep one feeling sleepy-eyed regarding the social and psychological context that is benefited by their slumber.

The use of addictive substances or habits is often about a need to surrender. In my study, food, unlike offending parents who are psychologically unavailable, is a right and ready object that one can invest with magical qualities. By orally ingesting the symbolically laden food, one surrenders to whatever has been projected onto it. Drugs and alcohol have a history of religious use as providing vehicles of transcendence from the self. Food behavior—whether fasting or feasting—provides its own mood-altering, religiously laden effects. The need to "let go" or escape is primary, especially for one plagued with grief, anxiety, despair.

But how one "lets go," and who benefits by the "letting go," are important questions to consider.

Finally, I noted a flatness in the theological discourse regarding hope and redemption as it is located in Christian theology and in Twelve-Step groups. This theological vapidity also has its roots in sexual trauma. The child who was betrayed by a caretaker has felt ultimate desertion. This caretaker betrayal feels like a God betrayal; thus, faith will never be easy and will always be shrouded by the dark cloud of those early experiences. Such a betrayal leaves a child in a chronic state of grief. It is a loss of her experience of bodily integrity and ability to trust. This inability to trust affects her future relationships, her connection to her own impulses, and her judgment regarding "trustworthy" others. Such a loss can never be returned to her in a patriarchal culture. Spinning out theologies of hope from abused or violated bodies is not the solution.[3]

Working toward naming not just the unnamed but the unnamable, speaking not just the unspoken but the unspeakable, have been part of moving toward a feminist political spirituality and psychology. Change involves replacing the arrogance and insecurity of the scrutinizing male gaze found in Western religious and secular society with the sharpness of inner vision. Seeing from the reference point of the "I" can be a new vehicle of empowerment for most survivors. Such a vision may enable the survivor to resist future dominance of her flesh by others and by herself. She can start by catching herself in the act of collusion by refusing to turn her aggression inward and refusing to avert her eyes as her culture has taught her to do.

The beginning of overcoming paralysis of power is action. This may mean participation in a discussion group or a consciousness-raising group, standing up to challenge a speaker who has expressed a biased opinion, or writing a letter to an editor, a politician, or even a friend. It may mean working against discrimination in laws, media, organized religion and/or educational institutions. Whatever the action chosen, it can engender a more authentic hope than waiting on transcendent miracles. Channeling aggressive energy outward rather than inward is a radical step that may be part of mending our divided selves. It may also connect us to the world—a move away from self-destructive isolation.

My project of interviewing nine eating-disordered survivors of incest has helped me discover the traumatic effects of incest in relation to faith.

My desire is that this work will help raise the consciousness of scholars of religion and society as well as secular and religious therapeutic helping professionals. I extend an invitation to all who are concerned to consider more closely the traumatic roots of eating problems and the complex meanings given by survivors to their trauma and eating problems as manifested in religious discourse. Taking such enculturated symptoms seriously is paramount.

By making these troublesome connections we realize that "treatment" for survivors with eating disorders must include psychologically empowering theory that takes seriously the sociopolitical role of spirituality in the survivor's journey to herself and to her community. Understanding a politically empowering spirituality can lead us to perceive food problems and self-abusive behavior in a new way—not as masochism, not as a defect or sin, nor even as an addiction/disease, or something to fear, but rather as an imbalance in individuals that signifies a tremendous gendered power imbalance in one's social system at large. Too often "eating disorders" have been approached as individual addictions or diseases to be cured. This acontextual analysis creates a duality and keeps the focus off culture and fixed on the individual. I believe that self and culture cannot be separated in a sound "recovery" model.

We need to go beyond the question of how we control addiction and ask, What is missing in our lives? Where is the sweetness and connectedness that can fill our spirits? What perpetuates the violence, greed, abuse, and prejudice that weaken our links to each other? What in our social system blocks so many people from feeling security and joy in their lives?[4]

As long as women are seen as less than fully human and conditioned as sex objects for fathers, bosses, brothers, and lovers, then women will somatize symptoms that both reveal and resist this dehumanization. They will literally *wear* their conflict in their relationship to their body and food. These secondary symptoms—an obsessive relation to her body, food, and weight—reveal how difficult it is to be embodied female in a patriarchal culture where sexual violence is acceptable. A woman who embodies patriarchal values through an eating disorder reveals a deep desire to be seen and yet to remain unseen, to be safe but not so safe as to sacrifice love, to have meaning at any price, and to be of value no matter what the cost. Being engendered female means overvaluing acceptance by others and knowing that it is through appearance and sexual compliance that one gains such acceptance. If a woman is a survivor of sexual abuse in her family, these empty female lessons are embedded even more deeply into her experience. Her relationship to her body is naturally fraught with conflict because she wants full subjectivity—to be recognized—as much as she wants to experience affection.

If the price for affection is the surrendering of her bodily (soul) integrity, then a body conflict will result. However, this is never a price she can live with. Something deep within each of the nine survivors resisted and still resists her objectification. Resistance for the eating-disordered survivor usually remains individual, silent, and something she only experiences when she feels control over her own body—a false victory. Until such bodily integrity is experienced in her present social context, this bodily hypervigilance will seem necessary to her. Facing this reality requires that we embrace our despair over living in a patriarchally skewed culture. We can no longer embrace a patriarchal theology that promises us an enchanted future if we only surrender our wills to "Him"—or any powerful other.

Resisting Christian misogyny includes exposing the politics behind the burdensome religious rhetoric that portrays women as dangerously appetitive and virtuous only insofar as they are self-depriving. When external salvation achieved through appeasing a magical masculine parental rescuer is recognized as a cultural, albeit seductive, myth, we see that the psychosocial gender arrangements which that myth supports need to be radically altered. Despair underlies the Christian theology of redemption—a despair masked as hope through a miracle man. When one is dependent on a transcendent miracle for "redemption," one is in crisis.

The crisis that incest survivors experience is both personal and cultural. They need support in working through the facts of their history: no one was there to protect them, no one is there to heal their grief and rage, and not even the best therapy or spirituality group can totally repair the emotional, physical, and social damage that they have suffered. There is no grand cure because incest is not a disease, it is a crime that too often has the sanction of cultural myths.[5] Only in the context of supportive and politically conscious advocacy can a survivor begin to accept that recovery is always partial in a patriarchal culture. With support, one can begin to work through the aftermath of trauma, focusing on constructively resisting and preventing abuse. As survivors take small steps toward their own partial wholeness, they often find connections that lead them to work for social change.

One necessary step in effecting broad cultural change is to expose the false theological underpinnings of "thin" myths, the messages our culture circulates about women's bodies. Both individually and socially, acknowledging the realities of our past and present circumstances forms a basis for making practical decisions as to where we want to go. Metahistorical solutions, saviors who love us so much they will die for us, paternal gods (or any powerful others) who promise to protect and heal us if we loyally surrender our wills are all patriarchally engendered false hopes. They may be seductive to those of us who have felt consistently hopeless, but they impede our authentic empowerment.

What Do You Want the Readers to Know?

I end with the survivors' last answers. I asked them, "What would you want people who are ignorant about incest to know?" This is what they said:

NATALIE: I want those who haven't experienced incest to know it's much more common and more devastating than anyone could ever tell you or ever imagine. The best thing that you could do for another person is to believe them.

HADDOCK: I want them to know child incest destroys adult lives. I want them to look for characteristics in children to spot incest early. You know, does the kid torture animals, is she seductive, does she isolate, is she daddy's little princess, are her drawings desperate? I also want people to explore who's abusing all the men who abuse children. I want insurance that would pay for rehabilitation and therapy—it has to stop. And there are even more of us walking wounded abusing themselves and their children. I was lucky to get help. But what about those wounded who don't have the money?

MELINDA: I want them to listen. Listen. Listen to the children. You know, pain isn't created in a vacuum. I want them to stop accusing the victim. To stop victimizing the victim.

CHERISE: I want people to know that sexual abuse may take anywhere from five minutes to three hours, but it lasts a lifetime, it takes its toll. I also want people to begin focusing on the perpetrator, like we've begun focusing on children and adult victims. Perpetrators need help too.

JANINE: I send the message that it's not okay to man-handle children or touch women without their permission in any way. It's never legitimate to sexually molest or abuse a child nor is it ever redeemable—in my mom's words, "Well at least you've drawn nearer to God as a result." It is a life damaging act.

That person who is compelled to do this needs help and should get it or lock themselves in a room and not allow themselves to go near children. Our legal system should mandate ongoing treatment for perpetrators because they're never cured. The damage they inflict takes a lifetime to undo—scratch that—there is no ultimate recovery from it. It wreaks havoc on one's spirituality, one's mentality, and one's capacity for connection. It needs to be stopped yesterday.

STEPHANIE: Don't trust anyone. Wait a minute, that's my pathology. I just want kids to know that sexual abuse happens. It happens a lot, it happens everywhere, it is devastating. You've got to protect yourselves and parents must protect those who cannot protect themselves.

MARGERY: I want people to believe it's more common than they know. I want the law to work in protecting victims and treating perpetrators alongside their jail sentences.

SAMANTHA: I want them to believe this happens and it happened to me. Too often people numb out and say, "It's too horrible, I can't deal with it. I can't believe it." I know that's what my mother did. She didn't want to believe anything could be wrong in *our* family. She's not alone. So many people just put their heads in the sand. You can't raise the consciousness of someone who refuses to see. But I want mothers to realize that some of the fault belongs to them for not protecting us.

RENITA: I want survivors to know that incest affects every aspect of your life, and don't kid yourself that it doesn't. Denial of this reality is what keeps me turning to food. I have to acknowledge that this really happened and it affects the way I work, the way I study, the way I move, the way I don't move, what I believe, and what I don't believe.

Appendix A
Sample Questionnaire (Voices)[1]

Your age _____   Your ethnic background _____

Your first name _____

Your phone # _____ (should I need clarification)

Please read carefully the following questions and answer them, giving as long an explanation as you need for me to understand your feelings (feel free to add longer answers by stapling extra sheets of paper headed by the number of and question you're answering).

If the question does not need an explanation, just write the answer.

Circle the name of the divine power that you feel most accurately describes what you're responding to in these questions.

The God/Goddess/Higher Power Questionnaire

I

1. I feel/do not feel close to God/Goddess/HP because . . .
2. The time of my life when I felt the closest to God/Goddess/HP . . .
3. I think that my life when I felt the closest to . . . God/Goddess/HP was when I was __ year old because . . .
4. I think that God/Goddess/HP wants/does not want me to be good because . . .
5. I believe/do not believe in a personal God/Goddess/HP because . . .

II

6. The time in my life when I felt the most distant from God/Goddess/ HP was when I was . . . because . . .
7. My most important duties toward God/Goddess/HP . . .

III

8. For me, the love of God/Goddess/HP toward me is/is not important because . . .
9. For me, my love for God/Goddess/HP is/is not important because . . .
10. The feeling I get/used to get from my relationship with God/Goddess/HP is one of . . . because . . .

IV

11. I feel that the fear of God/Goddess/HP is/is not important because . . .
12. What I like the most about God/Goddess/HP is . . . because . . .
13. What I resent the most about God/Goddess/HP is . . . because . . .
14. What I dislike the most about religion is . . . because . . .

V

15. Emotionally, I would like to have the . . . that God/Goddess/HP has because . . .

VI

16. Among all the religious characters I know, I would like to be like . . . because . . .

VII

17. My favorite person, saint or Bible character is . . . because . . .

VIII

18. I believe/do not believe in the devil because . . .
19. I think that the devil wants us to . . .
20. Sometimes I have/have not felt that I hated God/Goddess/HP

IX

21. I feel that what God/Goddess/HP expects from me is . . .
22. I feel that to obey the Commandments is/is not important because . . .
23. I pray/do not pray because I feel that God/Goddess/HP will . . .

X

24. I feel that God/Goddess/HP punishes/does not punish you if you . . . because . . .

25. I think God/Goddess/HP considers my sins/wrongdoings as . . . because . . .
26. I think the way God/Goddess/HP has to punish people is . . . because . . .
27. I believe that the way God/Goddess/HP rewards people is . . .

XI

28. I think that God/Goddess/HP provides/does not provide for my needs because . . .
29. The most important thing I expect from God/Goddess/HP is . . . because

XII

30. In my way of feeling, for me to full please God/Goddess/HP I would have to . . . because . . .
31. If I could change my past, I would like to change . . . because . . .
32. If I can change myself now, I would like to be . . . because . . .

    to change my . . .   because . . .
    to improve my . . .   because . . .
    to increase my . . .   because . . .

XIII

33. If I am in distress, I resort/do not resort to God/Goddess/HP because . . .
34. If I am happy, I thank/do not thank God/Goddess/HP because . . .
35. Religion has/has not helped me to live because . . .
36. If I receive absolute proof that God/Goddess/HP does not exist, I will . . . because . . .
37. Prayer is/is not important to me because . . .
38. I wish/don't wish to be with God/Goddess/HP after death because . . .

XIV

39. I think that God/Goddess/HP is closest to those who . . . because . . .

XV

40. I consider God/Goddess/HP as my . . . because . . .
41. I think God/Goddess/HP sees me as . . . because . . .

XVI

42. If I have to describe God/Goddess/HP according to experiences, I would say that God/Goddess/HP is . . . because . . .

XVII

43. The day I changed my way of thinking about God/Goddess/HP was . . . because . . .

XVIII

44. Religion was always/never/at one time important to me (during the years from . . . to . . .) because . . .
45. For me, the world has/has not an explanation without God/Goddess/HP because . . .

The "Family" Questionnaire

1. The member of my family to whom I felt the closest was my . . . because . . .
2. The member of my family to whom I felt the most distant was my . . . because . . .
3. The member of my family whom I loved the most was my . . . because she/he . . .
4. The member of my family whom I disliked the most was my . . . because she/he . . .
5. Physically I resemble my . . . because . . .
6. Emotionally I resemble my . . . because . . .
7. The favorite member of my family was my . . . because . . .
8. The member of my family whom I admired the most is my . . . because . . .
9. Please write down the names of the members of your family in order of preference according to how much you like them:
    1.   5.
    2.   6.
    3.   7.
    4.   8.
10. The member of my family whom I despised the most is . . . because . . .
11. The boss in my family was my . . . because . . .
12. The disciplinarian in my family was my . . . because . . .
13. The provider in my family was my . . . because . . .
14. If I could change myself I would like to be like my . . . because . . .
15. In my family we were close/very close/not close at all because . . .

16. My father was closest to me/to my . . . because . . .
17. My mother was closest to me/to my . . . because . . .
18. The most important person in my family was . . . because . . .
19. In my family the children were considered as . . . because . . .
20. If I described myself as I feel I actually am, I would say I am . . .

For Adults Sexually Abused as Children

1. What does the phrase "incest survivor" mean to you?
2. When and why did you become interested in your own recovery from childhood sexual abuse as an adult?
3. What is it about abuse recovery groups (if you are involved in one) that is important to you?
4. If you are a member of an Anonymous group:
    a. How did the group form?
    b. How does the group decide on its practices?
    c. Describe the group's practices.
    d. What are the benefits and/or drawbacks of being a group member?
5. How do you personally practice "recovery" from sexual/physical/emotional abuse?
6. What is the connection for you between being an incest survivor in recovery and your view of your body?
    a. Before I attended a recovery group I felt . . . about/in my body
    b. After participating in a recovery group for . . . months, I feel . . . about/in my body.
(Answer if [c & d] apply to you)
    c. I'd say I have an eating disorder (that began at age _____) because . . .
    d. I find that what helps my recovery from my eating disorder is . . . because . . .
7. What is the connection for you between being an incest survivor in recovery and your relationships to others?
    a. Before I attended a recovery group I felt this way about/in my relationships to:
        Men
        Women
        Children

b. After participating in a recovery group I feel this way about:
Men
Women
Children

8. What is the connection for you between being an incest survivor in recovery and your political views?

9. How does your recovery in group influence your sense of spirituality?
   a. My sense of spirituality means . . .
   b. I use another word for spirituality and that word is . . . because . . .

10. In general, how has abuse recovery influenced your life?

11. What do you see as the future of recovery groups for survivors of abuse?

Appendix B
Research Protocol for Interview Study: "Incest, Eating Disorders, and Religious Self-Descriptions"

I General Historical Frame

1. Would you tell me a little bit about your background? For instance: where you were born, your parents' ethnic heritage, class background, etc.
2. In brief, would you tell me about your family? For instance, who was around the most as you were growing up, how many siblings, what kinds of pressures did your family face?
3. Could you tell me about your schooling? Where you went to school and what it was like for you?
4. When and where did you first work? What has working (if you do work) been like for you?
5. When you were growing up, did church or synagogue have any place in your life? What place? (Denomination?)

II Abuse History

1. Being as specific or as general as you would like, please describe your experience of your history of being sexually abused.
   - How old, how often, how long at a time, in what setting?

- Was anyone else present/Did anyone else know?
- Any discernible pattern/ritual aspect?

2. If you have any discernible memories of the abuse events, could you tell me what went on inside while you were being abused, and after? For example:
   - Images
   - Feelings
   - Dissociation/numbness/splitting
   - Conflicting feelings

3. In response to being traumatized, many people say their life fundamentally changed. Did you notice the emergence of any different behaviors or coping patterns as a result of being sexually abused?
   - When did these patterns emerge?
   - Can you remember what you were trying to accomplish through your (different/coping) behaviors?
   - Were you ever abused in other relationships?
   - Have you ever been abusive to yourself and/or others?
   - As the result of being abused, did you ever have to take drugs or be hospitalized?

4. Can you tell me briefly about your experience with having an eating disorder?
   - What did you hope to accomplish by being thin?
   - When you felt *out of control* with food/weight, how did you see yourself? What kinds of things did you say to yourself?
   - When you felt *in control* with food/weight, how did you see yourself? What kinds of things did you say to yourself?
   - As the result of having an eating disorder, did you ever have to take drugs or be hospitalized?

III Religious Self-Descriptions

1. What connections, if any, do you see between your abuse history and your eating-disorder history?

2. Many survivors feel responsible for what happened to them. Did you ever blame yourself?
   - If yes, how did you handle the shame?

3. Did you ever feel that being female contributed to your abuse?
   - How?

4. Did you ever feel that your body size/shape had anything to do with your being abused?
5. How has your history of abuse affected your relationships with men/women/authority figures?
6. What does the world "spirituality" mean to you? How would you describe yourself spiritually?
7. Is there a god/goddess/higher power in your life? How does God/HP see you now? How would you say God saw you around the time that you were being abused?
8. In Twelve-Step groups they talk of "turning your life and will over to the care of God as you understand God." How would you say you understand God?
9. Do you see any relationship between your religious or spiritual concerns and your having been abused and/or your developing an eating disorder?
10. If you are in a spirituality group, how has it helped you heal from the pain of your past? What would you like to see improved in your spirituality group/church or synagogue that would help you heal the pain of your past?
11. If you could send a message to people who are ignorant about sexual abuse, what would you want them to know?

Appendix C
The Twelve Steps of Alcoholics Anonymous

1. We admitted we were powerless over alcohol—that our lives had become unmanageable.
2. Came to believe that a Power greater than ourselves could restore us to sanity.
3. Made a decision to turn our will and our lives over to the care of God *as we understood Him.*
4. Made a searching and fearless moral inventory of ourselves.
5. Admitted to God, to ourselves and to another human being the exact nature of our wrongs.
6. Were entirely ready to have God remove all these defects of character.
7. Humbly asked Him to remove our shortcomings.
8. Made a list of all persons we had harmed, and became willing to make amends to them all.
9. Made direct amends to such people wherever possible, except when to do so would injure them or others.
10. Continued to take personal inventory and when we were wrong promptly admitted it.
11. Sought through prayer and meditation to improve our conscious contact with God, *as we understood Him,* praying only for knowledge of His will for us and the power to carry that out.
12. Having had a spiritual awakening as the result of these steps, we tried to carry this message to alcoholics, and to practice these principles in all our affairs.

Appendix D
Brief History of Twelve-Step Groups

Alcoholic Anonymous (AA) was founded in 1935 by Bill Wilson in Akron, Ohio.[1] Bill, a successful stockbroker on Wall Street, had for many years drunk to excess and could never find a way of curing his addiction. He watched his life and work disintegrate before his eyes. At the depths of his powerlessness he was visited by an old drinking buddy who was now clean and sober. The friend, Ebby, was a member of a zealous religious sect called the Oxford Group that had helped him overcome his drinking problem.

The Oxford Group, a nondenominational evangelical movement and parent group of AA, dates back to 1908 but was primarily active in the 1920s and 1930s. It started as a small group of people—mostly men— who came from a strong Christian background and hoped to create a human chain of good relationships based on honesty and moral principles that would change the world. Unfortunately, the relationships were locked into sex-role stereotypes, so that women were taught to "serve" and take a secondary role.

The Oxford Group stressed principles that became essential parts of the Twelve-Step approach—deflation of the ego, humility, dependence on and guidance from a Higher Power, taking a moral inventory, confession of one's defects, and willingness to make restitution, as well as sharing the program with other alcoholics. The other four principles the Oxford Group espoused were "absolute honesty, absolute purity, absolute unselfishness, and absolute love."[2] Oxford groups operated throughout the United States until the 1930s and used the practice of "witnessing"[3] with the aim of helping other alcoholics become sober.

Eventually the meetings expanded from small intimate groups into large ones that took the name Moral Rearmament, with their goal the reforming of "drunken" countries rather than drunken individuals.[4]

Bill Wilson formulated the current Twelve Steps from 1938 to 1939, several years after meeting his ally, Dr. Bob Smith, who joined him in working toward the creation of anonymous support meetings.[5] The organization expanded rapidly, and has been worldwide since 1985, with over a million members and more than 58,000 chapters in over ninety countries.[6]

Al-Anon, the companion organization for family members of alcoholics, used the same steps, which its members applied to their own problems. By the 1970s, this technique had been so well received that it was being used for other problems. People addicted to gambling, narcotics, or overeating formed Twelve-Step groups.[7] Others, whose problems seemed to stem from their relationships to other people, started more groups: Adult Children of Alcoholics, Codependence Anonymous, Sex and Love Addicts Anonymous, and Workaholics Anonymous.

Most of the survivors I interviewed came from Overeaters Anonymous (OA), which was founded in 1961 by three women in Los Angeles who wanted to see if they could apply the Alcoholics Anonymous (AA) principles to help them with their eating disorders. Today, there are about 160,000 members in the OA fellowship in the United States, Canada, and internationally.[8]

Appendix E
The Feminist Steps

1. We affirm we have the power to take charge of our lives and stop being dependent on substances or other people for our self-esteem and security.
2. We come to believe that a trustworthy life-force awakens the healing wisdom within us if we open ourselves to this power.
3. We make a decision to become our authentic Selves and trust in the healing power of the truth.
4. We examine our beliefs, destructive habits, and dependent behavior in the context of living in a hierarchal, patriarchal culture.
5. We share with safe and self-selected others all those things inside of us for which we feel shame and guilt.
6. We affirm and enjoy our talents, strengths, and creativity, striving not to hide these qualities to protect others' egos.
7. We become willing to let go of our shame, guilt, and any behavior that keeps us from loving ourselves and others.
8. We make a list of people we have harmed and people who have harmed us, and take steps to clear out negative energy by making amends and sharing our grievances in a respectful way.
9. We express love and gratitude to others, and increasingly appreciate the wonder of life and the blessings we *do* have.
10. We continue to trust our reality and daily affirm that we see what we see, we know what we know, and we feel what we feel.
11. We promptly acknowledge our mistakes and make amends when

appropriate, but we do not say we are sorry for things we have not done, and we do not cover up, analyze, or take responsibility for the shortcomings of others.

12. We seek out jobs, and people that affirm our intelligence, perceptions, and self-worth and avoid situations or people who are hurtful, harmful, or demeaning to us.

13. We take steps to heal our physical bodies, organize our lives, reduce stress, and have fun.

14. We seek to find our inward calling, and develop the will and wisdom to follow it.

15. We accept the ups and downs of life as natural events that can be used as lessons for our growth.

16. We grow in awareness that we are interrelated with all living things, and we contribute to restoring peace and balance on the planet.

Appendix F
Profile of Male Perpetrators[1]

Sociologists David Finkelhor and Linda Meyer Williams have recently completed a thorough study of men who have sexually abused their daughters. The sample consisted of 118 incestuous fathers—fifty-five men in the U.S. Navy and sixty-three civilians from treatment centers around the country—and a carefully matched control group of nonincestuous fathers.

In this landmark study on the characteristics of incest offenders, Finkelhor and Williams set out to determine whether men are socialized to see all intimacy and dominance as sexual, whether fathers separated from their daughter for long periods soon after birth are more likely to molest her than fathers who have not been absent, and whether incestuous men had themselves been abused as children more often than had nonoffenders. The researchers also sought to learn each man's feelings about his daughter, his outlook on sex, and his attitudes toward incest.

Many theories have been advanced about why fathers molest their daughters. Everything from alcoholism to a frigid wife has been blamed. This study has brought to light new information. They found, for example, that there are distinct differences in the onset of abuse: daughters ranged in age from 4 weeks to 15 years old when the incest began. "Fathers were more likely to start abuse when their daughter was four to six years old or ten to twelve years old," the study reveals, "than to initiate abuse when she was seven, eight, or nine years old." Men reported various behaviors leading up to the abuse. Some of the fathers said they had masturbated while thinking of their daughter, had exposed themselves to her, or had made her touch their genitals before they began touching hers. A substantial percentage of the men—63 percent—had been sexually attracted to their daughter for a period of years before the abuse began. Most significantly, the findings reveal that there are many paths to incestuous behavior and that there is not just one type of man who commits such abuse.

Each man was interviewed for at least six hours and was asked hundreds of questions. The results presented here dispel some common myths and prompt the following typology.

Type 1: Sexually Preoccupied

Twenty-six percent of the fathers studied fell into this category. These men had "a clear and conscious (often obsessive) sexual interest in their daughters." When they talked about what attracted them to their daughter, they talked in detail about her physical qualities—the feel of her skin, for example, or the smell of her body.

Type 1 Subcategory: Early sexualizers

Among the sexually preoccupied fathers, many regarded their daughter as a sex object almost from birth. "One father reported that he had been stimulated by the sight of his daughter nursing and that he could never remember a time when he did not have sexual feelings for her. . . . He began sexually abusing her when she was four weeks old." Many of these offenders were sexually abused as children. "These men are so sexualized that they may simply project their sexual needs onto every-body and everything."

Type 2: Adolescent Regressives

About a third of the fathers—33 percent—became sexually interested in their daughter when she entered puberty. They said they were "trans-fixed" by her body's changes. For some the attraction began when the daughter started to act more grown up, before her body changed. Some of the fathers in this group became aroused by a daughter after having been away from her for a long time. Sometimes the fathers let the attraction build for years, masturbating to fantasies of the daughter, before they acted.

These men acted and sounded like young adolescents themselves when they talked about their daughter. One said, "I started to wonder what it would be like to touch her breasts and touch between her legs and wondered how she would react if I did."

"The father-adult in me shut down," said another offender, "and I was like a kid again."

Type 3: Instrumental Self-Gratifiers

These fathers accounted for 20 percent of the sample. They described their daughter in terms that were nonerotic. When they abused her, they thought about someone else—their wife, even their daughter as an adult. They blocked what they were doing from their minds: "They used their daughter's body as a receptacle."

While one man was giving his seven-year-old a bath, she rubbed against his penis. "I realized that I could take advantage of the situation," he said. "She wasn't a person to me." Another man said, "I abused her from behind so I wouldn't see her face."

Instrumental self-gratifiers abused sporadically, worried about the harm they were causing, and felt great guilt. To alleviate the guilt, some convinced themselves that their daughter was aroused.

Type 4: Emotionally Dependent

Just over 10 percent of the sample fit this category. These fathers were emotionally needy, lonely, and depressed. They thought of themselves as failures and looked to their daughter for "close, exclusive, emotionally dependent relationships," including sexual gratification, which they linked to intimacy and not to their daughter's real or imagined sexual qualities.

The average age of the daughter when the incest began was six to seven years. One man, separated from his wife, saw his five-year-old daughter only on weekends. "It was companionship," he said, "I had been alone for six months. We slept together and would fondle each other. The closeness was very good and loving. Then oral sex began."

Type 5: Angry Retaliators

About 10 percent of the men were in this category. These fathers were the most likely to have criminal histories of assault and rape. They abused a daughter out of anger at her or, more often, at her mother for neglecting or deserting them. Some denied any sexual feelings for the daughter. One father of a three-year-old said, "My daughter has no sex appeal for me at all. What I did was just an opportunity to get back at my daughter for being the center of my wife's life. There was no room for me."

Sometimes the daughter was abused because she resembled her mother, sometimes because of the father's desire to desecrate her or to possess her out of an angry sense of entitlement. Some angry retaliators tied up, gagged, beat, and raped their daughter and were aroused by the violence.

Other Findings

Alcohol and drugs. While 33 percent of the men reported being under the influence of alcohol when the abuse occurred, and 10 percent reported that they were using drugs, only 9 percent held alcohol or drugs responsible. It's more likely that alcohol or drugs are used to lower their inhibitions to abuse.

Marital discord. Forty-three percent of the men felt that their relationship with their wife was part of the reason for the incest. "However, the wife was rarely the only factor mentioned. . . . Different men probably come to incestuous acts as a result of different needs, motives, and impairments."

Sexual abuse of the offender as a child. Significantly, 70 percent of the men said they themselves had been sexually abused in childhood. Half were physically abused by their father and 44 percent had been physically abused by their mother. "Although not all who are abused go on to become perpetrators, it is critical that we learn more about how child sexual victimization affects male sexual development and male sexual socialization.

Profile of Female Perpetrators[2]

Women who abuse fall into four major categories according to psychologist Ruth Mathews. The first is a *teacher-lover*—usually made up of older women who seduce young adolescents. The second category is *experimenter-exploiter*, which encompasses girls from rigid families where sex education is proscribed. They may take baby-sitting as an opportunity to explore small children. The third category is the *predisposed*, meaning women who are predisposed to offend by their own history of severe physical and/or sexual abuse. The victims are often their own children or siblings. The final category is *male-coerced* women—women who abuse children because perpetrating men force them to.

Appendix G
Incest Laws[1]

Criminal Prosecution

The narrow legal definitions of incest, together with the strict requirements for proof, the meager punishments generally handed down, and the trauma for victims who must testify tend to make the criminal prosecution of incest unlikely and is sometimes an impossible enterprise.

In most cases criminal prosecution for incest can be undertaken only if the victim is a minor at the time the abuse is discovered. To complicate the issue, however, most incest is "blocked" from consciousness until one reaches adulthood and begins to remember what happened. By then, the statute of limitations on criminal offenses has usually long since expired.

Incest statutes. The states of Connecticut, Maine, Michigan, New Jersey, Ohio, Rhode Island, Vermont, and Virginia have no incest statutes. Incest cases in these states are prosecuted under other sexual-abuse statutes, which often carry a higher penalty.

Blood-relatedness. In California, the District of Columbia, Florida, Hawaii, Indiana, Kansas, Louisiana, Maryland, Minnesota, Nevada, New Mexico, New York, and North Dakota, blood relationship is a requisite to prosecute for incest. In all other states it is not.

Vaginal penetration. The following states deem vaginal penetration necessary in order for incest to have occurred: Alabama, Alaska, Arizona, Arkansas, California, Delaware, the District of Columbia, Florida, Georgia, Hawaii, Idaho, Indiana, Kentucky, Louisiana, Maryland, Massachusetts, Minnesota, Mississippi, Missouri, New Hampshire, Nevada, New Mexico, North Carolina, Oklahoma, Utah, and West Virginia.

Independent corroboration. The corroboration of an independent party is required only in Alabama, Arkansas (if the victim consented and is at least 16), California (if the victim consented and is of legal age), and Illinois (if the testimony is not clear and convincing).

Penalties for Incest

The penalties for the crime of incest vary from state to state, as the following examples show:

Indiana—imprisonment of up to 18 months, plus additional time for aggravating circumstances, or minus time for mitigating circumstances; a fine of less than $1,000.

Delaware—imprisonment of up to 2 years; a fine of not more than $1,000.

Kansas—imprisonment of 2 to 10 years.

Illinois—imprisonment of 4 to 15 years.

Alaska, Arizona, California, Florida, Hawaii, Iowa, Louisiana (if uncle-niece or aunt-nephew incest), Missouri, New Mexico, New York, North Dakota, Oregon, South Dakota, Utah, Wyoming—imprisonment of up to 5 years.

Alabama, Arkansas, Colorado, the District of Columbia, Georgia, Idaho, Kentucky, Louisiana (if other than uncle-niece or aunt-nephew incest), Maryland, Massachusetts, Minnesota, Mississippi, Montana, Nebraska, Nevada, New Hampshire, North Carolina, Oklahoma, Pennsylvania, Tennessee, Texas, Washington, West Virginia, Wisconsin—imprisonment of 5 years and up.

South Carolina—imprisonment of 10 years and up.

Civil Remedies

Many victims do not want to put their abuser in jail. Some want financial restitution for therapy and for other consequences of the abuse. Others just want a written apology or a court order compelling the abuser to get therapy. Civil remedies give victims a chance to tell their story in court and to be awarded punitive damages for the pain and injury suffered. For many victims, just lodging the complaint gives them a sense of empowerment that helps them heal.

Statutes of limitations generally are reckoned from the date of injury and run for a fixed period, often three years. But in child sexual-abuse cases, the statute of limitations is often more flexible. Thanks to the work of lawyers such as Shari Karney and Mary Williams of California, these statutes in some states begin when the victim remembers the abuse. The phenomenon is called delayed discovery and is based on the fact that someone who has no memory of an act cannot complain about it.

Appendix H
Letter to Politician[1]

Reform legislation is imperative if we are to protect children against incest and sexual abuse. I urge readers to send this letter, or some version of it, to their political representatives at the state level, including governors and legislators.

Dear

The children of our state need your help. According to the most reliable studies of the incidence of incest and child sexual abuse in the United States, at least one out of three girls and one out of seven boys will be sexually abused before the age of 18. Research has shown that 89 percent of these assaults are committed by someone the child knows, trusts, or loves. In spite of the crippling damage done to victims, incest often carries lighter penalties than other child sex-abuse crimes. I urge that all the laws in our state pertaining to incest and to any and all sexual assaults against children be viewed and strengthened, and ask you to take the following steps as soon as possible.

1. *Expand the definition of incest in our state in order to broaden the application of criminal statutes.* Most states require vaginal penetration (assumes victim is always female) and a close blood relationship to establish incest in a criminal prosecution. The definition should be ex-

panded to include any other acts of sexual assault by a parent or family member and any and all sexual assaults by any care giver—including stepparent, adoptive parent, and guardian of either sex—or any other person in a position of authority.

2. Increase criminal penalties for incest and child sexual abuse. Incest and sexual-abuse victims suffer long-lasting psychological and physical trauma. Penalties should be at least equal to those for capital crimes, and minimum sentences for perpetrators should be set by law. Persons convicted of incest and child sexual abuse should be denied custody and/ or visitation privileges.

3. Abolish or extend statutes of limitations for civil and criminal cases pertaining to incest and child sexual abuse. Some states have recently extended their statute of limitations for civil cases (see the California Code of Civil Procedure, Section 340.1). At least seven states have no statute of limitations in criminal cases, and legislation to abolish such statutes is pending in ten others. Because the victims are children and because they may be terrorized into silence and/or may repress memories of sexual assaults for many years (studies have shown the average age of discovery to be between 29 and 49), statutes of limitations should be based on the special circumstances of the crime or case.

I ask you to reform our laws and give our state prosecutors and child victims a real chance for justice.
Sincerely,

Appendix I
The Quality of Experience: A Feminist Method

In this section I will briefly familiarize the reader with the method used to interview, analyze, and theorize about the ways in which incested women preoccupied with their appetite, body, and weight reveal religious, psychological, and socially constructed conflicts. First, I will explore the general background of the nine women who were selected for this study. Then I will go into some detail as to the method of inquiry I have chosen and why.

The Interview

I conducted nine in-depth interviews and administered lengthy open-ended questionnaires to explore the social psychology and theology of female survivors of incest who identify themselves as having eating disorders. Typically, I had at least two prior contacts with the respondent before asking her if she would be interested in being interviewed. Having a prior contact—establishing some trust—was particularly important given the secrecy and shame associated with this topic and the necessity of survivors of incest, women of color, and lesbians to be discriminating about how their lives are studied.

To create analytical notes and conceptual categories from the data, I adopted Thompson's (1992)[1] and Glaser and Strauss's (1967)[2] technique of "theoretical sampling," which directs the researcher to collect, analyze, and test hypotheses during the sampling process (rather than imposing theoretical categories onto the data). I took my first samples in 1991 by attending a summer conference in Chicago called "Victims of Incest Can Emerge Survivors" (VOICES). At the conference I gave out a lengthy questionnaire[3] with a stamped, self-addressed envelope to be returned to me within a month after the conference. From this sample questionnaire I got a sense of some of the shared religious themes among over fifty survivors of incest (ages twenty to sixty-seven). Women who responded to the questionnaire inspired me to take seriously the links between what a woman believes about herself due to her sexually traumatic and theological past and how a woman relates to her body.[4]

Second, I attended OA for three months prior to setting up interviews.[5] During that time, I took ample notes and read the OA literature as well as conversed with women after the meetings. I was able not only to gather material for formulating my final open-ended questionnaire, but also to test my hypothesis about the connection among eating problems, incest, and religious discourse.

Demographics of the Women in the Study

Birthplace

Three of the incest survivors interviewed came from big cities: Pittsburgh, Pennsylvania; Philadelphia, Pennsylvania; and Baltimore, Maryland. Five came from smaller cities and towns: Cleveland, Ohio; Luddington, Michigan; Whittier, California; Metuchen, New Jersey; and Watseeka, Illinois. One of the women interviewed came from Bombay, India.

Religion

All of the women interviewed were at one time practicing Christians. Two of the women grew up in practicing Catholic families (both went to Catholic schools; one attended Mass six days a week until the age of fourteen, the other grew up with Hindu grandparents but with her siblings attended Catholic services). Five grew up in families that attended Sunday Protestant worship services: Episcopalian, Methodist, Southern Baptist, Unitarian, fundamentalist Presbyterian and mainline Presbyterian. Two grew up going to Protestant services on holidays only.

One grew up with parents and relatives who publicly attended Protestant worship services and privately participated in a sadistic cult.

Education

All of the survivors are college educated. Four hold graduate degrees.

Employment

Two of the nine survivors were unemployed at the time of the interview. Three held two or more jobs at once, "to make ends meet." Three of the survivors were administrative assistants. One survivor called herself a "recycler": "You know, I collect garbage and haul it in to be recycled." This same survivor graduated with honors from an Ivy League school.

Class

Two of the women interviewed may be considered as coming from working-class backgrounds, six may be considered middle-class, and one identifies herself as coming from an upper-class background: "We had a nanny and several hired-help."

Race

Six of the women are European-American. One woman is Indian-American. One woman has an African-American mother and a Native-American father. One woman's mother is Native-American and father is European-American.[6]

For some of the women of color, racism coupled with the stress resulting from class mobility related to the onset of their eating problems.[7] The woman born of an African-American mother and a Native-American father was frequently admonished for looking "dirty." Her father often humiliated her by "washing" her in a tub in the bathroom with a dry Brillo pad while reciting a degrading litany: "You're filthy, you're dirty, you're no good, just like your mother." He did not do this to her brother, who was lighter skinned. As a young child, this survivor began to think that although she could not change the color of her skin, she could at least try to be thin. However, her father, who was a working-class cook on a railroad, began bringing home food and insisting that his children were going to be "well fed." After her father incested her he would call her a "fat ugly pig." He would announce, "You're fat and disgusting and no one will ever love you." As a result, like many of the survivors interviewed, this survivor tried to "control" her eating in public and do most of her eating in secret—in her bedroom. By age eight, she weighed 250 pounds.

The fact that some of the women of color associated the ambivalent messages about food and eating with their family's class mobility and/or the demands of assimilation suggests that the added dimension of racism was connected to the imperative to be thin. Their parents class expectations exacerbated standards about weight that they inflicted on their daughters.[8]

Sexual Orientation

Five of the respondents identify themselves as heterosexual. One of the respondents identifies herself as lesbian and one as celibate. Two of the women were not comfortable affixing a label to their sexual preference. According to psychologist Elaine Westerlund, "Both confusion between affection and sex arising from the incest experience and confusion over the role of the incest in choice-making may contribute to self-doubts over sexual preference in women with incest histories."[9] Since I do not assume that lesbianism (or celibacy or bisexuality) is a "failure" of "normative" heterosexuality, it was not an intent of my study to investigate the role of the incest trauma in the establishment of a lesbian (or celibate or bisexual) identity.

Family Information

The size of the participants' families of origin vary from 2 children to 5 children. Five of the women are the oldest in the family. One is the middle child. Three are the youngest. Three of the survivors were one of two children. Two of the survivors were one of three children. Three of the survivors were one of four children. Only one of the survivors came from a family with five children. Most of the mothers of these women were exclusively "homemakers." Only two of them held paying jobs outside the home (one was an elementary school teacher, the other a legal secretary). Four of the survivors have mothers who have died (one of whom was a perpetrator). One woman's mother died when she was seven; the three other mothers died when the survivors were adults. Two of the survivors have fathers (both of whom were perpetrators) who have died. The father of one died when she was seventeen and the other when she was forty. One survivor's family lived with their paternal siblings' family and paternal grandparents; as she put it, "There were twenty of us living in 3 rooms."

Offenders

All of the survivors were abused by one or more older males in their family.[10] Two were abused by women as well. The paternal perpetrators may be professionally categorized as follows: cook, mechanic, fisherman, mechanical engineer, electrical engineer, traveling salesman, accountant, doctor, and attorney. In two cases the paternal grandfather was the perpetrator. Of the three female perpetrators one was the aunt and one was the mother of the child abused; the other was the nanny of the child-victim. Of the three male sibling perpetrators, each was at least four years older than the survivor. One brother was five years older (he was twelve and she was seven), another brother (who recently confessed his abuse of her) was four years older (he was thirteen and she was nine), and the other was 6 years older (he was seventeen and she was eleven) than the survivor upon the onset of sibling-sexual abuse.

The women I have interviewed represent diverse backgrounds and reveal that class, sexual preference, race, and ethnicity neither predispose a woman to nor protect her from developing an eating disorder in North America. Too often the epidemiological portrait of eating problems has been one of a white middle- and upper-class "illness." This model is more likely to reveal which populations of women have been studied rather than the actual prevalence.[11]

I am aware of the dangers of generalization that tend to go hand in hand with psychological readings of female predicaments—as if all women share the same experience. Each woman's story is her own. Yet, as a feminist, I am equally aware that no woman's story is just her own. I try to write from this dual perspective, following the style of Mary Daly, Karen Horney, Ellyn Kaschak, Judith Herman, Charlotte Davis Käsl, and other feminist theorists. Each woman leads a particular life determined by her own talents and temperament, her abilities and experiences, her ethnic and class membership. Yet all these experiences, I maintain, are centrally organized by gender, so that each woman's story of violence and consequent problem with food and identity may reflect many women's stories.

Feminist Qualitative Methodology

In feminist qualitative methodology one is concerned with the process of gathering data as well as the product of the research. Feminist methodology holds the belief that the personal and the political are very much connected. As a feminist researcher in psychology and religion, I see the sexual-abuse history of a woman not only as her personal history but also as a microcosmic portrait that cannot be separated from the larger reality of violence against women in culture. I am concerned with how women have been socialized to become victims, how men have been socialized to become aggressors, and what role religious discourse plays toward "normalizing" these ends.[12] The feminist methodological process that I employ is an interview method that is respectful of respondents' strengths and recognizes each respondent as an authority on her own experience. At times the reader may wonder why I quote the women at length—it is because I believe their theoretical insights into their history are just as valid as the ones being made about them by me or other theorists.

Because I understood the volatility of the questions that I was using for investigation, I took great pains to see that my respondents were not overtly or subtly victimized by the process. I made it clear that under no circumstances would her name or identifying characteristics be revealed. I informed her that she could "share her history" with as little or as much detail as she saw fit. I wanted her to know that she was in control of what she decided to share.

As the interviewer, I am collecting and relaying the respondent's interpretation of her own life history and present experience. I use social and self-psychological theory as well as feminist theology and philosophy to explore survivors' expressed experience throughout this book without ever presuming to be the authority on the respondents' "real" meaning in their self-descriptions.

I see women as an oppressed group. I seek to recognize the political and social context of what it means to be a woman in North American culture. Issues of race, class, age, and sexual orientation are, of course, relevant. For instance, the female respondents who are women of color and/or lesbians live within multiple webs of oppression. It is understood that in addition to what they have internalized because of their incest history, they may be feeling self-hatred as members of oppressed minorities. A survivor who is further marginalized by her race, class, or sexual preference may have internalized the racism or homophobia of Western culture, which may complicate her empowerment process. According to psychologist Christine Dinsmore, "Incest survivors, because of their childhood traumas, generally feel different from the rest of the world." [13] Classism, homophobia, sexism, and racism only further conspire to deepen a survivor's alienation.

As author and poet Margaret Randall writes, "The female child, double commodity in a consumer society, suffers her greatest invisibility at the hands of the male authority figure abusing her in incest. The reclamation of worth, with its accompanying reclamation of rights, must, in fact, include a reclamation of memory." [14]

I see the process of gathering data as facilitating the adult survivor's naming injuries of all kinds—sexism, classism, racism, and heterosexism. The interview process also enabled a reclamation of memory and, as such, possibly offered one of the many potential vehicles to her social and psychological empowerment.

Politics of Social Scientific Research

In asking each of the nine women if they were willing to be interviewed for my research on incest, I was careful to solicit her cooperation in a friendly and non-authoritarian manner. I worked to convey a sensitive approach because I knew personally the vulnerability of the subject as well as the volatility of my subject matter. I wanted each woman to know that I did not intend to exploit either her or her personal information. The attitude I conveyed may have had some influence in encouraging the women to regard me as an empathic observer rather than purely as an objective, scientific observer of a social phenomenon.

Ann Oakley writes in her essay, "Interviewing Women: A Contradiction in Terms," that in her previous interviewing experiences she found an attitude of refusing to answer questions or offer any kind of personal feedback was not helpful in terms of the traditional goal of promoting "rapport." A different role, that could be termed "no intimacy without reciprocity," seemed especially important in longitudinal in-depth interviewing. Without feeling that the interview process offered some personal satisfaction to them, interviewees would not be prepared to continue after the first interview. The interviewee's definition of the interview is important.[15]

Frequently researchers establish rapport not as scientists but as human beings yet proceed to use this knowledge for scientific ends, usually without the informants' knowledge. According to Oakley, ethical dilemmas are greatest when there is the least social distance between interviewer and interviewee. When both share the same gender socialization and critical life experiences, social distance can be minimal. When both interviewer and interviewee share membership in the same minority group, the basis for equality may impress itself even more urgently on the interviewer's consciousness. She quotes A. F. Mamak, who writes:

I found that my academic training in methodological views of Western social science and its emphasis on "scientific objectivity" conflicted with the experiences of my colonial past. The traditional way in which social science research is conducted proved inadequate for an understanding of the reality, needs and desires of the people I was researching.[16]

As interviewer, I informed all of the respondents about the nature of the interview and explained that the information gathered would be used for my research on incest, theology, and psychology. Before every interview I explained to the respondent that I was a fellow survivor and that I understood how difficult this subject matter is to talk about. I promised her name would be changed to preserve her anonymity. I also assured her that in the way I wrote up the findings her identity would be protected.[17]

My research is decidedly political; it offers women who were sexually violated by family members or "friends" a chance to unload themselves of the shame brought upon them by their perpetrators, as well as a chance to expose the patriarchal culture that licenses male domination in home, church, and state. Also, by sharing their "personal" stories while cognizant that others are doing the same, they have a sense that they are not alone—that this is not a unique female experience—that they are naming something political that has been a part of female experience and female gender construction for millennia.

Method of Case Presentation

The way the cases are presented in the book is at times analogous to a group-therapy interview—where each woman responds to the interviewer's questions from the written, open-ended questionnaire. The interviews were actually conducted not in a group setting but privately between the respondent and the interviewer, who taped and transcribed the session. At times I have chosen to quote from the interviews when I thought an illustration of a theoretical point might aid the reader.

Anonymity

One of the women interviewed wanted the tape-recorded version of the interview to be mailed directly to her after it was transcribed. Another asked me to destroy the tape after I had transcribed the interview. I obliged both of them. I also made written transcripts available to the three survivors who wanted them to better understand their own history of sexual abuse as well as how it related to their eating disorder and faith.

Nonhygienic Research

It is my belief that research cannot escape the researcher's personal history. As Helen Roberts claims, "All research is 'grounded' because no researcher can separate herself from personhood and thus deriving second order constructs from experience." [18] A feminist methodology for social science requires that this rationale of research be described and discussed not only in feminist research but in social science research in general. According to Roberts,

[Feminist methodology] requires, further, that the mythology of "hygienic research," with its accompanying mystification of the researcher and the researched as objective instruments of data production, be replaced by the recognition that personal involvement is more than a dangerous bias—it is the condition under which people come to know each other and to admit others into their lives. [19]

In qualitative research the self is always a nonhygienic "instrument" of observation. The data are always messy and require acute observation to winnow out. One needs to draw upon one's background and experience and imagination at all points in the process. As Grant McCracken has put it: "The diverse aspects of the self become a bundle of templates to be held up against the data until parallels emerge."[20]

Disciplined Subjectivity

In psychohistorical work, the "compost heap of today's interdisciplinary efforts,"[21] as Erik Erikson put it, there is, it seems, a unique burden on the part of the investigator to discipline her or his subjectivity. What that means for Erikson is a *specific self-awareness* that the observer must include in her or his own field of perception.[22] According to psychohistorian Charles Strozier, "Nothing else is really honest."[23] Strozier claims that "thoughtful psychologists and historians and social scientists in general have always had some sense of their own role in shaping what they are observing, but disciplined subjectivity necessarily sharpens such awareness."[24]

Because I am a survivor of incest as well as a woman who has struggled with the traumatic symptoms of food, body, and weight preoccupation, I bring empathy to the interviews as well as to the analysis of the data. *Empathy,* as Heinz Kohut has clarified, is the primary tool by which we gather psychologically meaningful data. Defined as "vicarious introspection," empathy is one of our best means of exploring psychological experience. Without empathy as a primary means of gathering data, we are left with little that reveals much of substance about the human world that is customarily the purpose of our inquiry.[25]

Specifics of Long-Interview Method

The *long interview* is one of the most powerful methods in qualitative research.[26] For psychologically descriptive and analytic purposes, no instrument of inquiry is more revealing. This method can take the investigator into the mental world of the individual, to expose categories of logic which she or he uses to make sense of the world. It can also take the investigator into the life-world of the individual to see the content and pattern of daily experience. The long interview gives us the opportunity to step into the minds of other people, to see and experience the world as they do themselves.[27]

The applications of the long interview method are many, but for my social-scientific area of study the method is used to get to a clearer understanding of the theological and psychosocial meaning behind the behaviors and beliefs of the women in question. Quantitative studies have been done on women with eating disorders[28] and with women who have suffered incest.[29] Quantitative research is often concerned with comprehending the breadth of a trend or problem rather than understanding the cultural and psychological underpinnings to that trend or problem. A focus on numbers alone may leave us with monocular vision when it could be binocular.[30] Without a qualitative understanding of how culture mediates human action, one can know only what the numbers reveal. The long qualitative interview is useful because it aids the investigator in situating these numbers in their fuller social and cultural context.[31]

Using a qualitative method has enabled me to inquire into how incest survivors who are food, weight, and body preoccupied define themselves in relation to their spirituality, their sense of agency, their bodies, their families, their relationships, and to those whom they hold in authority. The long interview lets me map out the organizing ideas of spirituality for the survivor and how these ideas enter into her values, her view of herself, and her world. The self-as-instrument process works most easily when it is used simply to search out a match in one's experience for ideas and actions that the respondent has described in the interview. In my research I have enabled the "fleshing out" of what the respondent may hint at by matching her comments with statements that show familiarity (but not necessarily similarity). For instance, when one respondent mentioned that having an alcoholic in the family made her able to read others' moods with great accuracy, I was able to rummage around in my own history for my own relationship with an alcoholic in my own extended family and the consequent feelings towards that person. This matching activity helped me to understand the combination of fear in relation to her alcoholic father—of not knowing who would show up, the sober one or the drunk one—and the powerful social skill she felt she had learned as a result. The matching process helped me fill in and develop what the respondent meant to say and enabled her to expand on the meanings behind the words she chose. My own experience serves as a bundle of possibilities, pointers, and suggestions that can be used to dive deeper into the remarks of the respondent. I worked never to assume but always substantiate and confirm the matches before I considered them thematically relevant.

Sometimes there was no match to be found in my own experience (e.g., I have never been gang-raped). In these cases I proceeded by fashioning an understanding of what was being said. According to McCracken, the process of *imaginative reconstruction* is somewhat more difficult than the matching technique: "It requires the investigator to build an alien, mysterious world of meaning out of assertions that are themselves unconnected, new, or strange. They must perform this task using their own categories of everyday thought, categories that neither anticipate nor welcome the new configuration of meaning."[32] The best technique of imaginative reconstruction is to hold whatever the respondent says (no matter how unfamiliar) as simply and utterly common and then ask oneself, "What does the world look like when I hold these things to be true?" When this process succeeds, the investigator succeeds in reconstructing a version of the respondent's view of the world by taking up and trying on her underlying assumptions and categories. Its results are often the real achievements of the qualitative methodology.

As I have said, qualitative methods are most useful and powerful when the are used to discover how the respondent sees herself and the world. This objective of the method makes it essential that testimony be elicited in as unobtrusive, nondirective manner as possible.[33] Before conducting the interviews I immersed myself in the literature of eating disorders and religion, and incest and religion, but did not find material exploring the connections among sexual abuse, eating problems, and religion. I became familiar with the theories in the literature, and then I worked to set them aside to better pay attention to the life stories and reflections of the subjects I was interviewing. I remembered that the law of the qualitative long interview is *nondirection:* one must avoid leading questions that interpret or proscribe feeling and intent. I felt it to be vitally important to allow the respondent to tell her own story in her own terms. I believe it is also just as important to give structure to the interview by providing a well-shaped protocol (questionnaire) with a well-constructed series of "prompts" that give the interview structure and focus.

Self-Interview

I interviewed myself on tape before interviewing any other respondent.[34] This process was both strange and enlightening. I found that I could play the part of interviewer by staying focused on the questionnaire. By pausing between asking and answering the question, I could switch into the role of respondent and tell my own story. After having the interview transcribed I was amazed by my candor and spontaneity. The process of sharing a side of myself to another side of myself proved worthwhile. In the writing up of the data for this project, I decided to quote my own case material just as I quote that of the other survivors. Overall, this act of interviewing myself helped me (therapeutically as well as professionally) to discern the differences among what I would hear over the following months as I interviewed the other eight survivors.

Questionnaire

For the purpose of giving focus and structure to the long interview process, I chose to use a open-ended questionnaire, which I formulated with the help of psychohistorian Charles Strozier. The open-ended questionnaire has several functions. First, it ensures that I cover all the terrain in the same order for each respondent in each interview. Second, since the respondent and I, the interviewer, are both survivors of incest, the questionnaire also facilitated some distance, giving the respondent room to articulate her story in her own language. Prompts were used to keep the respondent on the topics in question. The third function of the questionnaire is to establish channels for the direction and scope of discourse.[35] The fourth function of the questionnaire preserved the larger structure and objectives of the interview and therefore freed me to give all my attention to the respondent's testimony.

Because of the sensitive area of inquiry, incest and eating problems, trust had to be established before respondents would agree to be interviewed. None of the respondents were perfect strangers to me prior to the interview. They came from Twelve-Step, Feminist Step, or self-help spirituality groups in which I had been a participant-observer. I deliberately selected the respondent pool for contrasts in age, class, education, sexual preference, race, Christian denomination, and occupation.

I opened the interview carefully with a general inquiry section in which respondent anxieties about being interviewed were laid to rest. The questions and prompting strategies were then set in motion as I worked to identify key terms, chose the most promising avenues of inquiry, and listened for material that was indexed by respondent testimony but not made explicit in it. All of this activity was set in a generous time frame (at least two hours) in order to let respondents tell their own story in their own terms.

Analytic Categories

The analysis of qualitative data is perhaps the most demanding and least examined aspect of the qualitative research process.[36] There were several preliminary technical considerations to be considered. Interviews must be recorded on tape. Interviewers must transcribe a verbatim account of the interview testimony. For all nine of the interviews a transcript was created. If I interviewed a respondent for a second time, a transcript was also made. If I conversed with a respondent after a Twelve-Step or other spirituality meeting or came across her locally, I would make a written record of the content-rich information in writing.

The object of analysis was to determine the social, psychological, and religious, categories, relationships, and assumptions that informed the respondents' views of the world in general and in the topic in particular. I came to this undertaking with a sense of what the literature says ought to be there, a sense of how the topic at issue is constituted in my own experience, and a glancing sense of what took place in the interview themselves.

In a few instances, a follow-up interview was necessary to inquire about particular matters so that further narrowing and clarification could take place. In sum, the final step of the long qualitative interview called for the careful analysis of the verbatim transcription of interview data.

Quality Control

How does the investigator ensure the quality of her own qualitative research? There are no guarantees. Much of the difficulty surrounding this question stems from the tendency to judge qualitative research by quantitative standards. It is important to keep in mind the distinction between qualitative and quantitative research visible and clear. In the first, categories take shape in the course of research, whereas in the second, they are fixed from the beginning. The reader of qualitative research must keep in mind that such work is done to show shared themes among a group of particular women and as such may or may not be transferable to a larger population. I do make some general claims about culture that come from hearing the women's stories and coping history. I also qualify such claims when necessary.

I am convinced that this qualitative feminist method enabled me to draw out complex psychological themes, gendered cultural nuances, and religious layers of meaning that could not be reached with a "fill-in-the-blank" questionnaire. The open-ended protocol gave the survivor some control regarding disclosure.

My main intention was to understand the multilayered psychosocial "nature" of a survivor's relationship to food, her body, her past trauma, and her consequent faith. A focused open-ended interview was the ideal vehicle to gather such information. Because I have familiarity with the subject matter I believe I was able to design a sensitive questionnaire, to listen empathically, and to analyze data with greater perception than a quantitative study would have allowed. By using the long interview approach I was able to collect and analyze richly descriptive information. At the same time, with the help of the focused questionnaire, I was able to manage this incredibly full data. Too, a mutually respectful relationship during and prior to the interview appeared to facilitate positive results for my respondent, myself, and this study. Overall, I believe both respondent and interviewer were enriched by the process.

Notes

Notes to the Introduction

1. Hilde Bruch, *The Golden Cage: The Enigma of Anorexia Nervosa* (Toronto: Random House, 1979), ix. Elsewhere in this project I have used the term "relentless pursuit of thinness" in contrast to the medical term *anorexia nervosa*, in order to describe the behavior in a manner outside the disease model. See Matra Robertson, *Starving in the Silences: An Exploration of Anorexia Nervosa* (New York: New York University Press, 1992), xiv. No matter what the survivors' (those interviewed) habits were with food—binging (sometimes called "compulsive overeating"), binge-purging, starving, or chronic dieting—the common denominator was her pursuit of thinness as a key to power/escape. Exploring the "why" of this pursuit is the focus of my work.

2. G. Sloan and P. Leichner, "Is There a Relationship between Sexual Abuse or Incest and Eating Disorders?" *Canadian Journal of Psychiatry* 31 (1986): 656-60.

3. A. Abramson and Grace M. Lucido, "Childhood Sexual Experience and Bulimia," *Addictive Behaviors* 16 (1991): 529-32.

4. In a well-conducted study, 66 of 172 female purging bulimics interviewed had been physically victimized: 23 had been raped, 29 had been sexually molested, 29 had been physically abused as children, and 23 were battered in adult relationships. See Maria Root and Patricia Fallon, "Victimization Experiences as Contributing Factors in the Development of Bulimia in Women," *Journal of Interpersonal Violence* 3 (1988) no. 2: 161-73.

5. For descriptions of incestuous and other adverse sexual experiences in eating-disordered subjects see A. H. Crisp, "The Psychopathology of Anorexia Nervosa: Getting the 'Heat' Out of the System," in *Eating and Its Disorders*, ed. A. J. Stunkard and E. Stellar (New York: Raven Press, 1984), 209-34. See also R. Oppenheimer et al., "Adverse Sexual Experience in Childhood and Clinical Eating Disorders: A Preliminary Description," *Journal of Psychiatric Research* 19 (1985), no. 2/3: 357-61.

6. Much of my methodology has come from directly working with Charles Strozier, co-director, with Robert Lifton, of the Center on Violence and Human Survival at John Jay College of Criminal Justice, City University of New York. See Robert J. Lifton, *Home from the War* (New York: Simon and Schuster, 1973).

7. Conversation with Drorah O'Donnell Setel, 23 November 1992, the American Academy of Religion. See also Geneen Roth, *Feeding the Hungry Heart: The Experience of Compulsive Eating* (New York: Signet, 1982); Jane R. Hirschmann and Carol H. Munter, *Overcoming Overeating: A Revolutionary Approach to Curing Eating Problems* (New York: Fawcett Publishing, 1990).

8. See Appendix B.

9. Be warned that reading about sexual traumas can have disturbing effects.

Notes to Chapter I

1. "Rape in America: A Report to the Nation," prepared by the National Victim Center and Crime Victims Research and Treatment Center, 1992.

2. "The Mind of the Rapist," *Newsweek,* July 1990, quoting U.S. Bureau of Justice Statistics.

3. "Rape in America."

4. Mary Koss, Christine A. Gidycz, and Nadine Wisniewski, "The Scope of Rape: Incidence and Prevalence of Sexual Aggression and Victimization in a National Sample of Higher Education Students," *Journal of Consulting and Clinical Psychology* 55 (1987): 162-70, cited in Peggy Reeves Sanday, *Fraternity Gang Rape: Sex, Brotherhood, and Privilege on Campus* (New York: New York University Press, 1990), 26.

5. Diana E. Russell, *Rape in Marriage* (Bloomington: Indiana University Press, 1990).

6. National Clearinghouse on Marital and Date Rape flyer, Berkeley, California, and "The Myths about Acquaintance Rape" (n.d.), in *WAC Stats: The Facts about Women,* ed. Women's Action Coalition. (New York: New Press, 1993), 49-50.

7. Lorie Heise, "Violence against Women: The Missing Agenda," in *Women's Health: A Global View* (New York: Westview Press, 1992).

8. *WAC Stats,* 49-50.

9. Heise, "Violence against Women."

10. Adrienne Rich, *Of Woman Born: Motherhood as Experience and Institution* (New York: W. W. Norton, 1976), 33.

11. Naomi Wolf, *The Beauty Myth: How Images of Beauty Are Used against Women* (New York: William Morrow, 1991), 181-82.

12. Joanne Carlson Brown and Rebecca Parker, "For God So Loved the World," in *Christianity, Patriarchy, and Abuse: A Feminist Critique* (New York: Pilgrim Press, 1989), 1.

13. Ibid., 2.

14. Mary Daly, *Gyn/Ecology: The Metaethics of Radical Feminism* (Boston: Beacon Press, 1978), 39.

15. Charlotte Davis Käsl, *Many Roads, One Journey: Moving beyond the Twelve Steps* (New York: Harper Collins, 1992), 55.

16. *Jouissance* refers to the pleasure of connectedness where two become one and where the pleasure of the one is the pleasure of the other, a pleasure that transcends boundaries and revels in immediate, "naive" sensation, a pleasure that is unmediated by the social network of positions of the symbolic. See Tamsin E. Lorraine, *Gender, Identity, and the Production of Meaning* (Boulder: Westview Press, 1990), 83.

17. See Susan Faludi, *Backlash: The Undeclared War against American Women* (New York: Crown Publishers, 1991).

18. See Catharine MacKinnon, *Toward a Feminist Theory of the State* (Cambridge, Mass.: Harvard University Press, 1989).

19. "A backlash also exists in reaction to the civil rights movement where the eighties reflect an increasing decline in the gains of African Americans." See Käsl, *Many Roads, One Journey*, 55.

20. Margaret Randall, *This Is about Incest* (Ithaca, N.Y.: Firebrand Books, 1987), 25.

21. See Christine A. Courtois, *Healing the Incest Wound: Adult Survivors in Therapy* (New York: W. W. Norton, 1988).

22. American Psychological Association, *Diagnostic and Statistical Manual of Mental Disorders*, 3d ed., rev. (Washington, D.C.: American Psychiatric Association, 1987).

23. Michael Trimble, *Trauma and Its Wake: The Study and Treatment of Post-Traumatic Stress Disorder* (New York: Brunner/Mazel, 1985), cited in B. W. Thompson, " 'A Way Outa No Way': Eating Problems among African American, Latina, and White Women," *Gender and Society* 6 (December 1992): 559.

24. Thompson, "A Way Outa No Way," 559.

25. Taken from a transcribed conversation between Charles B. Strozier and Robert Lifton, co-directors of the Center for Violence and Human Survival, New York (spring 1992).

26. R. J. Lifton, *Life in Death: Survivors of Hiroshima* (New York: Random House, 1967), 484.

27. Wendy Simonds, *Women and Self-Help Culture: Reading between the Lines* (New Brunswick, N.J.: Rutgers University Press, 1992, 51).

Notes to Chapter 2

1. Barbara Kingsolver, *The Bean Trees* (New York: Harper and Row, 1988), 136.

2. Ellyn Kaschak, *Engendered Lives* (New York: Basic Books, 1992), 141.

See also Diana Russell, "The Incidence and Prevalence of Intrafamilial and Extrafamilial Sexual Abuse of Female Children," *Child Abuse and Neglect: The International Journal* 7 (1983): 133.

3. C. Dinsmore, *From Surviving to Thriving: Incest, Feminism, and Recovery* (Albany, N.Y.: SUNY Press, 1991), 21.

4. Ibid., 23.

5. J. L. Herman, *Trauma and Recovery: The Aftermath of Violence—From Domestic Abuse to Political Terror* (New York: Basic Books, 1992), 7.

6. Ibid., 5.

7. Ibid., 9.

8. Ibid., 9.

9. Ibid., 12.

10. P. Janet, *L'automatisme psychologique: Essai de psychologie expérimentale sur les formes inférieures de l'activité humaine* (Paris: Félix Alcan, 1889), cited in Herman, *Trauma and Recovery*, 12.

11. J. Breuer and S. Freud, "Studies on Hysteria" [1893-95], in *Standard Edition*, vol. 2, trans. J. Strachey (London: Hogarth Press, 1955), cited in Herman, *Trauma and Recovery*, 12.

12. Ibid.

13. Ibid.

14. Ibid.

15. Most therapists insist that therapeutic abreaction—reexperiencing a trauma with the help of the therapist so that feelings can be reprocessed in a less frightening way—is necessary to recovery. As Alice Miller says: "As long as feelings can be talked about, they cannot really be felt, the self-damaging blockages remain." See Miller, *Banished Knowledge: Facing Childhood Injuries*, trans. L. Vennewitz (New York: Doubleday, 1990), 181.

16. Miller, *Banished Knowledge*, 30.

17. S. Freud, "The Aetiology of Hysteria" [1896] in *Standard Edition*, vol. 3, trans. J. Strachey (London: Hogarth Press, 1962), 203.

18. M. Bonaparte, A. Freud, and E. Kris, eds., *The Origins of Psychoanalysis: Letters to Wilhelm Fliess, Drafts and Notes by Sigmund Freud* (New York: Basic Books, 1954), 215-16, cited in Herman, *Trauma and Recovery*, 14.

19. Janet Greeson, *Food for Love* (New York: Simon and Schuster, 1993), 114.

20. Herman, *Trauma and Recovery*, 30.

21. H. Russell, *Sexual Exploitation: Rape, Child Sexual Abuse, and Sexual Harassment* (Beverly Hills: Sage Publications, 1984), cited in Herman, *Trauma and Recovery*, 30.

22. R. Warshaw, *I Never Called It Rape: The Ms. Report on Recognizing, Fighting and Surviving Date and Acquaintance Rape* (New York: Harper and Row, 1988).

23. Lenore Walker, *The Battered Woman* (New York: Harper and Row, 1979).

24. David Finkelhor and K. Yllo, *License to Rape: Sexual Abuse of Wives* (New York: Holt, Rinehart and Winston).

25. "Violent Death Rate Cited as U.S. Health Concern," *New York Times,* 28 November 1984, A-14.

26. See Homeless Women's Rights Network, "Victims Again: Homeless Women in New York City Shelter System" (1989), cited in Carol J. Adams, "Toward a Feminist Theology of Religion and the State," paper read at the American Academy of Religion, 22 November 1992, San Francisco.

27. "Violent Death Rate Cited as U.S. Health Concern."

28. L. Heise, "Abuse," *This World* (Sunday suppl.), *San Francisco Chronicle,* 2 July 1989, 12.

29. "Crimes of Gender," *Z Magazine,* July/August 1989, 61.

30. Kaschak, *Engendered Lives,* 118.

31. Heinz Kohut, *The Analysis of the Self: A Systematic Approach to Psychoanalytic Treatment of Narcissistic Personality Disorders* (New York: International Universities Press, 1971), and idem, *The Restoration of the Self* (New York: International Universities Press, 1977).

32. "Tragic Man" struggles for creativity and self-realization against despair, and is at once a pathological narcissistic personality and a representative of the modern human condition. Modern literature repeatedly describes "Tragic Man's" problems with fragmentation, "the falling apart of the self and of the world and the task of reconstituting the self and the world." Kohut's views can thus be seen as mother-blaming in practice, though this is not necessary to his theories. See Judith Kegan Gardiner, "Self-Psychology as Feminist Theory," *Signs: Journal of Women in Culture and Society* 12, no. 4 (1987): 761-80.

33. Gardiner, "Self-Psychology as Feminist Theory," 780.

34. Writing in the 1930s-1950s in Great Britain, Vienna-born psychoanalyst Melanie Klein (1882-1960) breaks away from the solo-focused, drive-centered theory of Freud to a variety of subsequent approaches that give primacy instead to interpersonal relations. Objecting to Freud's notion of *primary narcissism,* defined as an objectless state, Klein argues that the drives (instincts) are associated from the beginning with certain objects, a priori knowledge of which is a constitutive part of their nature. Others, greatly stimulated by Klein's work, abandoned the drive model altogether, placing relations with others, real and imaginary, at the heart of their theories. In addition to Klein, the psychoanalysts most prominently associated with object-relations thinking include Ronald Fairbairn (1889-1964), Harry Guntrip (1901-1975), and D. W. Winnicott, (1896-1971). Each of these British analysts has written sympathetically about religion. See David M. Wulff, "The Object-Relations Perspective," in *Psychology of Religion: Classic and Contemporary Views* (New York: John Wiley and Sons, 1991), 327.

35. Alice Miller, *The Drama of the Gifted Child: How Narcissistic Parents Form and Deform the Emotional Lives of Their Children* (New York: Basic Books, 1981), 6. See also idem, *For Your Own Good: Hidden Cruelty in Child-*

Rearing and the Roots of Violence (New York: Farrar, Straus and Giroux, 1984), and idem, *Thou Shalt Not Be Aware: Society's Betrayal of the Child* (New York: Farrar, Straus and Giroux, 1984).

36. Miller, *Drama of the Gifted Child*, 6.

37. W. R. D. Fairbairn, "The Repression and the Return of Bad Objects (With Special Reference to the 'War Neuroses')," *British Journal of Medical Psychology* 19 (1943): 327-41.

38. Ibid.

39. Ibid., 332.

40. Ibid., 333.

41. According to psychotherapist E. Sue Bloom, "Ritual abuse—also called cult abuse and Satanic abuse—is a phenomenon whose pervasiveness is only now becoming clear to those who deal with child sexual abuse. The chilling stories told by unrelated victims around the country are virtually identical. The truths of this abuse are so shocking to society that the victimizers are protected by our disbelief." *Ceremonies* are used as a form of indoctrination into various ideologies. The victims are often told they have a bond with the devil, which may be enforced through "marriage" or "bridal" ceremonies. See E. Sue Bloom, *Secret Survivors: Uncovering Incest and Its Aftereffects in Women* (New York: Ballantine Books, 1990), 60.

42. Judith Herman, "The Abuses of Memory," *Mother Jones*, March/April 1993, 3-4.

43. Courtois, *Healing the Incest Wound*, 68. See Appendix G for profiles of male and female perpetrators.

44. Roland Summit, "Beyond Belief: The Reluctant Discovery of Incest," in *Sexual Assault and Abuse: A Handbook for Clergy and Religious Professionals*, ed. Mary D. Pellauer, Barbara Chester, and Jane Boyajian (San Francisco: Harper and Row, 1987), 173.

45. J. L. Herman, *Father-Daughter Incest* (Cambridge, Mass.: Harvard University Press, 1981), 49.

46. Herman, *Trauma and Recovery*, 52. See also Toni Horwitz, "Balkan Death Trip: Scenes from a Futile War," *Harper's*, March 1993, 35-45.

47. Herman, *Trauma and Recovery*, 52.

48. Summit, "Beyond Belief," 173.

49. Courtois, *Healing the Incest Wound*, 153-54.

50. L. Shengold, "Child Abuse and Deprivation: Soul Murder," *Journal of the American Psychoanalytic Association* 27 (1979): 533-59.

51. Courtois, *Healing the Incest Wound*, 155.

52. Herman, *Trauma and Recovery*, 53.

53. Ibid.

54. David Finkelhor finds Post-Traumatic Stress Disorder symptoms in the majority of victims of child sexual abuse but he believes clinicians should be leery of relying on PTSD symptomatology for diagnosing a history of sexual abuse. He has urged researchers to come up with diagnostic categories that see sexual abuse as a process rather than simply a violent event that results in PTSD.

This process involves the context in which the abuse occurs, the victim's shame is maintained, and the violator is protected. See David Finkelhor, "The Trauma of Child Sexual Abuse," *Journal of Interpersonal Violence* 2 (December 1987), no. 4: 348-66.

55. Finkelhor, "Trauma of Child Sexual Abuse," 361.

56. Sylvia B. Patten et al., "Posttraumatic Stress Disorder and the Treatment of Sexual Abuse," *Social Work*, May 1989, 197-203.

57. H. B. Lewis, *Shame and Guilt in Neurosis* (New York: International Universities Press, 1971).

58. Frank Ochberg, *Post-Traumatic Therapy and Victims of Violence* (New York: Brunner/Mazel, 1988), 10-12.

59. D. Doolittle, "Transitional Phenomena in Child Molesters," paper read at the annual conference of the Boston Institute for the Development of Infants and Parents, Pine Manor College, Chestnut Hill, Massachusetts (1988); T. K. Seghorn, R. A. Prentky, and R. J. Boucher, "Childhood Sexual Abuse in the Lives of Sexually Aggressive Offenders," *American Academy of Child and Adolescent Psychiatry* 26 (1987): 262-67, cited in Gail M. Price, "Guilt in Victims of Trauma," *Dissociation* 3 (September 1990), no. 3: 160-64.

60. M. J. Lerner, *The Belief in a Just World* (New York: Plenum Press, 1980).

61. R. Janoff-Bulman, "The Aftermath of Victimization: Rebuilding Shattered Assumptions," in *Trauma and Its Wake: The Study and Treatment of Post-Traumatic Stress Disorder,* ed. C. R. Figley, (New York: Brunner/Mazel, 1985), 15-35.

62. Patten et al., "Posttraumatic Stress Disorder and the Treatment of Sexual Abuse," 199.

63. Finkelhor, "Trauma of Child Sexual Abuse," 363.

64. Most research around incest is done on survivors and offenders. When it comes to mothers, more often than not, stereotypes substitute for data. See "Another Side of the Story," a review of Sandi Ashley's *The Missing Voice: Writings by Mothers of Incest Victims* (Dubuque, Iowa: Kendall/Hunt, 1992), and Janis Tyler Johnson's *Mothers of Incest Survivors: Another Side of the Story* (Bloomington: Indiana University Press, 1992), in *The Women's Review of Books* 10 (April 1993), no. 7: 24.

65. Herman, *Father-Daughter Incest*, 49.

66. Bloom, *Secret Survivors*, 169.

67. P. M. Coons, "Child Abuse and Multiple Personality Disorder: Review of the Literature and Suggestions for Treatment," *Child Abuse and Neglect* 10 (1986): 455-62.

68. F. W. Putnam, "The Clinical Phenomenology of Multiple Personality Disorder: Review of 100 Recent Cases," *Journal of Clinical Psychiatry* 47 (1986): 285-93, cited in Herman, *Trauma and Recovery*, 126.

69. Linda Alcoff and Laura Gray, "Survivor Discourse: Transgression or Recuperation?" *Signs: Journal of Women in Culture and Society* 18 (1993), no. 2: 274.

70. Herman, *Trauma and Recovery*, 125.

71. Otto Kernberg, "Borderline Personality Organization," *Journal of the American Psychoanalytic Association* 15 (1967): 641-85.

72. F. Putnam, *Diagnosis and Treatment of Multiple Personality Disorder* (New York: Guilford Press, 1989); E. L. Bliss, *Multiple Personality, Allied Disorders, and Hypnosis* (New York: Oxford University Press, 1986), cited in Herman, *Trauma and Recovery,* 126.

73. Herman, *Trauma and Recovery,* 126.

74. See also Kaschak, *Engendered Lives,* 99.

75. Personal communication with Charles B. Strozier, April 20, 1992.

76. Sometimes called *psychogenic amnesia,* which includes a sudden inability to recall important personal behavior or events (not due to an organic mental disorder) that is too extensive to be explained by ordinary forgetfulness. See Courtois, *Healing the Incest Wound,* 154.

77. Herman, *Trauma and Recovery,* 52.

78. Ibid., 35.

79. Ibid.

80. L. C. Kolb and L. R. Multipassi, "The Conditioned Emotional Response: A Subclass of Chronic and Delayed Post-Traumatic Stress Disorder," *Psychiatric Annals* 12 (1982): 979-87; T. M. Keane, R. T. Zimmering, and J. M. Caddell, "A Behavioral Formulation of Posttraumatic Stress Disorder in Vietnam Veterans," *Behavior Therapist* 8 (1985): 9-12, cited in Herman, *Trauma and Recovery,* 36.

81. "Rape in America: A Report to the Nation."

82. Lifton, *Death in Life,* 484.

83. Clinicians working in the field of childhood abuse should be alerted to the connection between the survivor characteristics of chronic depression, revictimization, sexual compulsivity, and substance abuse and HIV high-risk behaviors. See C. T. Allers, K. J. Benjack, J. White, and J. T. Rousey, "HIV Vulnerability and the Adult Survivor of Childhood Sexual Abuse," *Child Abuse and Neglect* 17 (1993): 291-98.

84. Summit, *Beyond Belief,* 173.

85. See Herman, *Father-Daughter Incest,* 99-100.

86. See Marc Galanter, "The End of Addiction," *Psychology Today,* November/December 1992, 64-70, 90.

87. L. Rew, "Long-term Effects of Childhood Sexual Exploitation," *Issues in Mental Health Nursing* 10 (1989): 229-44.

88. See C. T. Allers, K. J. Benjack, J. White, and J. T. Rousey, "HIV Vulnerability and the Adult Survivor of Childhood Sexual Abuse," *Child Abuse and Neglect* 17 (1993): 291-98.

89. B. A. van der Kolk et al., "Childhood Origins of Self-Destructive Behavior," *American Journal of Psychiatry* 148 (1991): 1665-71.

90. Wolf, *The Beauty Myth,* 161.

91. Herman, *Trauma and Recovery,* 109.

92. Van der Kolk et al., "Childhood Origins of Self-Destructive Behavior," 1665-71.

93. Herman, *Trauma and Recovery*, 109.

94. Though 80 to 90 percent of sexual abuse is committed by men, the emotional damage and pain of male and female survivors who were abused by women is equally traumatic and equally criminal. In a patriarchal culture, women are socially ostracized for expressing displeasure or anger. They are socialized to tolerate pain in an effort to please others. Often such repression of anger manifests in self-destructive behavior. All too often this violence is released through physical, verbal, or sexual violence toward herself or toward a less powerful social group, namely, children or other women. It is my belief that anyone who sexually abuses children is breaking the law and in serious need of a sex-offender rehabilitation program. See Charlotte Davis Käsl, *Women, Sex, and Addiction: A Search for Love and Power* (New York: Harper and Row, 1989).

95. G. Brown and B. Anderson, "Psychiatric Morbidity in Adult Inpatients with Childhood Histories of Sexual and Physical Abuse," *American Journal of Psychiatry* 148 (1991): 55-61.

96. Christina Thürmer-Rohr, *Vagabonding: Feminist Thinking Cut Loose* trans. Lise Weil (Boston: Beacon Press, 1991), 167.

97. Herman, *Trauma and Recovery*, 111.

98. D. Russell, *The Secret Trauma* (New York: Basic Books, 1986).

99. This is not to say that sexual arousal and violence never merge together for the survivor. In fact, many survivors do have sexual feelings when they see or think about violence. This is most often a source of great conflict for the survivor when she is unaware that such coalescing is due to the early conditioning that merged the two together.

100. Herman, *Trauma and Recovery*, 112.

Notes to Chapter 3

1. A. H. Crisp, *Anorexia Nervosa: Let Me Be* (London: Academic Press, 1980). See also P. E. Garfinkel and D. M. Garner, *Anorexia Nervosa: A Multidimensional Perspective* (New York: Brunner/Mazel, 1982). Both cited in Palmer et al., "Childhood Sexual Experiences," 670.

2. Studies show one in three females and one in six or seven males experiences sexual abuse before age eighteen. See D. Finkelhor, *Sexually Victimized Children* (New York: Free Press, 1979).

3. See note 4, chapter 1.

4. G. Sloan and P. Leichner, "Is There a Relationship between Sexual Abuse or Incest and Eating Disorders?" *Canadian Journal of Psychiatry* 31 (1986): 656-60.

5. Abramson and Lucido, "Childhood Sexual Experience and Bulimia," 529-32.

6. For descriptions of incestuous and other adverse sexual experiences in eating-disordered subjects see Crisp, "Psychopathology of Anorexia Nervosa," 209-34. See also R. Oppenheimer et al., "Adverse Sexual Experience in Child-

hood and Clinical Eating Disorders: A Preliminary Description," *Journal of Psychiatric Research* 19 (1985), no. 2/3: 357-61.

7. Ochberg, *Post-Traumatic Therapy*, 7-8.

8. Ibid.

9. Over 300 million dollars is spent a year on cosmetic surgery. The diet industry grosses 35 billion dollars. See Jenefer Shute, *Life Size* (Boston: Houghton Mifflin, 1992).

10. Rita Freedman, *Bodylove: Learning to Like Our Looks—and Ourselves* (New York: Harper and Row, 1988), 82.

11. See Wolf, *The Beauty Myth*, 192. See also S. Kano, *Making Peace with Food* (Boston: Amity Publishing Co., 1985).

12. Kaschak, *Engendered Lives*, 89.

13. See Judith Butler's *Gender Trouble*, 137.

14. Men also have embodied parts to learn within the gender hierarchy, but for them the physical is characteristically organized around the ability to act upon the environment in much less physically restricted ways. A man can sit and move openly, spread his legs when he sits (thus taking up more space), make noises, and, in general, allow his presence to be felt directly by others and by himself. See Kaschak, *Engendered Lives*, 89.

15. M. P. P. Root, "Persistent, Disordered Eating as a Gender Specific, Post-Traumatic Stress Response to Sexual Assault," *Psychotherapy* 28 (Spring 1991), no. 1: 96-104.

16. Ibid., 98.

17. One-third of all female college students are thought to engage in the habitual use of laxatives, vomiting, and diuretics in order to rid their bodies of unwanted food and weight. See Wolf, *The Beauty Myth*, 181.

18. H. B. Lewis, *Psychic War in Men and Women* (New York: New York University Press, 1976).

19. Paul Ricoeur, *The Symbolism of Evil* (Boston: Beacon Press, 1967), 100-39.

20. R. P. Bulka, "Guilt From, Guilt Towards," *Journal of Psychology and Judaism* 11 (1987): 71-90.

21. Gail M. Price, "Guilt in Victims of Trauma," *Dissociation* 3 (September 1990), no. 3: 160-64.

22. Ibid., 163.

23. L. Damon and J. Todd, "Letter to the Editor," *American Journal of Orthopsychiatry* 56 (1986): 460-61.

24. See D. W. Winnicott, "Transitional Objects and Transitional Phenomena," in *Through Paediatrics to Psycho-Analysis* (New York: Basic Books, 1975), 229-42. See also Richard Ulman and Harry Paul, "A Self-Psychological Theory and Approach to Treating Substance Abuse Disorders: The 'Intersubjective Absorption' Hypothesis," *New Therapeutic Visions* 8 (1992): 121-41.

25. Sometimes perpetrators threaten children they abuse by saying, "If you tell anyone, they'll take me (or your mother, or you) away. And no one will ever love or protect you."

26. I use the word "natural" to mean spontaneous expression. Too often, in a patriarchal culture such expression is also culturally constructed. According to Judith Butler, "any conception of the 'natural' is a dangerous 'illusion' of which we must be 'cured.' See Butler, *Gender Trouble*, 93. Also see Susan Bordo, *Unbearable Weight* (Berkeley: University of California Press, 1993), 290.

27. Rita Nakashima Brock, *Journeys by Heart: A Christology of Erotic Power* (New York: Crossroad Press, 1988), 13.

28. Miller, *Thou Shalt Not Be Aware*, 318.

29. See my chapter 2. Dissociation has been found to be on a continuum, with a range from healthy to unhealthy, from dreaming and fantasies to multiple personality and amnesia. See also R. Price, "Dissociative Disorders of the Self: A Continuum Extending into Multiple Personality," *Psychotherapy* 24 (1987): 387-91. "Addictive patterns of food, alcohol, and drug intake can provide a means of chemical dissociation. . . . Dissociative reactions are complex psychological mechanisms characterized by an alteration of normal integrated awareness and self-identity. Certain faculties, functions, feelings, and memories are split off from immediate awareness or consciousness and compartmentalized in the mind, where they become separate entities. This process can be conceptualized as a form of autohypnosis." See Courtois, *Healing the Incest Wound*, 99, 154.

30. Kaschak, *Engendered Lives*, 219.

31. I have found that dreams are usually the worst during the first two years of memory retrieval and taper off in direct relation to feeling some power in one's life, or through an ability to manage the backlog of emotions.

32. Root. "Persistent, Disordered Eating," 99.

33. H. Kohut, "The Addictive Need for an Admiring Other in Regulation of Self-Esteem," in *The Kohut Seminars on Self-Psychology and Psychotherapy with Adolescents and Young Adults*, ed. M. Elson (New York: W. W. Norton, 1987), 131.

34. D. Brenner, "Self-Regulatory Functions in Bulimia," *Contemporary Psychotherapy Review* 1 (1960): 79-93, quoted from paper read by Donna Fellenberg, Training Institute in Self Psychology (TRISP), New York, February 5, 1993.

35. Herman, *Father-Daughter Incest*, 43-44.

36. "Indeed, the daughter does become a 'woman' in a sense, but she is initiated into a patriarchally defined adult sexual negotiation that confuses the nature of the child-parent relationship and permits his colonization of her body. She is, then, the perfect patriarchal woman, a child-woman: humiliated, defeated, and powerless." See Susan Osborn, "The Trouble with Being a Woman: Anne Sexton's Incest Poetry" (forthcoming), 20.

37. Osborn, "Trouble with Being a Woman," 20.

38. Wolf, *The Beauty Myth*, 161-62.

39. J. K. Chardone, "Eating Disorders: Their Genesis in the Mother-Infant Relationship," *International Journal of Eating Disorders* 4 (1985): 15-39.

40. This sentence could be read as *mother bashing*, which is not my intention.

It is my belief that no individual should be held solely responsible for another's well-being. It is a cultural and filial responsibility that must be shared. See Rich, *Of Woman Born*, 232-33. It is no wonder more women are in therapy than men. Women have been systematically enculturated to believe they are valuable to the degree that they sacrifice/give of themselves, to men, but especially to children.

41. D. Fellenberg quoting Brenner, "Self-Regulatory Functions in Bulimia," 1983. Fellenberg recognizes that one who does walk away from the binger, either literally or figuratively, is the mother. It is my belief, in these scenarios, that the father often capitalizes on tensions between mother and daughter. He seduces the daughter to believing that "he's the good parent" and is then relied upon to fulfill *selfobject* needs. He fails his daughter by experiencing his daughter's need for nurturance (and consequent desire for physical affection or pleasurable emotional intensity) as "sexual." See Phyllis Chesler, *Women and Madness* (New York: Harcourt Brace Jovanovich, 1972), 19.

42. Compulsive behavior and obsessive thoughts of food and/or thinness work to prevent fragmentation in all nine of the case studies. According to Freud, much of obsessive ideation and ritual is in the service of controlling danger/death or managing the feelings of falling apart—an impossible struggle. These are defense mechanisms: *isolation* (the separation of idea or image from affect or emotional content), *displacement* (the shifting of feeling or energy from one image or idea to another), and *undoing* (the wiping out of a prior thought or action, or counteraction, to create the sense that the original action did not occur). All of these have to do with numbing; in particular, undoing attempts not only to stop time and action but to reverse their flow. See R. J. Lifton, *The Broken Connection: On Death and the Continuity of Life* (New York: Basic Books, 1980), 211. See also Josef Breuer and Sigmund Freud, "Studies on Hysteria," *Standard Edition*, vol. 2 (1983), 3-17.

43. Root, "Persistent, Disordered Eating," 100.

44. Ibid.

45. Ibid.

46. Elaine Westerlund, *Women's Sexuality After Childhood Incest* (New York: W. W. Norton, 1992), 126.

Notes to Chapter 4

1. The term *spiritualize* here refers to a method of using religious discourse to gloss over atrocious political and personal conditions. See example in M. Daly, *Beyond God the Father* (Boston: Beacon Press, 1973), 5.

2. Herman, *Father-Daughter Incest*, 108.

3. Even if the environment of the child-victim is not a religious one, she will discern misogynous messages about females being the sexual and *touchable class*, just through living in a modern Western society. Secular and Christian categories are difficult to distinguish in North America. For how children from

religious homes are affected by sexual abuse, see Sheila A. Redmond, "Christian *Virtues* and Child Sexual Abuse," in *Christianity, Patriarchy and Abuse: A Feminist Critique*, ed. Joanne Carlson Brown and Carole R. Bohn (New York: Pilgrim Press, 1989), 73.

4. See James G. Williams, *The Bible, Violence and the Sacred: Liberation from the Myth of Sanctioned Violence* (New York: Harper Collins, 1991); Robert Hamerton-Kelly, *Sacred Violence: Paul's Hermeneutic of the Cross* (Minneapolis: Fortress Press, 1992); R. Schwager, *Must There Be Scapegoats? Violence and Redemption in the Bible* (San Francisco: Harper and Row, 1987); James Poling, *The Abuse of Power: A Theological Problem* (Nashville: Abingdon, 1991); see also A. Imbens and I. Jonker, *Christianity and Incest*, trans. Patricia McVay (Minneapolis: Fortress Press, 1992).

5. For information on Hinduism and treatment of women, see Julia O'Faolain and Lauro Martine, *Not in God's Image* (New York: Harper Torchbooks, 1973); Katherine Mayo, *Slave of the Gods* (New York: Harcourt, Brace and Co., 1929); Evelyn Sullerot, *Women, Change and Society* (New York: McGraw-Hill, 1971); Daly, *Gyn-Ecology;* Florence Rush, *Best Kept Secret: Sexual Abuse of Children* (New York: McGraw-Hill, 1981).

6. Herman, *Father-Daughter Incest,* 50-52.

7. Ibid., 60.

8. Ibid., 52.

9. Imbens and Jonker, *Christianity and Incest,* 282. See also Redmond, "Christian *Virtues* and Child Sexual Abuse," 76.

10. See Daly, *Beyond God the Father,* 77. See also Rosemary Radford Ruether, *Sexism and Godtalk: Toward a Feminist Theology* (Boston: Beacon Press, 1983), 116-38.

11. Redmond, "Christian *Virtues* and Child Sexual Abuse," 76.

12. I have included self-sacrifice in this category because I believe it is a primary form of female suffering.

13. Redmond, "Christian *Virtues* and Child Sexual Abuse," 76.

14. Deborah J. Pope-Lance and Joan Chamberlain Engelsman, *Domestic Violence: A Guide for Clergy* (Lawrenceville: New Jersey Department of Community Affairs, 1987), 29.

15. See Brown and Parker, "For God So Loved the World," and Rita Nakashima Brock, "And a Little Child Will Lead Us: Christology and Child Abuse," both in *Christianity, Patriarchy, and Abuse,* ed. Joanne Carlson Brown and Carole R. Bohn (New York: Pilgrim Press, 1988).

16. St. Anselm, "Curs Deus Homo," in *St. Anselm: Basic Writings,* 2d ed., trans. S. N. Deane (La Salle, Ill.: Open Court Publishing, 1962), chap. 9.

17. Most currently available data indicate that perpetrators of incestuous abuse are predominantly male. Even if the offender is not the father, insofar as the offender is male, he is perceived as belonging to the entitled class—the group you don't refuse. See Courtois, *Healing the Incest Wound,* 18. See also Russell, "Incidence and Prevalence," 133-46.

18. Karen Horney, *Neurosis and Human Growth* (New York: W. W. Norton, 1950); idem, *The Adolescent Diaries of Karen Horney* (New York: Basic Books, 1980).

19. Marcia Weskott, *The Feminist Legacy of Karen Horney* (New Haven: Yale University Press, 1986), 163-64.

20. In some cases a survivor "surrenders" to protect her life. Some survivors are terrorized by their perpetrator and are promised they will die if they disclose the incest. Not all incest perpetrators are pedophiles. See Appendix F for perpetrator profiles.

21. Redmond, "Christian *Virtues* and Child Sexual Abuse," 73.

22. M. J. Lerner, *The Belief in a Just World* (New York: Plenum Press, 1980).

23. Root, "Persistent, Disordered Eating," 99.

24. Adapted from Rabbi Julie Ringold Spitzer's work, *Spousal Abuse in Rabbinic and Contemporary Judaism* (New York: National Federation of Temple Sisterhoods, 1985).

25. *Greek New Testament,* 3d ed., ed. K. Aland, M. Black, C. M. Martini, B. M. Metzger, and A. Wikgren (Münster: Institute for New Testament Textual Research, 1983), 115.

26. Parts of this section are adapted from the Reverend Marie M. Fortune and Denise Hormann's work, *Family Violence: A Workshop Manual for Clergy and Other Service Providers* (Seattle: Center for the Prevention of Sexual and Domestic Violence, 1980). See also a manual that I co-researched, *Domestic Violence: A Guide for Clergy,* by Joan Engelsman and the Reverend Deborah Pope-Lance (Trenton: New Jersey Department of Community Affairs, 1986).

27. Matthew 5:39, Revised Standard Edition.

28. For notions that "true forgiveness comes as a by-product of recovery," among the many, see Beverly Engel, *The Right to Innocence: Healing the Trauma of Childhood Sexual Abuse* (New York: Ivy Books, 1989), 173; and Betsy Petersen, *Dancing with Daddy: A Childhood Lost and a Life Regained* (New York: Bantam Books, 1991), 144.

29. More research needs to be done on recidivism and rehabilitation of perpetrators. See Herman, *Father-Daughter Incest,* 158.

30. Before 1978, when Congress passed the first federal law prohibiting the production and sale of child pornography, it was possible in the United States to purchase more than 250 different magazines filled with pornographic pictures of young children, most of the illustrations imported from abroad. Most pedophiles spend a better part of their waking hours fantasizing about children. What pornography does for those kinds of fantasies is reinforce them. Though as one psychiatrist, Rob Freeman-Longo, has said, "Pornography is in the eye of the beholder. . . . A pedophile can look at the children's underwear section of a Sears catalogue and become aroused." The argument that Freeman-Longo and ACLU groups have made is that the resources necessary to broaden the battle against child porn might be better spent in arresting the child molesters. See John Crewdson, *By Silence Betrayed: Sexual Abuse of Children in America* (New York: Harper and Row, 1988), 246-47.

31. Kathleen Z. Young, "The Imperishable Virginity of Saint Maria Goretti," *Gender and Society* 3 (December 1989), no. 4: 474-82.

32. "Address Delivered to the Young People of Catholic Action from Sengallia Diocese on the Modernness of Saint Maria Goretti's Message," *Oxford Review* 47 (24 November 1980): 88-99. See also Redmond, "Christian *Virtues* and Child Sexual Abuse," 74-75.

33. In a recent article a father of one of the eight teenage boys (of the gang called Spur Posse) accused of raping and molesting several "girls as young as 10" defended his son's right to have sex on his terms. Mr. Belman said, "The girls that Kris had sex with were *giving it away.*" He added, "There wouldn't be enough jails in America, if boys were imprisoned for doing what mine has done." Mr. Belman went on to describe his son as being "all man." See Jane Gross, "Where *Boys Will Be Boys* and Adults Are Befuddled," *New York Times,* 29 March 1993, A-1, A-13.

34. A modern (1989-1993) example of holding a woman accountable for rape (in court proceedings) because she was not a virgin is the case of a gang rape (with a baseball bat, a stick, and a broomstick, as well as forced fellatio) of a retarded seventeen-year-old (with an IQ of 64) in Glen Ridge, New Jersey. See Karen Houppert, "Baseball Bats and Broomsticks," *Village Voice,* 16 March 1993, 29-33.

35. Sherry Ortner has stated that all complex agrarian societies have forms of the "virginity complex." The complex is found in societies in which inheritance is associated with legitimate birth and is the basis of status inequalities. Legitimate inheritance and status or place in society are dependent on the social perception of female chastity. The appropriate construction of female sexuality is linked to preservation of the social order and legitimate inheritance. A man's honor rests upon the control of his female relatives. See Sherry Ortner, "The Virgin and the State," *Feminist Studies* 4 (1978): 19-37. See also Jane F. Collier, "From Mary to Modern Woman: The Material Basis of Marianismo and Its Transformation in a Spanish Village," *American Ethnologist* 13 (1986): 100-107.

36. Price, "Guilt in Victims of Trauma," 160-64.

37. Terrorizing a child, or any person (with emotional desertion or physical injury) has been found to lead to the rapid internalization of the thinking, affect and intentionality of the perpetrator. This phenomenon, termed the Stockholm Syndrome, was observed in bank employees taken hostage in Sweden in 1973 and has been seen in victims of all forms of violence. See D. Lang, "A Report at Large (Swedish Hostages)," *New Yorker,* 25 November 1974, 56-126. The Stockholm Syndrome differs from *identification with the aggressor* in that not only the behavior, but also the entire worldview, including the disavowed guilt of the perpetrator is incorporated. See Price, "Guilt in Victims of Trauma," 162.

38. Redmond, "Christian *Virtues* and Child Sexual Abuse," 77.

39. Sheila Rowbotham, *Woman's Consciousness, Man's World* (Harmondsworth, U.K.: Penguin, 1973), 29-30.

40. Herman, *Trauma and Recovery,* 210.

41. Deuteronomy 5:16, *The Bible,* Revised Standard Edition.

42. Miller, *For Your Own Good.*

43. J. A. Phillips, *Eve: The History of an Idea* (San Francisco: Harper and Row, 1984). Phillips has made one of the most succinct and sound analyses of the development of God as male and father, and the impact it has had on the consciousness of a people. See Redmond, "Christian *Virtues* and Child Sexual Abuse," 87.

44. Carol Saussy, *God Images and Self Esteem: Empowering Women in a Patriarchal Society* (Louisville, Ky.: Westminster/John Knox, 1991), 17. See also Carol Christ and Judith Plaskow's *Women's Spirit Rising: A Feminist Reader in Religion* (San Francisco: Harper and Row, 1979) and Sally McFague's *Models of God: Theology for an Ecological, Nuclear Age* (Philadelphia: Fortress Press, 1987).

45. Susan Bordo, "Reading the Slender Body," in *Body/Politics: Women and the Discourse of Science,* ed. Mary Jacobus, Evelyn Fox Keller, and Sally Shuttleworth (London: Routledge, 1990), 83.

46. Rich, *Of Woman Born,* 78.

47. S. Ortner, "Is Female to Male as Nature Is to Culture?" in *Woman, Culture and Society,* ed. M. Z. Rosaldo and L. Lamphere (Stanford, Calif.: Stanford University Press, 1974).

48. Ruether, "Woman, Body, and Nature: Sexism and the Theology of Creation," in *Sexism and God-Talk* (see n. 10 above), 72.

49. Nel Noddings, *Women and Evil* (Berkeley: University of California Press, 1989), 36.

50. See Hermigild Dressler et al., eds., *The Fathers of the Church* (Washington, D.C.: University Press of America, 1959).

51. Kaschak, *Engendered Lives,* 55-56.

52. Ruether, "Western Tradition," 32.

53. Conversation with Judith Walker (summer 1987).

54. Augustine, *De Trinitate* 7.7.10., cited in Ruether, "Western Tradition," 32.

55. According to Aristotle the woman, by nature, was "inferior in her capacity for thought, will, and physical activity." In his "Politics," Aristotle taught that women were "natural slaves"; it was their nature to be obedient servants in all things to their heads and masters, men. See Aristotle, "Politics," trans. Benjamin Jowett, in *The Complete Works of Aristotle,* ed. Jonathan Barnes (Princeton, N.J.: Princeton University Press, 1984), 1.1-2.

56. Thomas Aquinas, *Summa Theologica,* pt. 1., Q. 91, "On the Production of Woman"; pt. 3, Q. 39, Ar. 1, "Whether the Female Sex Is an Impediment to Receiving Orders," cited in Ruether, "Western Tradition," 32.

57. Martin Luther, "Lectures on Genesis," in *Luther's Works,* ed. Jaroslav Pelikan, vol. 1 (St. Louis: Concordia Publishing House, 1955), 68-69.

58. See Elizabeth Clark and Herbert Richardson, "The Puritan Transformation of Marriage," in *Women and Religion,* ed. R. R. Ruether (New York:

Harper and Row, 1977), 144-45. For a more recent look at Christian dread of female equality, see the speech given at the 1992 Republican convention by televangelist Pat Robertson, who spoke on the proposed equal rights amendment: "It is about a socialist, anti-family political movement that encourages women to leave their husbands, kill their children, practice witchcraft, destroy capitalism and become lesbians."

59. See *The 'Malleus Maleficarum' of Heinrich Kramer and James Sprenger,* trans. Montague Summers (New York: Dover Publications, 1971), 47 [1928]. This infamous manual for witch hunters was inspired by a 1484 bull of Pope Innocent VIII and approved by the Faculty of Theology of the University of Cologne. See D. M. Wulff, *Psychology of Religion* (New York: John Wiley and Sons, 1991), 332.

60. Although not all victims of witchcraft persecution were women, overwhelmingly women were targets. Moreover, the official image of the witch was female. In fact, witch hunting tended to stop when this image was violated and men of some social standing came to be accused. See Ruether, "Western Tradition," 36. See also H. C. E. Midelfort, *Witch Hunting in South West Germany, 1563-84* (Stanford, Calif.: Stanford University Press, 1972). See also Marion L. Starkey, *The Devil in Massachusetts* (New York: Alfred A. Knopf, 1949).

61. Weskott, *Feminist Legacy of Karen Horney,* 94-95.

62. Kaschak, *Engendered Lives,* 68.

63. See Susan Bordo, "Anorexia Nervosa: Psychopathology as the Crystallization of Culture," in *Feminism and Foucault: Reflections on Resistance,* ed. Irene Diamond and Lee Quinby (Boston: Northeastern University Press, 1988), 101. See also Sandra Bartky, "Foucault, Femininity, and the Modernization of Patriarchal Power," in *Femininity and Domination: Studies in the Phenomenology of Oppression* (New York: Routledge, 1990), cited in Anne Marie Hunter, "Numbering the Hairs of Our Heads: Male Social Control and the All-Seeing Male God," paper read at the American Academy of Religion, 23 November 1991, Kansas City, Missouri.

64. Bruch, *Golden Cage,* 58 cited in Hunter, "Numbering the Hairs of Our Heads," 8.

65. Karen Horney wrote, "The neurotic is not mad but *supranormal:* the paragon of what neurotogenic culture produces." In her view therapy was deconstruction of the neurotic (culture) type as a condition of social change. See K. Horney, "Maturity and the Individual," *American Journal of Psychoanalysis* 7 (1947), 85-87, cited in Weskott, *Feminist Legacy of Karen Horney,* 13.

66. Religious food offered women not only the sweetness of Christ's body (the Eucharist) but the identification with the suffering of the cross, thus a holy marker. See Carol Walker Bynum, *Holy Feast and Holy Fast* (Berkeley: University of California Press, 1987), 119.

67. Roundness in female flesh is not universally (cross-culturally) disdained. Some cultures aesthetically prefer fleshy females. Most often her weightiness symbolizes her family's greater material wealth and her reproductive potential.

For more on the historical trend toward thinness, see Joan J. Brumberg, *Fasting Girls: The History of Anorexia Nervosa* (New York: New American Library, 1988).

68. Rudolph Bell, *Holy Anorexia* (Chicago: University of Chicago, 1985), 149. The male-dominated hierarchy of the church determined whether the fasting nun was a heretic, a witch, or a saint. After the Reformation such fasting began to be regarded regularly as insane behavior. The concept of illness, rather than piety, became the explanation of women's ascetic practices. See Matra Robertson, *Starving in the Silences* (New York: New York University Press, 1992), 25-26.

69. Bynum, *Holy Feast and Holy Fast*, 62.

70. Ibid. I went to Siena, Italy (summer of 1992), to learn about popular perceptions of St. Catherine of Siena, who was likely the most famous and rigorous of fasting holy women. I was amazed by what I found. Her home had been turned into a church and chapel for visitors. Her narrow, cement, prayer-cell had hundreds of bills (currency of many different nations), trinkets, jewelry, valentines, and pictures of wounded children, thrown into it. On the walls of the chapel, paintings of Catherine, though not in relief, pop out at onlookers. The renderings depict a sickly woman so weak that she needed to be carried by others. Other images depicted Catherine with eyes and head cast down (much like Jesus on the Cross) as she looked dully at a lily-of-the-valley. Being frail and near death seems to mark her saintliness. Even modern-day religious folk appear inspired by this quintessentially feminine self-starver.

71. Bell, *Holy Anorexia*, 20-21, 135.

72. Teresa of Avila, *The Life of Saint Teresa of Jesus*, trans. and ed. E. Allison Peers (Garden City, N.Y.: Doubleday/Image, 1960), 165.

73. Catherine of Siena, *The Dialogue* in *Classics of Western Spirituality*, trans. S. Noffke (New York: Paulist Press, 1980), 243, cited in Gail Corrington, "Anorexia, Asceticism, and Autonomy: Self-Control as Liberation and Transcendence," *Journal of Feminist Studies in Religion* 2 (1986): 51.

74. Bynum, *Holy Feast and Holy Fast*, 212.

75. Themes of *imitatio Christi* include suffering as Christ suffered—stigmata, through self-sacrificial acts of charity, and healing the sick with no thought of one's self. Suffering like Christ was that which enabled merging with Christ's essence and thus healing others as Christ did through his suffering flesh. See Bynum, *Holy Feast and Holy Fast*, 245-50.

76. See case of Henriette A., in Helmut Thöma, *Anorexia Nervosa*, trans. Gillian Brydone (New York: International Universities Press, 1967), 98-99.

77. Thomas of Cantimpré, *Life of Lutgard*, bk. 1, chap. 2, par. 21, 194-95, and bk. 1, chap. 1, par. 12, 193, cited in Bynum, *Holy Feast and Holy Fast*, 213.

78. André Vauchez, *La Sainteté en Occident aux derniers siècles du moyen âge d'après les procès de canonisation et les documents hagiographiques* (Bibliothèque des Ve'tudes française de Rome, 1981), 406. And see Donald Weinstein and Rudolph M. Bell, *Saints and Society: The Two Worlds of Western Chris-*

tendom, 1000-1700 (Chicago: University of Chicago Press, 1982), 33-36, cited in Bynum, *Holy Feast and Holy Fast*, 213.

79. On touch in Lutgard's Life, see Martinus Cawley, "Life and Journal of Lutgard," 20-48. Columba of Rieti, like Lutgard, experienced attempted rape and her body went rigid in response; see "Life of Columba," chap. 8, trans. J. Bollandus and G. Henschenius, in *Acta sanctorum . . . editio novissima*, ed. J. Carnandet et al. (Paris: Palmé, etc., 1863), vol. 5, 169-70, cited in Bynum, *Holy Feast and Holy Fast*, 213. See also Bell, *Holy Anorexia*, 151-79.

80. Kaschak, *Engendered Lives*, 191.

81. Mary Douglas, *Purity and Danger: An Analysis of the Concepts of Pollution and Taboo* (Boston: Ark Paperbacks, 1985).

82. Douglas, *Purity and Danger*, cited in Martha J. Reineke, "Abjection, Anorexia, and Women Mystics," *Journal of the American Academy of Religion* 58 (Summer), no. 2: 249.

83. Ibid.

84. Kaschak, *Engendered Lives*, 191.

Notes to Chapter 5

1. Herman, *Trauma and Recovery*, 95.

2. Fairbairn, "Repression and the Return of Bad Objects," 331.

3. Shengold, *Soul Murder*, 315, cited in Herman's *Trauma and Recovery*, 193.

4. Herman, *Trauma and Recovery*, 193. See also James W. Fowler, *Stages of Faith* (San Francisco: Harper and Row, 1981).

5. Kaschak, *Engendered Lives*, 143.

6. This statement is advice given the virgin Eustochium by the fourth-century Latin church father, Jerome, *Epistle* 22. 10-11 *(Ad Eustochium)*, "Select Letters of Saint Jerome," Eng. trans. F. A. Wright, Loeb Classical Library (New York: Putnam, 1933), cited in Gail, "Anorexia, Asceticism, and Autonomy," 52-61.

7. Women such as Ida of Louvain, Elsbet Achler, and Columba of Rieti were reported by their hagiographers to "snatch up the eucharist and [eat] without knowing they were doing so." See Bynum, *Holy Feast and Holy Fast*, 213.

8. Conversation with Charles B. Strozier, 6 March 1993.

9. A. Rizzuto, *The Birth of a Living God* (Chicago: University of Chicago Press, 1979), x.

10. Saussy, *God Images and Self Esteem*, 49.

11. See Redmond, "Christian *Virtues*."

12. Richard B. Ulman and Harry Paul, "Dissociative Anesthesia and the Transitional Selfobject Transference in the Intersubjective Treatment of the Addictive Personality" in *New Therapeutic Visions* ed. Arnold Goldberg (Hillsdale, N.J.: Analytic Press, 1992), 8. See also Richard B. Ulman and Doris Brothers, "A Self-Psychological Reevaluation of Posttraumatic Stress Disorder (PTSD)

and Its Treatment: Shattered Fantasies" *Journal of the American Academy of Psychoanalysis* 2 (1987), no. 15: 175-203.

13. Paul Tillich, *The Courage to Be* (New Haven: Yale University Press, 1952), 47.

14. Ibid.

15. Many survivors do not report having any positive sensations in their bodies during the abuse. But some do and this knowledge confounds them. It is important to know that our bodies are most sensitive around our genitals and orifices. When these are stimulated, through thought or physical sensation, our nerves respond. Sexual responses can be automatic. High stress and anxiety can themselves trigger sexual responses. Abuse is abuse whether or not one responded sexually. See Wendy Maltz, *The Sexual Healing Journey: A Guide for Survivors of Sexual Abuse* (New York: Harper Perennial, 1991), 44.

16. Donna F. LaMar, *Transcending Turmoil: Survivors of Dysfunctional Families* (New York: Plenum/Insight, 1992).

17. Winnicott believes that a memory of a good-enough *mothering-parent—* any consistent caretaker—is projected onto an object and thus is able to aid the child through the difficult process of separation-individuation. See D. W. Winnicott, "Transitional Objects and Transitional Phenomena," *Playing and Reality* (London: Routledge, 1971). For Paul Pruyser, "Most psychoanalysts believe this capacity to be alone is dependent on the individual having within the self, with trust and reliance, a dynamic image of the benevolent mother, which not only sees one through times when she must be physically absent, but functions as an auxiliary ego that enhances the child's mastery of his or her impulses." In Paul W. Pruyser, *The Play of Imagination: Towards a Psychoanalysis of Culture* (New Haven: International Universities Press, 1983), 174.

18. Alice Miller, *The Untouched Key: Tracing Childhood Trauma in Creativity and Destructiveness* (New York: Doubleday, 1988), 148.

19. J. V. Becker et al., "Time-Limited Therapy with Sexually Dysfunctional Sexually Assaulted Women," *Journal of Social Work and Human Sexuality* 3 (1984): 97-115, cited in Herman, *Trauma and Recovery*, 69.

20. See Appendix G.

21. Herman, *Trauma and Recovery*, 178.

22. Women's Action Alliance is an excellent activist and resource organization based in New York. Their phone number is 212/532-8330.

23. See Appendix H for a sample letter to your local and state representative.

24. Daly, *Beyond God the Father*, 50.

25. Audre Lorde, *Sister Outsider* (Freedom, Calif.: Crossing Press, 1984), 55.

26. Daly, *Beyond God the Father*, 50.

27. Marie Fortune, *Sexual Violence: The Unmentionable Sin* (New York: Pilgrim Press, 1983), 81-87.

28. Martin Buber saw the moral need for community to be built on the basis of a strong sense of relational bonding between persons, and between persons and other creatures, such as trees. See Martin Buber, *I and Thou*, trans. Walter Kaufman (New York: Charles Scribner's Sons, 1970), cited in Carter Heyward,

Touching Our Strength: The Erotic as Power and the Love of God (New York: Harper and Row, 1989), 14.

29. Tillich, *The Courage to Be*, 32-63.

30. Daly, *Pure Lust* (Boston: Beacon Press, 1984), 223.

Notes to Chapter 6

1. Herman, *Trauma and Recovery*, 133.

2. Ibid.

3. Conversation with feminist scholar Susan Osborn, 29 March 1993.

4. A feminist approach to eating disorders and incest is taken at The Renfrew Center, a treatment facility with twelve centers on the East Coast. For more information, call 1-800-RENFREW. See also Overcoming Overeating Newsletter (created by Jane Hirschmann and Carol Munter) c/o Jade Publishing, 935 W. Chestnut, Suite 420, Chicago, IL 60622. To order tapes call 1-800-468-0464.

5. See Wulff, *Psychology of Religion*, Glossary, 30.

6. "A *transitional sphere* is a unique pattern of dynamic relation in which certain things and certain attachments are held to be of incontestable value. The *transitional object* is not a thing in an ordinary sense, but a quasi-sacred entity, that is constituted by a process of make believe in which the rest of the [group or] family conspire. . . . In a word, the *transitional object* is a product of active imagining on the part of the child, reinforced by the [group or] family's participatory creation of a *transitional sphere* which has all the features of play." See Paul Pruyser on D. W. Winnicott in *Play of Imagination*, 58-59. D. W. Winnicott, *The Maturational Process and the Facilitating Environment* (New York: International Universities Press, 1972), 181.

7. Arnold Van Gennep, *The Rites of Passage,* trans. Monika B. Vizedom and Gabrielle L. Caffee (Chicago: University of Chicago Press, 1960).

8. The Serenity Prayer is: "God grant me the serenity to accept the things I cannot change, the courage to change the things I can, and the wisdom to know the difference." An earlier version is rumored to have originated with Reinhold Niebuhr who supposedly based it on a prayer by St. Francis of Assisi.

9. Kenneth L. Schmitz, "Ritual Elements in Community," *Religious Studies* 7 (January 1979): 166.

10. Van Gennep, *Rites of Passage*, 117.

11. Victor Turner, *Dramas, Fields, and Metaphors* (Ithaca, N.Y.: Cornell University Press, 1974).

12. Jerome Frank, *Persuasion and Healing* (New York: Schocken Books, 1974), 27.

13. For Campbell, "A hero ventures forth from the world of common day into a region of supernatural wonder: fabulous forces are there encountered and a decisive victory is won: the hero comes back from this mysterious adventure with the power to bestow boons on his fellow man." In Joseph C. Campbell, *The Hero with a Thousand Faces* (Princeton, N.J.: Princeton University Press,

1973), 30. Also see the word *monomyth* used in James Joyce's *Finnegans Wake* (New York: Viking Press, 1939), 581.

14. See Appendix E for the Feminist Steps. It is a format that works to make the invisible meanings (regarding the politics of recovery) visible. I have been using this format with survivors of incest since 1990.

15. Ronald L. Grimes, *Beginnings in Ritual Studies* (Lanham, Md.: University Press of America, 1982), 149.

16. Victor Turner, *The Ritual Process: Structure and Anti-Structure* (Chicago: Aldine Press, 1969), 122.

17. See James Joyce's character Leopold Bloom and his "community of exiles," in "Cyclops," in *Ulysses* (New York: Vintage Books, 1986), 240-84.

18. Turner, *Dramas, Fields, and Metaphors*, 238.

19. Ibid. 232.

20. Lorde, *Sister Outsider*.

21. See Matthew Fox, *Original Blessing: A Primer in Creation Spirituality* (Santa Fe: Bear and Co., 1983).

22. In the *Big Book* (sourcebook of Alcoholics Anonymous) people are warned against becoming sexually involved with group members, especially sponsoring members of one's sexual preference group. Such a relationship is dubbed "Thirteen Stepping."

23. C. D. Käsl, *Many Roads, One Journey* (New York, Harper Collins, 1992), 292.

24. Paolo Freire, *Pedagogy of the Oppressed* (New York: Seabury Press, 1969), cited in Kaschak, *Engendered Lives*, 214.

25. Ellen Herman, *Out/Look: National Lesbian and Gay Quarterly* (Summer 1988), excerpted in *Utne Reader*, November 1988, 60.

26. Herman, *Utne Reader*, 60.

27. It is not my intention to pretend the views expressed by the women interviewed, and my analysis of their experiences, are representative of the majority of "Twelve-Steppers." I have been reminded more than a few times to acknowledge that "the anonymous organizations have a huge membership that spans a range of opinion from the profound to the pathological, that groups differ tremendously and that members speak as individuals only." See Kate Gilpin, "Taking Inventory," *On the Issues*, Spring 1993, 52-53; see also Marc Galanter, "The End of Addictions," *Psychology Today*, November/December 1992, 64-70, 90.

28. Gilpin, "Taking Inventory," 53.

29. Polly Young-Eisendrath, "Entanglements: Food, Sex, and Aggression in Female Development," paper quoted in *Perspective*, Winter 1993, 3.

30. Ibid.

31. See *The Twelve Steps of Overeaters Anonymous* (Torrance, Calif.: Overeaters Anonymous, 1980), 6.

32. See step 12 in Appendix C.

33. Käsl, *Many Roads, One Journey*, 83-84.

34. See traditions 1 and 10 in *The Twelve Steps of Overeaters Anonymous,* 115.

35. Fowler, *Stages of Faith.*

36. See ibid. See also Kenneth Stokes, *Faith Is a Verb: The Dynamics of Adult Faith Development* (Mystic, Conn.: Twenty-Third Publications, 1989), cited in Käsl, *Many Roads, One Journey,* 30.

37. At Twelve-Step business meetings members discuss shifting needs or conflicts that arise. Yet such groups are often full of the most *loyalistic* members.

38. Herman, *Trauma and Recovery,* 196.

39. Nelle Morton, *The Journey Is Home,* (Boston: Beacon Press, 1985), 202.

40. "No cross-talking" means no advice giving. After one hears a speaker one cannot comment on the content using "you" statements. Only "I" statements are encouraged.

41. In some incest groups, perpetrators of incest, even incest survivors who have perpetrated sexually against another, are asked to leave (and not come back) at the beginning of the meeting. Some are referred to Parents Anonymous meetings which aid perpetrators.

42. Käsl, *Many Roads, One Journey,* 313.

43. Ibid., 314.

44. Ibid., 87.

45. L. J. Tess Tessier, "Women Sexually Abused as Children: The Spiritual Consequences," *Second Opinion* 17 (January 1992) 3: 11-13. See also Carter Heyward, *Touching Our Strength: The Erotic as Power and the Love of God* (San Francisco: Harper and Row, 1989); Rita Nakashima Brock, *Journey by Heart: Christology of Erotic Power* (New York: Crossroad Press, 1988). Lorde, "Uses of the Erotic: The Erotic as Power," in *Sister Outsider.*

46. For new approaches to eating disorders, see Gayle Lacks, "Women and Food: The Stone Center Perspective on Women's Psychological Development," *Perspective,* Winter 1993, 7. In Lacks's words, "For most women in this society, food is used to stay in unhealthy [abusive] relationships."

47. Imbens and Jonker, *Christianity and Incest,* 280.

48. Conversation with Annie Imbens on 22 November 1992, the American Academy of Religion, San Francisco.

49. This idea follows the battered women's discourse coming out of the 1970s, which did not address battered women as victims but as female subjects and "potential feminist activists, members of a politically constituted collectivity." Through the support and consciousness-raising of former residents of battered women's shelter, many are inspired to work toward finding freedom from dependence on batterers, not just through finding temporary shelter but also finding jobs paying a "family wage," day care, and affordable permanent housing. See Nancy Fraser, *Unruly Practices: Power, Discourse, and Gender in Contemporary Social Theory* (Minneapolis: University of Minnesota Press, 1989), 176-177.

Notes to Chapter 7

1. I am not referring here to sexually innocent play among "curious peers" (of which I am skeptical); rather, I am referring to what the offender may call the abuse in order to manipulate the child into participating and/or minimizing its effects. See Appendix G for a profile of perpetrators.

2. Roy F. Baumeister, *Escaping the Self: Alcoholism, Spirituality, Masochism, and Other Flights from the Burden of Selfhood* (New York: Basic Books, 1991), 198.

3. Too often erotic feminist theologies come from disembodied states. Paper given by Adams, "Toward a Feminist Theology of Religion and the State."

4. Käsl, *Many Roads, One Journey,* 87.

5. Though incest is illegal in all fifty states, it is one of the most underreported crimes committed. When cases do come to court, only a fraction of the offenders are given jail sentences. The ones who are imprisoned rarely serve full sentences. See Appendix H for laws regarding incest.

Notes to Appendix A

1. Sample questionnaires were left on a questionnaire table at a Chicago VOICES conference in July 1990. It is based on the questionnaire Ana-Maria Rizutto used with mentally disturbed patients to discern their God imagery.

Notes to Appendix D

1. See "Bill's Story," in *Alcoholics Anonymous* (New York: AA World Services, 1976 [1939]), 1-16. This is affectionately referred to in AA circles as "the big book."

2. These last four principles were not adopted directly by AA because they were seen as too rigid. See Käsl, *Many Roads, One Journey,* 139-40.

3. "Witnessing" here means telling one's story of recovery and how one's sobriety comes through practicing the spiritual principles of the program.

4. Käsl, *Many Roads, One Journey,* 141.

5. Ibid.

6. Galanter, *Cults: Faith, Healing, and Coercion,* 178.

7. See Gilpin, "Taking Inventory," 52-53.

8. See Annette Price, "Are You Ruled by Food," *New Woman,* February 1993, 45-50.

Notes to Appendix F

1. All information taken directly from Heidi Vanderbilt's "Incest: A Chilling Report," *Lear's,* February 1992.

2. Ibid.

Notes to Appendix G

1. All the information below is gathered from Vanderbilt's "Incest: A Chilling Report."

Notes to Appendix H

1. This letter is taken from Vanderbilt's "Incest: A Chilling Report."

Notes to Appendix I

1. Thompson, "A Way Outa No Way," 547.

2. Barney G. Glaser and Anselm L. Strauss, *The Discovery of Grounded Theory: Strategies for Qualitative Research* (New York: Aldine DeGruyter, 1967).

3. See Appendix A for *sample questionnaire*. Adapted from Rizzuto, *Birth of a Living God.*

4. The VOICES questionnaire helped me to see that eating disorders are basically caricatures of the most misogynous messages of Christian theology. The incested daughter is often accused of being seductive. She is blamed for her enticing sexuality, and is encouraged to feel ashamed for any sexual reaction(s) she has. It is as if she carries the historical shame that has been lumped onto Eve for being appetitive, curious, and sensual—leading men into acting out animal-like/sinful behavior.

5. I also have been a participant observer since 1986 in the following Twelve-Step groups: Adult Children of Alcoholics, Survivors of Incest Anonymous, Al-Anon, Codependents Anonymous, Sex and Love Addicts Anonymous, and since 1991 Feminist Steps Anonymous.

6. A handful of researchers have given significant attention to how race, class, and sexuality influence women's understanding of their bodies and appetites. See Arnold Andersen and Andy Hay, "Racial and Socioeconomic Influences in Anorexia Nervosa and Bulimia," *International Journal of Eating Disorders* 4 (1985): 479-87; James Gray, Kathryn Ford, and Lily M. Kelly, "The Prevalence of Bulimia in a Black College Population," *International Journal of Eating Disorders* 6 (1987): 733-40; George Hsu, "Are Eating Disorders Becoming More Common in Blacks?" *International Journal of Eating Disorders* 6 (1987): 113-24; Shoshana Nevo, "Bulimic Symptoms: Prevalence and Ethnic Differences among College Women," *International Journal of Eating Disorders* 4 (1985): 151-68; Tomas Silber, "Anorexia Nervosa in Blacks and Hispanics," *International Journal of Eating Disorders* 5 (1986): 121-28, all cited in Thompson, "A Way Outa No Way," 546-61.

7. Conversation with B. W. Thompson, October 1992.

8. See Thompson, "A Way Outa No Way," 557.

9. Westerlund, *Women's Sexuality after Childhood Incest,* 72.

10. One of the offenders was a male babysitter twelve years older than the child victim.

11. See Thompson, "A Way Outa No Way," 554.

12. See Michel Foucault, *Discipline and Punish: The Birth of the Prison,* trans. Alan Sheridan (New York: Vintage Books, 1979); Jana Sawicki, *Disciplining Foucault: Feminism, Power, and the Body* (New York: Routledge, 1991).

13. Dinsmore, *From Surviving to Thriving,* 5.

14. Randall, *This Is about Incest,* 20.

15. Ann Oakley, "Interviewing Women: A Contradiction in Terms," in *Doing Feminist Research,* ed. Helen Roberts (London: Routledge and Kegan Paul, 1981), 47-49.

16. A. F. Mamak, "Nationalism, Race-Class Consciousness and Social Research on Bougainville Island, Papua New Guinea" in *Inside the Whale,* ed. C. Bell and S. Encel (Oxford: Pergamon Press, 1978).

17. Robert K. Yin, *Case Study Research: Design and Methods* (Newbury Park, Calif: Sage Publications, 1984), 143.

18. Roberts, *Doing Feminist Research,* 57.

19. Ibid.

20. Grant McCracken, *The Long Interview* (Newbury Park, Calif.: Sage Publications, 1988), 19.

21. Erik Erikson, *Young Man Luther: A Study in Psychoanalysis and History* (New York: W. W. Norton, 1958), 16.

22. Erik Erikson, *Insight and Responsibility* (New York: W. W. Norton, 1964), 52.

23. Charles B. Strozier, Robert J. Lifton, and Michael Perlman, *Nuclear Threat and the American Self* (forthcoming).

24. See Erik Erikson, *Dimensions of a New Identity: The 1973 Jefferson Lectures in the Humanities* (New York: W. W. Norton, 1974), 15. Heinz Kohut also made this notion a central part of his concerns. See the interviews in Heinz Kohut, *Self Psychology and the Humanities: Reflections on a New Psychoanalytic Approach* ed. C. B. Strozier (New York: W. W. Norton, 1985) cited in C. B. Strozier et al., *Nuclear Threat and the American Self.*

25. H. Kohut, "Introspection, Empathy, and Psychoanalysis: An Examination of the Relationship between Mode of Observation and Theory," in *The Search for the Self: Selected Writings of Heinz Kohut,* 4 vols., ed. Paul H. Ornstein (New York: International Universities Press, 1978 [1959]), vol. 1, 205-32.

26. McCracken, *Long Interview,* 9.

27. Ibid.

28. Brumberg, *Fasting Girls.*

29. Herman, *Father-Daughter Incest.* See also Russell, "The Incidence and Prevalence of Intrafamilial and Extrafamilial Sexual Abuse of Female Children," 133-46. See also Westerlund, *Women's Sexuality after Childhood Incest.*

30. McCracken, *Long Interview,* 9.

31. Ibid.

32. Ibid., 20.

33. "Intensive Interviewing," in *The Research Interview: Uses and Approaches,* ed. M. Brenner, J. Brown, and D. Canter (London: Academic Press, 1985), cited in McCracken, *Long Interview,* 21.

34. C. G. Jung was one of the first analysts to record an interview of himself for his book, *Memories, Dreams, Reflections* (New York: Random House/ Vintage Books, 1961); conversation with Jungian scholar Michael Perlman, 4 April 1993.

35. McCracken, *Long Interview,* 24.

36. See M. B. Miles, "Qualitative Data as an Attractive Nuisance: The Problem of Analysis," *Administrative Science Quarterly* 24 (December 1979): 590-601, cited in McCracken, *Long Interview,* 41.

Selected Bibliography

Abramson, A., and G. Lucido. "Childhood Sexual Experience and Bulimia." *Addictive Behaviors* 16 (1991): 529-32.

Adams, C. "Toward a Feminist Theology of Religion and the State." Paper read at the American Academy of Religion, 22 November 1992, San Francisco.

Aland, K., M. Black, C. M. Martini, B. M. Metzger, and A. Wikgren, eds. *New Testament*. 3d ed. Münster: Institute for New Testament Textual Research, 1983.

Alcoff, L., and L. Gray. "Survivor Discourse: Transgression or Recuperation?" *Signs: Journal of Women in Culture and Society* 18 (1993), no. 2: 274.

Allers, C. T., K. J. Benjack, J. White, and J. T. Rousey. "HIV Vulnerability and the Adult Survivor of Childhood Sexual Abuse." *Child Abuse & Neglect* 17 (1993): 291-98.

American Psychological Association. *Diagnostic and Statistical Manual of Mental Disorders*. 3d ed., rev. Washington, D.C.: American Psychiatric Association, 1987.

Andersen, A., and A. Hay. "Racial and Socioeconomic Influences in Anorexia Nervosa and Bulimia." *International Journal of Eating Disorders* 4 (1985): 479-87.

Anselm of Canterbury. "Curs Deus Homo." *St. Anselm: Basic Writings*. 2d ed. Trans. S. N. Deane. La Salle, Ill.: Open Court Publishing, 1962.

Aristotle, "Politics." *The Complete Works of Aristotle*. Trans. B. Jowett. Ed. Jonathan Barnes. Princeton, N.J.: Princeton University Press, 1984.

Ashley, S. *The Missing Voice: Writings by Mothers of Incest Victims*. Dubuque, Iowa: Kendall/Hunt, 1992.

Bartky, S. "Foucault, Femininity, and the Modernization of Patriarchal Power." In *Femininity and Domination: Studies in the Phenomenology of Oppression*. New York: Routledge, 1990.

Baumeister, F. *Escaping the Self: Alcoholism, Spirituality, Masochism, and Other Flights from the Burden of Selfhood*. New York: Basic Books, 1991.

Becker, J., et al. "Time-Limited Therapy with Sexually Dysfunctional Sexually Assaulted Women." *Journal of Social Work and Human Sexuality* 3 (1984): 97-115.

Bell, R. *Holy Anorexia.* Chicago: University of Chicago Press, 1985.

Benedict, R. *Virgin or Vamp: How the Press Covers Sex Crimes.* New York: Oxford University Press, 1992.

Bloom, E. S. *Secret Survivors: Uncovering Incest and Its Aftereffects in Women.* New York: Ballantine Books, 1990.

Bonaparte, M., A. Freud, and E. Kris, eds. *The Origins of Psychoanalysis: Letters to Wilhelm Fliess, Drafts and Notes by Sigmund Freud.* New York: Basic Books, 1954.

Bordo, S. "Anorexia Nervosa: Psychopathology as the Crystallization of Culture." In *Feminism and Foucault: Reflections on Resistance.* Ed. Irene Diamond and Lee Quinby. Boston: Northeastern University Press, 1988.

———. "Reading the Slender Body." In *Body/Politics: Women and the Discourse of Science.* Ed. by Mary Jacobus, Evelyn Fox Keller, and Sally Shuttleworth. London: Routledge, 1990.

———. *Unbearable Weight: Feminism, Western Culture, and the Body.* Berkeley: University of California Press, 1993.

Brenner, D. "Self-Regulatory Functions in Bulimia." *Contemporary Psychotherapy Review* 1 (1960): 79-93.

Brenner, M., J. Brown, and D. Canter, eds. *The Research Interview: Uses and Approaches.* London: Academic Press, 1985.

Breuer, J. and S. Freud. "Studies on Hysteria." In *Standard Edition.* Vol. 2. Trans. J. Strachey. London: Hogarth Press, 1955.

Brown, G., and B. Anderson. "Psychiatric Morbidity in Adult Inpatients with Childhood Histories of Sexual and Physical Abuse." *American Journal of Psychiatry* 148 (1991): 55-61.

Brown, J. C., and R. Parker. "For God So Loved the World." In *Christianity, Patriarchy, and Abuse: A Feminist Critique.* Ed. J. C. Brown and C. R. Bohn. New York: Pilgrim Press, 1989.

Browne, A., and D. Finkelhor. "Initial and Long-Term Effects: A Review of the Research." In *Sourcebook on Child Sexual Abuse.* Ed. David Finkelhor. Beverly Hills: Sage Publications, 1986.

Bruch, H. *Eating Disorders: Obesity, Anorexia and the Person Within.* New York: Basic Books, 1973.

———. *The Golden Cage: The Enigma of Anorexia Nervosa.* Toronto: Random House, 1979.

Brumberg, J. J. *Fasting Girls: The History of Anorexia Nervosa.* New York: New American Library, 1988.

Buchwald, E., P. R. Fletcher, and M. Roth. *Transforming a Rape Culture.* Minneapolis: Milkweed Editions, 1993.

Bulka, R. "Guilt from, Guilt Towards." *Journal of Psychology and Judaism* 11 (1987): 71-90.

Bynum, C. W. *Holy Feast and Holy Fast: The Religious Significance of Food to Medieval Women.* Berkeley: University of California Press, 1987.

Campbell, J. *The Hero with a Thousand Faces.* Princeton, N.J.: Princeton University Press, 1973.

Caplow, T. "The Dynamics of Information Interviewing." *American Journal of Sociology* 62 (1956) 2: 165-71.

Chardone, J. "Eating Disorders: Their Genesis in the Mother-Infant Relationship." *International Journal of Eating Disorders* 4 (1985): 15-39.

Chesler, P. *Women and Madness.* New York: Harcourt Brace Jovanovich, 1972.

Christ, C., and J. Plaskow. *Women's Spirit Rising: A Feminist Reader in Religion.* San Francisco: Harper and Row, 1979.

Clark, E., and H. Richardson. "The Puritan Transformation of Marriage." In *Women and Religion.* Ed. Rosemary Radford Ruether. New York: Harper and Row, 1977.

Collier, J. F. "From Mary to Modern Woman: The Material Basis of Marianismo and Its Transformation in a Spanish Village." *American Ethnologist* 13 (1986): 100-107.

Coons, P. "Child Abuse and Multiple Personality Disorder: Review of the Literature and Suggestions for Treatment." *Child Abuse and Neglect* 10 (1986): 455-62.

Corrington, G. "Anorexia, Asceticism, and Autonomy: Self-Control as Liberation and Transcendence." *Journal of Feminist Studies in Religion* 2 (1986), no. 2: 52-61.

Courtois, C. A. *Healing the Incest Wound: Adult Survivors in Therapy.* New York: W. W. Norton, 1988.

Crewdson, J. *By Silence Betrayed: Sexual Abuse of Children in America.* New York: Harper and Row, 1988.

Crisp, A. H. *Anorexia Nervosa: Let Me Be.* London: Academic Press, 1980.

———. "The Psychopathology of Anorexia Nervosa: Getting the 'Heat' Out of the System." In *Eating and Its Disorders.* Ed. A. Stunkard and E. Stellar. New York: Raven Press, 1984.

Daly, M. *Beyond God the Father: Toward a Philosophy of Women's Liberation.* Boston: Beacon Press, 1973.

———. *Gyn/Ecology: The Metaethics of Radical Feminism.* Boston: Beacon Press, 1978.

———. *Pure Lust: Elemental Feminist Philosophy.* Boston: Beacon Press, 1984.

Damon, L., and J. Todd. "Letter to the Editor." *American Journal of Orthopsychiatry* 56 (1986): 460-61.

"Death Rate Cited as U.S. Health Concern." *New York Times,* 28 November 1984, A-14.

Dinsmore, C. *From Surviving to Thriving: Incest, Feminism, and Recovery.* Albany, N.Y.: SUNY Press, 1991.

Doolittle, D. "Transitional Phenomena in Child Molesters." Paper read at Boston Institute for the Development of Infants and Parents, Pine Manor College,

Chestnut Hill, Massachusetts (1988). In T. K. Seghorn, R. A. Prentky; and R. J. Boucher, eds., "Childhood Sexual Abuse in the Lives of Sexually Aggressive Offenders." *American Academy of Child and Adolescent Psychiatry,* 26 (1987): 262-67.

Douglas, M. *Purity and Danger: An Analysis of the Concepts of Pollution and Taboo.* Boston: Ark Paperbacks, 1985.

Dressler, H., et al., eds. *The Fathers of the Church.* Washington, D.C.: University of America Press, 1959.

Engel, B. *The Right to Innocence: Healing the Trauma of Childhood Sexual Abuse.* New York: Ivy Books, 1989.

Erikson, E. *Childhood and Society.* 2d ed. New York: W. W. Norton, 1963.

———. *Dimensions of a New Identity: The 1973 Jefferson Lectures in the Humanities.* New York: W. W. Norton, 1974.

———. *Insight and Responsibility.* New York: W. W. Norton, 1964.

———. *Young Man Luther: A Study in Psychoanalysis and History.* New York: W. W. Norton, 1958.

Fairbairn, W. R. D. "The Repression and the Return of Bad Objects (With Special Reference to the 'War Neuroses')." *British Journal of Medical Psychology* 19 (1943): 327-41.

Faludi, S. *Backlash: The Undeclared War against American Women.* New York: Crown Publishers, 1991.

Finkelhor, D. "The Trauma of Child Sexual Abuse." *Journal of Interpersonal Violence* 2 (December 1987), no. 4: 348-66.

Finkelhor, D., and K. Yllo. *License to Rape: Sexual Abuse of Wives.* New York: Holt, Rinehart and Winston, 1988.

Fortune, M. *Sexual Violence: The Unmentionable Sin.* New York: Pilgrim Press, 1983.

Foucault, M. *Discipline and Punish: The Birth of the Prison.* Trans. A. Sheridan. New York: Vintage Books, 1979.

Fowler, J. *Stages of Faith.* San Francisco: Harper and Row, 1981.

Fox, M. *Original Blessing: A Primer in Creation Spirituality.* Santa Fe, N.M.: Bear and Co., 1983.

Frank, J. *Persuasion and Healing.* New York: Schocken Books, 1974.

Fraser, N. *Unruly Practices: Power, Discourse, and Gender in Contemporary Social Theory,* 176-77. Minneapolis: University of Minnesota Press, 1989.

Freedman, R. *Bodylove: Learning to Like Our Looks—and Ourselves.* New York: Harper and Row, 1988.

Freire, P. *Pedagogy of the Oppressed.* New York: Seabury Press, 1969.

Freud, S. "The Aetiology of Hysteria." In *Standard Edition.* Vol. 3. Trans. J. Strachey. London: Hogarth Press, 1962.

Galanter, M. *Cults: Faith, Healing, and Coercion.* New York: Oxford University Press, 1989.

diner, J. K. "Self-Psychology as Feminist Theory." *Signs: A Journal of Women in Culture and Society* 12 (1987), no. 4: 761-80.

Garfinkel, P., and D. M. Garner. *Anorexia Nervosa: A Multidimensional Perspective.* New York: Brunner/Mazel, 1982.

Gilpin, K. "Taking Inventory." *On the Issues,* Spring 1993, 52-53.

Glaser, G., and A. L. Strauss. *The Discovery of Grounded Theory: Strategies for Qualitative Research.* New York: Aldine DeGruyter, 1967.

Gray, J., K. Ford, and L. Kelly. "The Prevalence of Bulimia in a Black College Population." *International Journal of Eating Disorders* 6 (1987): 733-40.

Grimes, R. L. *Beginnings in Ritual Studies.* Lanham, Md.: University Press of America, 1982.

Gross, J. "Where *Boys Will Be Boys* and Adults Are Befuddled." *New York Times,* 29 March 1993, A-1, A-13.

Hamerton-Kelly, R. *Sacred Violence: Paul's Hermeneutic of the Cross.* Minneapolis: Fortress Press, 1992.

Heise, H. "Abuse." *This World (Sunday suppl.), San Francisco Chronicle,* 2 July 1989, 12.

Herman, E. *Out/Look: National Lesbian and Gay Quarterly,* Summer 1988. In *Utne Reader,* November 1988, 60.

Herman, J. L. "The Abuses of Memory." *Mother Jones,* March/April 1993, 3-4.

———. *Father-Daughter Incest.* Cambridge, Mass.: Harvard University Press, 1981.

———. *Trauma and Recovery: The Aftermath of Violence—From Domestic Abuse to Political Terror.* New York: Basic Books, 1992.

Herman, J. L., J. C. Perry, and A. B. Van der Kolk. "Childhood Trauma in Borderline Personality Disorder." *American Journal of Psychiatry* 146 (1989): 490-95.

Heyward, C. *Touching Our Strength: The Erotic as Power and the Love of God.* San Francisco: Harper and Row, 1989.

Hirschman, J. R., and C. H. Munter. *Overcoming Overeating: A Revolutionary Approach to Curing Eating Problems.* New York: Fawcett, 1990.

Horney, K. "Maturity and the Individual." *American Journal of Psychoanalysis* 7 (1947): 85-87.

———. *Neurosis and Human Growth.* New York: W. W. Norton, 1950.

———. *The Adolescent Diaries of Karen Horney.* New York: Basic Books, 1980.

Houppert, K. "Baseball Bats and Broomsticks." *Village Voice,* 15 March 1993, 29-33.

Hsu, G. "Are Eating Disorders Becoming More Common in Blacks?" *International Journal of Eating Disorders* 6 (1987): 113-24.

Hunter, A. M. "Numbering the Hairs of Our Heads: Male Social Control and the All-Seeing Male God." Paper read at the American Academy of Religion, 23 November 1991, Kansas City, Missouri.

Imbens, A., and I. Jonker. *Christianity and Incest.* Minneapolis: Fortress Press, 1992.

Janet, P. *L'automatisme psychologique: Essai de psychologie expérimentale sur les formes inférieures de l'activité humaine.* Paris: Félix Alcan, 1889.

Janoff-Bulman, R. "The Aftermath of Victimization: Rebuilding Shattered Assumptions." In *Trauma and Its Wake: The Study and Treatment of Post-Traumatic Stress Disorder*. Ed. C. Figley. New York: Brunner/Mazel, 1985.

Jerome, St. "Select Letters of Saint Jerome." In *Epistle*. Trans. F. A. Wright. New York: Putnam, 1933.

Johnson, J. *Mothers of Incest Survivors: Another Side of the Story*. Bloomington: Indiana University Press, 1992.

Joyce, J. *Finnegans Wake*. New York: Viking Press, Inc., 1939.

Jung, C. G. *Memories, Dreams, Reflections*. New York: Random House/Vintage Books, 1961.

Kano, S. *Making Peace with Food*. Boston: Amity Publishing Co., 1985.

Kaschak, E. *Engendered Lives: A New Psychology of Women's Experience*. New York: Basic Books, 1992.

Käsl, C. D. *Many Roads, One Journey: Moving Beyond the Twelve Steps*. New York: Harper Collins, 1992.

———. *Women, Sex, and Addiction: A Search for Love and Power*. New York: Harper and Row, 1989.

Keane, T., R. Zimmering, and J. M. Caddell. "A Behavioral Formulation of Posttraumatic Stress Disorder in Vietnam Veterans." *The Behavior Therapist* 8 (1985): 9-12.

Kernberg, O. "Borderline Personality Organization." *Journal of the American Psychoanalytic Association* 15 (1967): 1-85.

Kingsolver, B. *The Bean Trees*. New York: Harper and Row, 1988.

Kirk J., and M. Miller. *Reliability and Validity in Qualitative Research*. Beverly Hills: Sage Publications, 1986.

Kluft, P., ed. *Childhood Antecedents of Multiple Personality Disorder*, 197-238. Washington, D. C.: American Psychiatric Press, 1984.

Kohut, H. "The Addictive Need for an Admiring Other in Regulation of Self-Esteem." In *The Kohut Seminars on Self-Psychology and Psychotherapy with Adolescents and Young Adults*. Ed. M. Elson. New York: W. W. Norton, 1987.

———. *The Analysis of the Self: A Systematic Approach to Psychoanalytic Treatment of Narcissistic Personality Disorders*. New York: International Universities Press, 1971.

———. "Introspection, Empathy, and Psychoanalysis: An Examination of the Relationship between Mode of Observation and Theory." In *The Search for the Self: Selected Writings of Heinz Kohut*. Vol. 4. Ed. Paul H. Ornstein. New York: International Universities Press, 1978.

———. *The Restoration of the Self*. New York: International Universities Press, 1977.

———. *Self Psychology and the Humanities: Reflections on a New Psychoanalytic Approach*. Ed. C. Strozier. New York: W. W. Norton, 1985.

Kolb, L., and L. R. Multipassi. "The Conditioned Emotional Response: A

Subclass of Chronic and Delayed Post-Traumatic Stress Disorder." *Psychiatric Annals* 12 (1982): 979-87.

Koss, M., et al. "The Scope of Rape: Incidence and Prevalence of Sexual Aggression and Victimization in a National Sample of Higher Education Students." *Journal of Consulting and Clinical Psychology* 55 (1987): 162-70.

Lacks, G. "Women and Food: The Stone Center Perspective on Women's Psychological Development." *Perspective,* Winter 1993, 7.

LaMar, F. *Transcending Turmoil: Survivors of Dysfunctional Families.* New York: Plenum/Insight, 1992.

Lang, D. "A Report at Large (Swedish Hostages)." *New Yorker,* 25 November 1974, 56-126.

Lerner, M. *The Belief in a Just World.* New York: Plenum Press, 1980.

Lewis, H. B. *Psychic War in Men and Women.* New York: New York University Press, 1976.

———. *Shame and Guilt in Neurosis.* New York: International Universities Press, 1971.

Lifton, R. J. *The Broken Connection: On Death and the Continuity of Life.* New York: Basic Books, 1981.

———. *Home from the War.* New York: Simon and Schuster, 1973.

———. *Life in Death: Survivors of Hiroshima.* New York: Random House, 1967.

Lorde, A. "Uses of the Erotic: The Erotic as Power." In *Sister Outsider: Essays and Speeches.* Freedom, Calif.: Crossing Press, 1984.

MacKinnon, C. *Toward a Feminist Theory of the State.* Cambridge, Mass.: Harvard University Press, 1989.

Maltz, W. *The Sexual Healing Journey: A Guide for Survivors of Sexual Abuse.* New York: Harper Perennial, 1991.

Mamak, A. F. "Nationalism, Race-Class Consciousness and Social Research on Bougainville Island, Papua New Guinea." In *Inside the Whale.* Ed. C. Bell and S. Encel. Oxford: Pergamon Press, 1978.

Mayo, K. *Slave of the Gods.* New York: Harcourt, Brace and Co., 1929.

McCracken, G. *The Long Interview.* Newbury Park, Calif.: Sage Publications, 1988.

McFague, S. *Models of God: Theology for an Ecological, Nuclear Age.* Philadelphia: Fortress Press, 1987.

Midelfort, H. *Witch Hunting in South West Germany, 1563-84.* Stanford, Calif.: Stanford University Press, 1972.

Miedzian, M. *Boys Will Be Boys: Breaking the Link between Masculinity and Violence.* New York: Anchor Books/Doubleday, 1991.

Miles, M. "Qualitative Data as an Attractive Nuisance: The Problem of Analysis." *Administrative Science Quarterly* 24 (December 1979): 590-601.

Miller, A. *Banished Knowledge: Facing Childhood Injuries.* Trans. L. Vennewitz. New York: Doubleday, 1990.

———. *The Drama of the Gifted Child: How Narcissistic Parents Form and*

Deform the Emotional Lives of Their Children. New York: Basic Books, 1981.

————. *For Your Own Good: Hidden Cruelty in Child-Rearing and the Roots of Violence.* New York: Farrar, Straus and Giroux, 1984.

————. *The Untouched Key: Tracing Childhood Trauma in Creativity and Destructiveness.* New York: Doubleday, 1988.

————. *Thou Shalt Not Be Aware: Society's Betrayal of the Child.* New York: Farrar, Straus and Giroux, 1984.

Morrison, N. "Shame in the Treatment of Schizophrenia: Theoretical Considerations with Clinical Illustrations." *Yale Journal of Biology and Medicine* 58 (1985): 189-97.

Morton, N. *The Journey Is Home.* Boston: Beacon Press, 1985.

Nakashima Brock, R. *Journeys by Heart: A Christology of Erotic Power.* New York: Crossroad Press, 1988.

Nevo, S. "Bulimic Symptoms: Prevalence and Ethnic Differences among College Women." *International Journal of Eating Disorders* 4 (1985): 151-68.

Noddings, N. *Women and Evil.* Berkeley: University of California Press, 1989.

Noffke, S. *Classics of Western Spirituality.* New York: Paulist Press, 1980.

Oppenheimer, R., et al. "Adverse Sexual Experience in Childhood and Clinical Eating Disorders: A Preliminary Description." *Journal of Psychiatric Research* 19 (1985), nos. 2/3: 357-61.

Oakley, A. "Interviewing Women: A Contradiction in Terms." In *Doing Feminist Research.* Ed. H. Roberts. London: Routledge and Kegan Paul, 1981.

Ochberg, F. *Post-Traumatic Therapy and Victims of Violence.* New York: Brunner/Mazel, 1988.

O'Faolain, J., and L. Martine. *Not in God's Image.* New York: Harper Torchbooks, 1973.

Ortner, S. "Is Female to Male as Nature Is to Culture?" In *Woman, Culture and Society.* Ed. M. Z. Rosaldo and L. Lamphere. Stanford, Calif.: Stanford University Press, 1974.

————. "The Virgin and the State." *Feminist Studies* 4 (1978): 19-37.

Osborn, S. "The Trouble with Being a Woman." Forthcoming.

Palmer, R., et al. "Childhood Sexual Experiences with Adults Reported by Women with Eating Disorders: An Extended Series." *British Journal of Psychiatry* 156 (1990): 669-703.

Patten, B., et al. "Posttraumatic Stress Disorder and the Treatment of Sexual Abuse." *Social Work,* May 1989, 197-203.

Peers, E. *The Life of Saint Teresa of Jesus.* Garden City, N.Y.: Doubleday/Image, 1960.

Perry, C., and J. Laurence. "Mental Processing Outside of Awareness: The Contributions of Freud and Janet." In *The Unconscious Reconsidered.* Ed. K. Bowers and D. Meichenbaum. New York: John Wiley and Sons, 1984.

Petersen, B. *Dancing with Daddy: A Childhood Lost and a Life Regained.* New York: Bantam Books, 1991.

Phillips, J. *Eve: The History of an Idea.* San Francisco: Harper and Row, 1984.

Pope-Lance, J., and J. C. Engelsman. *Domestic Violence: A Guide for Clergy.* Lawrenceville: New Jersey Department of Community Affairs, 1987.

Price, A. "Are You Ruled by Food." *New Woman*, February 1993, 45-50.

Price, G. "Guilt in Victims of Trauma." *Dissociation* 3 (September 1990), no. 3: 160-64.

Price, R. "Dissociative Disorders of the Self: A Continuum Extending into Multiple Personality." *Psychotherapy* 24 (1987): 387-91.

Pruyser, P. W. *The Play of Imagination: Towards a Psychoanalysis of Culture.* New Haven: International Universities Press, 1987.

Putnam, F. "The Clinical Phenomenology of Multiple Personality Disorder: Review of 100 Recent Cases." *Journal of Clinical Psychiatry* 47 (1986): 285-93.

Randall, M. *This Is about Incest.* Ithaca, N.Y.: Firebrand Books, 1987.

Redmond, S. "Christian *Virtues* and Child Sexual Abuse." In *Christianity, Patriarchy and Abuse: A Feminist Critique.* Ed. J. Carlson Brown and C. R. Bohn. New York: Pilgrim Press, 1989.

Reeves Sanday, P. *Fraternity Gang Rape: Sex, Brotherhood, and Privilege on Campus.* New York: New York University Press, 1990.

Reineke, M. "Abjection, Anorexia, and Women Mystics." *Journal of the American Academy of Religion* 58 (Summer) 2: 249.

Rew, L. "Long-term Effects of Childhood Sexual Exploitation." *Issues in Mental Health Nursing* 10 (1989): 229-44.

Rich, A. "In the Wake of Home." *The Fact of a Doorframe: Poems Selected and New, 1950-1984.* New York: W. W. Norton, 1984.

———. *Of Woman Born: Motherhood as Experience and Institution.* New York: W. W. Norton, 1976.

Ricoeur, P. *The Symbolism of Evil.* Boston: Beacon Press, 1967.

Ringold Spitzer, J. *Spousal Abuse in Rabbinic and Contemporary Judaism.* New York: National Federation of Temple Sisterhoods, 1985.

Rizzuto, A. M. *The Birth of a Living God.* Chicago: University of Chicago Press, 1979.

Robertson, M. *Starving in the Silences: An Exploration of Anorexia Nervosa.* New York: New York University Press, 1992.

Root, M. P. P. "Persistent, Disordered Eating as a Gender Specific, Post-Traumatic Stress Response to Sexual Assault." *Psychotherapy* 28 (Spring 1991), no. 1: 96-104.

Root, M. P. P., and P. Fallon. "Victimization Experiences as Contributing Factors in the Development of Bulimia in Women." *Journal of Interpersonal Violence* 3 (1988), no. 2: 161-73.

Roth, G. *Feeding the Hungry Heart: The Experience of Compulsive Eating.* New York: Signet, 1982.

Rowbotham, S. *Woman's Consciousness, Man's World.* Harmondsworth, U.K.: Penguin, 1973.

Ruether, R. R. "Can a Male Savior Save Women?" *Sexism and Godtalk: Toward a Feminist Theology.* Boston: Beacon Press, 1983.

Ruether, R. R. "The Western Tradition and Violence against Women." In *Christianity, Patriarchy, and Abuse: A Feminist Critique.* Ed. J. C. Brown and C. Bohn. New York: Pilgrim Press, 1989.

Rush, F. *Best Kept Secret: Sexual Abuse of Children.* New York: McGraw-Hill, 1981.

Russell, D. "The Incidence and Prevalence of Intrafamilial and Extrafamilial Sexual Abuse of Female Children." *Child Abuse and Neglect: The International Journal* 7 (1983): 133-46.

———. *The Secret Trauma.* New York: Basic Books, 1986.

Russell, H. *Sexual Exploitation: Rape, Child Sexual Abuse, and Sexual Harassment.* Beverly Hills: Sage Publications, 1984.

Saussy, C. *God Images and Self Esteem: Empowering Women in a Patriarchal Society.* Louisville, Ky.: Westminster/John Knox, 1991.

Sawicki, J. *Disciplining Foucault: Feminism, Power, and the Body.* New York: Routledge, 1991.

Schmitz, L. "Ritual Elements in Community." *Religious Studies* 7 (January 1979): 166.

Schwager, R. *Must There Be Scapegoats? Violence and Redemption in the Bible.* San Francisco: Harper and Row, 1987.

Sgroi, M. *Handbook of Clinical Intervention in Child Sexual Abuse.* Lexington, Ky.: D. C. Heath Publishers, 1982.

Shengold, L. "Child Abuse and Deprivation: Soul Murder." *Journal of the American Psychoanalytic Association* 27 (1979): 533-59.

———. *Soul Murder: The Effects of Childhood Abuse and Deprivation.* New Haven: Yale University Press, 1989.

Shute, J. *Life Size.* Boston: Houghton Mifflin, 1992.

Silber, T. "Anorexia Nervosa in Blacks and Hispanics." *International Journal of Eating Disorders* 5 (1986): 121-28.

Simonds, W. *Women and Self-Help Culture: Reading between the Lines.* New Brunswick, N.J.: Rutgers University Press, 1992.

Sloan G., and P. Leichner. "Is There a Relationship between Sexual Abuse or Incest and Eating Disorders?" *Canadian Journal of Psychiatry* 31 (1986): 656-60.

Starkey, M. *The Devil in Massachusetts.* New York: Alfred A. Knopf, 1949.

Stebbins, R. "The Unstructured Research Interview as Incipient Interpersonal Relationship." *Sociology and Social Research* 56 (1972), no. 2: 164-77.

Stokes, K. *Faith Is a Verb: The Dynamics of Adult Faith Development.* Mystic, Conn.: Twenty-Third Publications, 1989.

Strozier, C. B., M. Perlman, and R. J. Lifton. *Nuclear Threat and the American Self.* Forthcoming.

Sullerot, E. *Women, Change and Society.* New York: McGraw-Hill, 1971.

Summers, M. *The 'Malleus Maleficarum' of Heinrich Kramer and James Sprenger.* New York: Dover Publications, 1971.

Summit, R. "Beyond Belief: The Reluctant Discovery of Incest." In *Sexual Assault and Abuse: A Handbook for Clergy and Religious Professionals.* Ed.

M. Pellauer, Barbara Chester, and Jane Boyajian. San Francisco: Harper and Row, 1987.

Tessier, J. "Women Sexually Abused as Children: The Spiritual Consequences." *Second Opinion* 17 (January 1992), no. 3: 11-13.

Thöma, H. *Anorexia Nervosa.* Trans. G. Brydone. New York: International Universities Press, 1967.

Thompson, B. W. " 'A Way Outa No Way': Eating Problems among African-American, Latina, and White Women." *Gender and Society* 6 (December 1992), no. 4: 546-61.

Thürmer-Rohr, C. *Vagabonding: Feminist Thinking Cut Loose.* Trans. L. Weil. Boston: Beacon Press, 1991.

Tillich, P. *The Courage to Be.* New Haven: Yale University Press, 1952.

Trimble, M. *Trauma and Its Wake: The Study and Treatment of Post-Traumatic Stress Disorder.* New York: Brunner/Mazel, 1985.

Turner, V. *Dramas, Fields, and Metaphors.* Ithaca, N.Y.: Cornell University Press, 1974.

———. *The Ritual Process: Structure and Anti-Structure.* Chicago: Aldine Press, 1969.

The Twelve Steps of Overeaters Anonymous. Torrance: Overeaters Anonymous, 1980.

Ulman, R., and D. Brothers. "A Self-Psychological Reevaluation of Posttraumatic Stress Disorder (PTSD) and Its Treatment: Shattered Fantasies." *Journal of the American Academy of Psychoanalysis* 2 (1987), no. 15: 175-203.

Ulman, R., and H. Paul. "A Self-Psychological Theory and Approach to Treating Substance Abuse Disorders: The 'Intersubjective Absorption' Hypothesis." *New Therapeutic Visions* 8 (1992): 121-41.

Vanderbilt, H. "Incest: A Chilling Report." *Lear's,* February 1992.

Van Der Kolk, A. B., et al. "Childhood Origins of Self-Destructive Behavior." *American Journal of Psychiatry* 148 (1991): 1665-71.

Van Gennep, A. *The Rites of Passage.* Trans. M. B. Vizedom and G. L. Caffee. Chicago: University of Chicago Press, 1960.

Vauchez, A. *La Sainteté en Occident aux derniers siècles du moyen âge d'après les procès de canonisation et les documents hagiographiques.* Bibliothèque des Ve'tudes française de Rome, 1981. In H. Weinstein and R. Bell. *Saints and Society: The Two Worlds of Western Christendom, 1000-1700.* Chicago: University of Chicago Press, 1982.

Von Feldt, K. "Untitled." *The Chorus* 5 (March/April 1993), no. 2: 8.

Walker, L. *The Battered Woman.* New York: Harper and Row, 1979.

Warshaw, I. *Never Called It Rape: The Ms. Report on Recognizing, Fighting and Surviving Date and Acquaintance Rape.* New York: Harper and Row, 1988.

Weskott, M. *The Feminist Legacy of Karen Horney.* New Haven: Yale University Press, 1986.

Westerlund, E. *Women's Sexuality after Childhood Incest.* New York: W. W. Norton, 1992.

Williams, J. *The Bible, Violence and the Sacred: Liberation from the Myth of Sanctioned Violence.* New York: Harper Collins, 1991.

Wilson, B. *Twelve Steps and Twelve Traditions.* New York: Alcoholics Anonymous, 1952.

Winnicott, D. W. "Transitional Objects and Transitional Phenomena." In *Through Paediatrics to Psycho-Analysis.* New York: Basic Books, 1975.

———. "Transitional Objects and Transitional Phenomena." In *Playing and Reality.* London: Routledge, 1971.

———. *The Maturational Process and the Facilitating Environment.* New York: International Universities Press, 1972.

Women's Action Coalition. *WAC Stats: The Facts about Women.* New York: The New Press, 1993.

Wolf, N. *The Beauty Myth: How Images of Beauty Are Used against Women.* New York: William Morrow, 1991.

Wulff, D. "The Object-Relations Perspective." In *Psychology of Religion: Classic and Contemporary Views.* New York: John Wiley and Sons, 1991.

Young, K. Z. "The Imperishable Virginity of Saint Maria Goretti." *Gender and Society* 3 (December 1989), no. 4: 474-82.

Young-Eisendrath, P. "Entanglements: Food, Sex, and Aggression in Female Development." Paper quoted in *Perspective,* Winter 1993, 3.

Index

Abandonment: concerns of, 93; death and, 36; emotional, 47, 68; feelings of, 81; second, 84

Abuse: animal, 30; backgrounds of respondents, xii, 7–9, 18–41, 161–75; chronic, 28–32; destroyed by, 101; discovered, 156; of drugs, 144; family, 75; frequency of, 4, 13; Freud and, 11–13; history, 144; key findings, 127–36; of others, 144; paradigm, xiii; and religion, 59–78; repeated, 41; resolution of, 68; self-, 97–144; substance, 36. *See also* Sexual abuse

Addiction: addictive trigger mechanisms, 90; alcohol, 7–9; behavior, 103, 121; to cope with abuse, 55; curing, 147–48; and cycle of shame, 128; as disease, 132; drug, 8, 35; food, 8, 115, 148; groups, 101; to heal from, 100; and incest recovery, 106–7; object of, 53; psychosocial problems seen as, 84; to recovery, 115; "sex and love," 109–10, 148; substance, 130; and suffering, 113; sugar, 8; Twelve Steps, 102, 147–48; understanding, 110; variety of, 148

AIDS: and anorexic deaths, 3; risk for HIV/AIDS among survivors, 36, 41

Alcohol: and drugs, 90, 154; and family, 171; histories, 7–9, 95; and incest, 151; respondents susceptibility to addiction, 66; and Twelve Steps, 146

Alcoholics Anonymous: Adult Children of Alcoholics (ACOA), 40, 117; Alanon, 116; founders of, 147–48; groups, 7, 35–36, 100, 109–10, 121; history of, 147–48; Twelve Steps of, 146

Alienation: from body, 89; in response to abuse, 23; in response to narcissistic parenting, 15–16

Amnesia: and dissociation, 25; following trauma, 11, 19; psychic, 6

Anonymity: defense of author's, 2; and groups, 101–2, 141, 148; and interview method 169; politics of, 2; preservation of, 168; and Twelve-Step programs, 84, 106

Anorexia, ix, 5–9, 42–58, 74–76; definition, 42; holy, 74; imagery, 70; and saints, 75; self-starvation, 7–9; sexual abuse, 37, 42

Appetite: and body, 54, 89, 126; control of, 58; cues, x, 42; as dangerous, 70; and hypervigilance, 26; meaning, 127; policing, 74; preoccupation with, 161; religious symbolism of, 71, 74–78; and saints, xii, 75–78; sexual, 110; shame and, 88; at war with, 50

Aristotle, 71

Atonement: and eating behavior, 92, 103, 128–29; Jesus as model of, 62; sanity and, 112

Augustine, 72

Authority: displaced, 112; exerted over female, 77; father God's, 87; figures, 102,

217

127–36; letter to politician, 159–60; and methodology, 161–75; "not a disease," 133; questionnaire, 141–44; and religion, 79–99; and religious discourse, 59–78; sin of, 128; and trauma overview, 10–41; and Twelve Steps, 100–126; U.S. laws on, 156–58. *See also* Sexual abuse
Indulgence, 88

Janet, P., 11–13
Jesus, 61–63, 71, 76, 87, 94, 125
Jonker, I., 62
Jouissance, 4
Kaschak, E., 44, 165
Kasl, C. D., 113, 165
Kohut, H., 15–16, 170
Kramer, H., 72

LeMar, D., 92
Lesbians: as survivors, 109–10, 164; and trust, 161
Lifton, R. J., 5–7
Lorde, A., 97, 106
Luther, M., 72

Masculinist: gaze, xii, 83; God, 81; society, xxi; worldview, 84
Masochism, 41, 132
Matthews, R., 155
McCracken, G., 170
Meaning: appetite and body, 127; betrayal and, 130; between food and incest, 42–58; core, 73; existential, 77, 83; food rituals, 79; God as source of, 80, 83; hunger for, 76; meaninglessness, 87–88, 129; political, 90; religious, 2, 7, 22, 59, 64, 91; spiritual, 81, 92; and victimization, 64; of weight, 77
Medical model, 7
Memory/memories: act of, 158; body, 12, 21; connecting to, 123; delayed, 158; discern, 144; emotional, 130; erase, 38; "False Memory Syndrome," 19; few, 94; flashbacks, 40, 43, 51, 55, 109, 117, 128; haunting, 45, 128; horrors

of, 81; and hysteria, 12; and incest, 37, 95; mistrust, 109; precious, 93; and PTSD, 6, 33–39, 128; reclamation of, 167; "recovery" or, 117; of respondents, 17–41; retrieving, 125; self-soothing, 54. *See also* Nightmares
Methodology, 161–75
Miller, A., 15–16, 49, 94
Molestation, x, 4, 83, 118–41, 151–55
Mother: background of, 163–66; closest to, 141; daughter resembles, 154; and eating disorders, 53; etymology, 70; honor thy, 69; I/eye-less, 99; and incest, 23, 28, 53, 82; sick, 94; single, 111; survivors, 20–23, 28, 35, 82, 134–35
Multiple Personality Disorder: as adaptive, 17, 28–31; alters, 29

Narcissism/narcissistic: as disorder, 15–17; and fantasies, 90; and food as object, 52; parents, 28, 90; recovery, 122; and Twelve Steps, 121; wounding, 15, 20, 53, 103–4
Nightmares, 117
Norms: and eating disorders, 43; thinness, 44
Numb, 6, 43, 109, 144; emotional anesthesia, 18; shame, 92
Nurturing: counterfeit, 6, 81; courage, 84, 99; domestic labor, 71; food, 52, 55; goddess imagery, 69; inner authority, 114; protection and, 94; relationships, 123; repair, 92; self-compassion, 123; and support, 125; and Twelve-Step programs, 111

Obedience: and Christianity, 62–64; daughterly, 84; reinforces, 119; submission and, 99; value of, 69
Object/objectification, 30, 48; of children, 20, 25; feeling like an, 40; politics of, 20, 126; resisting, 133; sexual, xi, 20, 25, 40, 48, 54, 58, 76, 78, 123–24, 132, 151–55
Obsession: with pursuit of thinness, 5; with weight, 5
Ortner, S., 70